URBAN TEXAS

NUMBER EIGHT
Texas A&M Southwestern Studies
Robert A. Calvert and Larry D. Hill
General Editors

URBAN TEXAS

POLITICS AND DEVELOPMENT

Edited by Char Miller and Heywood T. Sanders

TEXAS A&M UNIVERSITY PRESS : COLLEGE STATION

The paper used in this book meets the minimum requirements of the American National Standard for Permanence
of Paper for Printed Library Materials, Z39.48-1984. Binding materials have been chosen for durability.

Library of Congress Cataloging-in-Publication Data

Urban Texas : politics and development / edited by
Char Miller and Heywood Sanders. — 1st ed.
    p. cm. — (Texas A&M southwestern studies : no. 8)
    Includes index.
    Contents: The rise of urban Texas / by Char Miller
and David Johnson — Frugal and sparing : interest
groups, politics, and city building in San Antonio,
1870–85 / by David Johnson — Boss Tweed and
V. O. Key in Texas / by Amy Bridges — Woman,
religion, and reform in Galveston, 1880–1920 / by
Elizabeth Hayes Turner — The emergence of a Black
neighborhood : Houston's Fourth Ward, 1865–1915 /
by Cary D. Wintz — Olmos Park and the creation
of a suburban bastion, 1927–39 / by Char Miller
and Heywood Sanders — Protecting community and
property values : civic clubs in Houston, 1909–70 /
by Robert Fisher — Dallas in the 1940s : the challenges and opportunities of defense mobilization /
by Robert B. Fairbanks — Building a new urban
infrastructure : the creation of postwar San Antonio / by Heywood T. Sanders.
    ISBN 0-89096-397-5 (alk. paper)
    1. Urbanization—Texas—History.   2. Metropolitan
areas—Texas—History.   3. Real estate development—
Texas—History.   4. Capitalists and financiers—
Texas—History.   5. Urban policy—Texas—Citizen
participation—History—Case studies.   I. Miller, Char.
II. Sanders, Heywood T., 1948– . III. Series.
HT384.U52T487   1990
307.76'09764—dc20   89-33948
                                  CIP

Contents

Tables

Figure

Introduction

The history of Texas has largely been written in rural terms. The opening of the frontier, the image of the cowboy, the tales of land conquered and tamed into productivity for farming and ranching, and the boom of oil *cotton* all dominate our images of the state's past and evolution. Yet contemporary Texas is very much an urban state, boasting three of the nation's ten largest cities, an expanding set of metropolitan corridors, and an economy increasingly linked to the services and technological innovation that are *urban* products.

The creation of urban Texas and its major centers did not happen overnight. Dallas, Houston, San Antonio, Galveston, Arlington, and Austin have developed through a complex web of politics, society, and economics. These communities have long served as the markets of the state's natural resources and the service centers for its rural areas. But they have also grown through the aggressive actions of urban entrepreneurs and promoters, intent on control of an ever-widening urban hinterland and the boosting of land values. The twentieth-century histories of Texas' dominant urban centers — Dallas, Houston, and San Antonio — reflect very different patterns of growth, expansion, and regional dominance. The varying success of urban entrepreneurs reflects both large-scale economic forces and the very particular skills and innovativeness of individuals. The first essay, by Char Miller and David Johnson, presents an overview of the urban development process in the state's largest urban centers.

Their analysis, while noting the relevance of location, markets, and regional geography, lays particular stress on local entrepreneurship as the central element in urban growth and economic success. Both Dallas and Houston took advantage of private entrepreneurial activity in attracting new urban activities and gaining a competitive edge over urban rivals. The efforts of private entrepreneurs were also supported and enhanced by public investment, including the federal government's development of the Houston Ship Channel, and the attraction of a new aircraft manufacturing complex to Dallas during the Second World War. In this intercity battle for economic expansion, San Antonio, once the state's leading urban center, lagged far behind.

Chapter 2, by David Johnson provides a broader historical explanation of San Antonio's comparative failure at the business of urban growth. Although a number of students of urban development have described the dominance of a local "growth coalition" of government officials and business people in decisions about local development and public spending, San Antonio in the latter half of the nineteenth century was quite divided in political and fiscal terms. Indeed, its most influential business and civic leaders fought to restrain the growth of government and maintained a striking aversion to city taxation. The result was a limited public sector that could, among other things, pave streets only when all affected property owners agreed. Control over the city's politics proved a point of contention that effectively limited the development of a broad, community-oriented, and prodevelopment elite.

Although political division continued to characterize San Antonio into the twentieth century, other Texas cities often submerged overt political conflict as new "reform machines" emerged in Austin, Dallas, and Houston. The chapter by Amy Bridges notes the unusual success of municipal government reform in southwestern cities. But the adoption of the city manager plan and nonpartisan elections did not eliminate local politics. Indeed, cities like Dallas and Houston, as well as their counterparts in California and New Mexico, witnessed a local politics of factions and factional alliances, personalistic followings, and overt political involvement by city employees. Under the sway of longtime mayor Oscar Holcombe, Houston saw both the creation of public benefits for the working class and minorities and continuing support for the economic expansion sought by most of the city's business interests.

The success of municipal reform was nowhere more apparent than in Galveston, source of the city commission movement that swept Texas and the South. While the adoption of the commission plan was credited with saving the city after its devastation by hurricane and tidal wave in 1900, Elizabeth Turner argues in chapter 4 that much of the progressive character of the city was the product of its women activists. From a base in local churches, Galveston's women pressed for a substantial expansion of social services and health care. Their efforts did not merely seek to aid the worthy poor, but to alter the priorities and functions of the public sector in the areas of public health and welfare. Women's organizations succeeded in the improvement of sanitation and building ordinances and in the establishment of public playgrounds and tuberculosis treatment centers. Yet these upper-middle- and upper-income women did little to threaten the city's established economic and political elites and their interests, or to alter the position of minorities.

The process of urban development and growth also affected the circumstances of blacks and other minorities who had long found a home in Texas cities. Cary Wintz's examination of Houston's Fourth Ward, long known as the "mother ward" and the center of the city's black community, traces its development back to the 1840s. From modest beginnings, the black population boomed as a result of rural to urban migration in the wake of emancipation. But despite its evolution as the locus for black professionals and a host of religious, educational, and political institutions, the Fourth Ward came under increasing pressure from outside forces. A change in the form of city government that eliminated the ward's representation, new city programs, and the expansion of the downtown business district all operated to reduce the black community's political impact and its security. Thus the cost of urban progressivism and growth was borne directly by the city's least visible and least politically effective citizens, a pattern that has been repeated often in the twentieth century.

The character of urban Texas in the early twentieth century was shaped by a series of forces that affected the nation as a whole. The increasing wealth of urban citizens, the new mobility provided by the automobile, and the desire to shape a new kind of urban residential environment led to the emergence of automobile suburbs in Dallas, Houston, and San Antonio. These exclusive enclaves offered the security of racial, ethnic, and class homogeneity (enforced by restrictive convenants) and minimal taxes. Thus the new urban elite was able to escape the social problems and needs of the city, as well as the vagaries of its politics, even as it directed and profited from urban growth and expansion. As Char Miller and Heywood Sanders indicate in chapter 6, Olmos Park, now surrounded by the city of San Antonio, provided just this sort of suburban bastion, a bastion that enforced growing differences in urban wealth and political influence.

The boom times of the 1920s and the expansion after the Second World War saw the creation of a vast new set of residential neighborhoods, which remained part of major cities. In Houston, Robert Fisher argues in chapter 7, these in-city suburbs often sought organizational and political means for ensuring public services in a community without ward or district representation. Neighborhood clubs offered a vehicle for lobbying public officials and pursuing local objectives. They also provided a means of organizing residents and defending against racial change, although often without success. These neighborhood organizations represented an economic and political adaptation to a city with limited services and a limited public sector and, enabled the more affluent residents of Houston, like those in other Texas cities, to cope with the problems of urban life while avoiding responsibility to the larger community.

The urban Texas of the latter half of the twentieth century represents very much an *intended* product, if not necessarily a *planned* one. Population growth, outward expansion, and the achievement of national recognition were the products of entrepreneurial and political savvy, aided by national policies during the Second World War. Houston saw new investment in synthetic rubber and petrochemicals; San Antonio witnessed the expansion of its air bases and aircraft maintenance installations; and Dallas garnered a new industrial base with the coming of airplane manufacturing from the North. Robert Fairbanks's chapter portrays an organized and politically powerful business that set out to attract jobs and industry at a time of national mobilization. Dallas's success was rooted in a combination of economic and political strength that coupled the city's sales pitch with city and county investments in new runways, streets, water, and sewer. Dallas's success thus reflected not merely a meshing of public and private entrepreneurship, but a singular commitment of local government and its fiscal resources to industrial development and growth. But that commitment was not without its costs. The city's black citizens, poorly housed and poorly served, saw little improvement in their circumstances. And even the city's modest investment in public housing served the dual objectives of improving housing and maintaining black invisibility and obvious racial segregation.

San Antonio lagged behind both Dallas and Houston in growth and population expansion during the 1930s, 1940s, and 1950s. Its political system remained "unreformed," combining the manipulation of minority votes with persistent conflict over issues of taxing and spending. The combination of economic and political power that nourished Dallas's boom proved unattainable, with the result that public investment policies did little to support growth and industrial attraction, although they did provide improvements in black and Hispanic neighborhoods. The year 1955 saw the emergence of a new regime that combined the newly adopted city manager government form, a business-dominated local political party (the Good Government League), and a majority voting coalition centered in the Anglo neighborhoods of San Antonio's North Side. The result was apparently a reduction in overt political conflict and a more efficient, rational allocation of city services and spending. The reality was rather different, as the city's electorate fragmented along racial and ethnic lines and public investments were skewed to providing an urban infrastructure that served downtown, growth, and the promise of new industry.

The basic processes of urbanization and urban development in Texas cities are little different from those of other states and regions. Yet in the accommodation of public and private interests and the singular pursuit of urban expansion, the major cities of Texas constitute a unique group. While the rhetoric of individual initiative and risk taking dominates the state's folklore, urban Texas has been shaped by both private entrepreneurs and local governments that mirrored the entrepreneurs' goals and financially sustained their efforts. That coincidence of interest and effort has been neither consistent nor pervasive, as San Antonio's history suggests. The apparently ceaseless forward march of urban progress has been interrupted by divisions within local business communities, by factional politics, and by the occasional recalcitrance of urban voters. Yet one cannot help but conclude that the governments of urban Texas have largely succeeded in mirroring, sustaining, and financing the largely private initiatives of development entrepreneurs since the nineteenth century.

During the 1970s and much of the 1980s, the older cities of the East and Midwest looked at their Texas counterparts and envied their capacity to attract population and business. The magic formula appeared to be a combination of low taxes, few unions, abundant natural resources, and a government that served the interests of business and development. As one study of public-private partnership notes, "To many, Dallas epitomizes public-sector managerial efficiency and unfettered private sector development."[1] But for Dallas and Houston and San Antonio, managerial efficiency and development have provided only modest rewards and advantages for those with low incomes or minority status, who are unable to afford exclusive suburbs or the protection of private security forces. Indeed, for much of the twentieth century, the machinery of urban government has been employed to direct public resources and investment away from the neediest urban neighborhoods and the least advantaged. If the history of urban Texas has been one of boom and expansion, it has also been one of inequity and disadvantage. Today's central cities face not only the constraints of a time of economic downturn, but the inheritance of this history of bias. The result is a powerful lesson in one means of generating growth, coupled with an equally powerful conclusion about its ultimate costs and limits.

Part I.

Historical Overview

1. The Rise of Urban Texas

Char Miller and David R. Johnson

Texas contains three of the nation's ten largest cities, but their existence has not yet affected the hold that the state's rural heritage has on Texas' imagination — or so Texans' attachment to two nineteenth-century cultural landmarks, the Alamo and the Chisholm Trail, would suggest. As the shrine of Texas liberty, the Alamo continually generates elegies to the manly courage and bravery of the fallen heroes of 1836. It was on that hallowed ground, now trod by millions of tourists each year, that the "Trans-Appalachian American" reached his apogee: "The Texans had no bayonets, but by Mexican standards they were enormous men, towering a head higher or more. They smashed, butted, used tomahawks and knives. They fought as paladins . . . they died as paladins, each with his ring of surrounding dead." In death, of course, these tall men triumphed, a triumph that has reverberated across time and has done much to shape contemporary Texas myth and lore.[1]

The "immortal frontier" of the late nineteenth century spawned its share of Texas heroes, too: burly men who rode the range and drove cattle north from South Texas along the Chisholm Trail to Abilene, Kansas. That bit of economic activity has also been invested with great cultural significance. As the writings of Walter Prescott Webb and T. R. Fehrenbach and the cinematic marvels of John Ford demonstrate, those Texans who struggled to establish a cattle empire were also central participants in a dramatic transformation of national character, for it was only on the Plains that the "sun burned through the fogs and lifted the burdens of southern history."[2] As the mists dissipated, a new American — "neither Yankee nor southern" — emerged. And this new man, this Texan, "shot not only a business but a form of culture across the American west," forever altering life beyond the ninety-eighth meridian. The Lone Star State's exceptional past and unique contributions, Fehrenbach concludes, have set it apart from all other members of the American union: "We have a history; other states have records of economic development."[3]

The rural character of Texas' past — and its influence on the state's sense of self — cannot be denied. But such influences are not paramount (nor ever were) and are frequently overdrawn. Certainly Fehrenbach is not alone in his assumption that the Lone Star is a singular jewel in the American crown. Indeed, one of the fundamental ironies of the rural emphasis on the state's historiography and lore, and especially the focus on the Alamo and the cattle industry, is that these historical events depended heavily on urban environments for their impetus and ultimate success as symbols. The Alamo, for instance, may have been the scene of frontier heroics, but these heroics were played out on an urban stage. Set within what in 1836 was one of the largest cities west of the Mississippi River, Mission San Antonio de Valero's site plan and architectural form were legacies of Spanish colonial policies articulated in the Law of the Indies of 1583. Combining a mission, *villa* (civil settlement), and *presidio* (military encampment), this plan, put into effect in San Antonio beginning in the 1720s, proved a powerful symbol of its inhabitants' shared destiny, one that reflected the efforts of metropolitan Spain and, later, Mexico to subdue the rural hinterland. A little more than a century later, that settlement pattern took on another meaning: the Alamo was chosen by the Texans who would die within its compound precisely because it was an urban fortress, the most strategic spot from which to harass and delay the northern thrust of Santa Ana's army. It is not a little ironic, then, that the Battle of the Alamo has come to stand as the apotheosis of rural virtue and valor.[4]

The urban orientation of the cattle industry, of cattle drives (and drovers), is just as clear. Walter Prescott Webb argued, for example, that the origins of the industry lay in the region "south of San Antonio and west of the Colorado River," but then defined its geographical limits in a revealing manner: "We may describe the territory in question as a diamond-shaped area, elongated North and South. . . . San Antonio, Old Indianola, Brownsville and Laredo form the four points of the diamond. This restricted area was the cradle of the western cattle business."[5] An *urban* cradle, it should be noted, for what Webb described was the rural hinterland and its economic resource, which the four emerging urban centers would over time seek to develop and dominate. A map of the Chisholm trail provides added evidence for the significant role such communities played in the cattle business, the central foci of which were the commercial entrepôts of San Antonio, Austin, Waco, and Fort Worth. These towns served as collection points for north-bound cattle, as convenient fords across a variety of rivers and streams and, not incidentally, as outfitting centers, offering "saddles, rope, six-shooters, groceries and other supplies" to the drovers. And the longhorns' final destination was, of course, the burgeoning urban populations of the Middle West and the Northeast, whose demand for meat did much to trigger the exploitation of the western range by the cattle industry, and thus helped set into motion the long drive itself. The influence of the urban heritage of Texas has indeed been rich, deep, and pervasive.[6]

The demographic dimensions of that influence are manifest most readily in the data culled from the federal census (see figure 1.1). Although Texas was not classified officially as an urban state until the 1950 census — at which point nearly 60 percent of its population lived in communities of twenty-five hundred or more — a sizable minority had resided in urban areas since

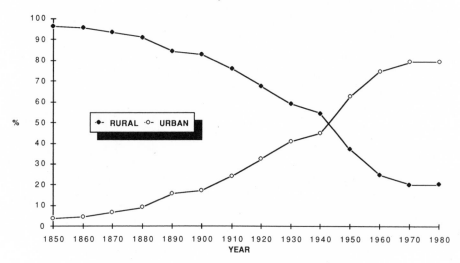

Fig. 1.1.
Texas Population: Rural and Urban Percentages.
Source: U.S. Census

the early twentieth century. Moreover, when one examines the rate of growth that the major cities of Texas have experienced since the 1870s, it is clear that the process of urbanization is not just a post–World War II phenomenon, a pattern commonly associated with the emergence of the Sunbelt. Instead, its roots extend back into the nineteenth century; strikingly, some of the largest percentile gains were recorded well in advance of the much-heralded Sunbelt explosion.

Houston's rate of growth is a case in point. The average decennial rate of increase in the city's population between 1860 and 1930 was 83 percent; between 1940 and 1980, the rate fell to 41 percent, or a bit less than half the earlier figures. Admittedly, these percentile rates of change mask the impact that changes in raw population figures would have had (Houston absorbed almost as many people in the decade after 1940 as it had throughout the rest of its existence), but neither should the escalating growth of the Bayou City's population after World War II obscure the importance and effect of the city's century-long pattern of sustained population increases. That rising curve laid the foundation for the mid-century takeoff.

And for the state as a whole, the impact of urban development can be assessed by comparing the differences in the rate of growth experienced in the urban and rural areas. Again, in terms of aggregate numbers, the critical turning point occurred between the 1940 and 1950 censuses, when more than 1.7 million people were added to the urban population rolls, while the rural population plunged by more than 400,000.

Table 1.1
Texas' Population Growth

City						Population							
	1860	1870	1880	1890	1900	1910	1920	1930	1940	1950	1960	1970	1980
Austin	3,494	4,428	11,013	14,575	22,258	29,860	34,976	53,120	87,930	132,459	186,545	251,868	345,496
Dallas	—	—	10,358	38,067	42,638	92,104	158,976	260,475	297,734	434,462	679,684	844,401	904,078
Fort Worth	—	—	6,663	23,076	26,668	73,312	106,482	163,447	177,662	278,778	356,268	393,476	385,164
Galveston	7,307	13,818	22,248	29,084	37,789	36,981	44,255	52,938	60,862	66,568	67,175	61,809	61,902
Houston	4,845	9,382	16,513	27,557	44,633	78,800	138,276	292,352	384,514	596,163	938,219	1,232,802	1,595,138
San Antonio	8,235	12,256	20,550	37,673	53,321	96,614	161,379	231,542	253,854	408,442	587,718	654,153	785,880

SOURCE: U.S. Censuses.
NOTE: — means data not available.

Table 1.2
Percentage Change in Texas' Urban Population

City						% Change							
	1860 (%)	1870 (%)	1880 (%)	1890 (%)	1900 (%)	1910 (%)	1920 (%)	1930 (%)	1940 (%)	1950 (%)	1960 (%)	1970 (%)	1980 (%)
Austin	455.5	26.7	148.7	32.3	52.7	34.2	16.8	52.3	65.5	50.6	40.0	35.0	36.3
Dallas	—	—	—	265.5	12.0	116.0	72.6	63.8	13.2	47.4	56.4	24.2	7.1
Fort Worth	—	—	—	246.3	15.6	174.7	45.2	53.5	8.7	56.9	27.8	10.4	-2.1
Galveston	74.9	89.1	61.0	30.7	29.9	-2.1	19.7	19.6	15.0	9.4	0.9	-8.0	0.2
Houston	102.2	93.6	76.0	66.9	62.0	76.6	75.5	111.4	31.5	55.0	57.4	31.4	29.3
San Antonio	136.1	48.8	67.7	83.3	41.5	81.2	67.0	43.5	9.6	60.9	43.9	11.3	20.1

SOURCE: U.S. Censuses.

But that transition was not quite as abrupt as the data suggest. A closer examination reveals, for instance, that in both aggregate and percentile terms, Texas' rural growth reached its peak in 1880, and with the exception of the 1900 and 1930 census returns, it has diminished ever since, a decline that parallels that of the national experience. In contrast, the state's urban population, always on the rise, surged forward between 1900 and 1910, and in 1920 the increase in urban population outstripped that of the rural for the first time. If in this sense Texas lagged behind the nation, which officially became urban in 1920, the key indicators signaled that the gap was not substantial and that it was narrowing. In the end, the census data underscore another pattern: urban Texas made its presence felt early in the state's history, during the very period when its most important legends were evolving. The heroic, basically rural imagery of Texas has thus obscured the fundamental role that urban Texans have played in organizing the state's economic and political structures.[7]

Population statistics indicate the broad outlines of urban development, but in and of themselves, they can neither describe fully its complex nature and timing in particular cities, nor address the equally complicated process whereby the various urban centers interacted and competed with one another across time. This poses a methodological problem. Until recently, urban historians have tended to rely on the case study method to describe the emergence of a particular city in hopes of illuminating the developmental process in general. But since urban development does not take place in a vacuum, indeed, because one community's rise is in part predicated on its relations with a host of other cities and depends, too, on a complex set of external forces beyond its control, a more comprehensive approach to the question of how cities expand and contract is required. A number of scholars have adopted a regional perspective to explore and explain the emergence of urban systems, a task that is frankly complicated. "We must learn," Timothy Mahoney has averred, "how [a] town has interacted with and functioned within the regional system of towns of which it is a part." This is a proposition that will lead historians to assess not only "the interaction of the town with the system, [but] its responses to larger forces of economic change, and responses of townsmen to the disruption caused by such external forces of change."[8]

Mahoney's arguments are informative and important, but embracing such a regional perspective does not necessarily resolve the urban historian's methodological problems. Still under debate is how to delineate those interactions with precision and how to determine what historical evidence best captures the fluid character of urban growth and regional development typified by the history of Texas urbanization. Much of the work to date has emphasized charting economic interdependencies, an effort that has helped clarify patterns of economic exchange but that has been unable to push beyond that model and determine convincingly what ought

Table 1.3
Population of Texas to 1980

	The State			Urban			Rural			% of Total	
		Change from Preceding Census			Change from Preceding Census			Change from Preceding Census			
	Population	Number	%	Population	Number	%	Population	Number	%	Urban	Rural
Current urban definition											
1980	14,229,191	3,022,461	27.1	11,333,017	2,412,071	27.0	2,896,174	620,390	27.3	79.6	20.4
1970	11,196,730	1,617,053	16.9	8,920,946	1,733,476	24.1	2,275,784	−116,423	−4.9	79.7	20.3
1960	9,579,677	1,868,483	24.2	7,187,470	2,349,410	48.6	2,392,207	−480,927	−16.7	75.0	25.0
1950	7,711,194	1,296,370	20.2	4,838,060	—	—	2,873,134	—	—	62.7	37.3
Previous urban definition											
1960	9,579,677	1,868,483	24.2	6,963,114	2,350,448	51.0	2,616,563	−481,965	−15.6	72.7	27.3
1950	7,711,194	1,296,370	20.2	4,612,666	1,701,277	58.4	3,098,528	−404,907	−11.6	59.8	40.2
1940	6,414,824	590,109	10.1	2,911,389	522,041	21.8	3,503,435	68,068	2.0	45.4	54.6
1930	5,824,715	1,161,487	24.9	2,389,348	876,659	58.0	3,435,367	284,828	9.0	41.0	59.0
1920	4,663,228	766,686	19.7	1,512,689	574,585	61.2	3,150,539	192,101	6.5	32.4	67.6
1910	3,896,542	847,832	27.8	938,104	417,345	80.1	2,958,438	430,487	17.0	24.1	75.9
1900	3,048,710	813,183	36.4	520,759	171,248	49.0	2,527,951	641,935	34.0	17.1	82.9
1890	2,235,527	643,778	40.4	349,511	202,716	138.1	1,886,016	441,062	30.5	15.6	84.4
1880	1,591,749	773,170	94.5	146,795	92,274	169.2	1,444,954	680,896	89.1	9.2	90.8
1870	818,579	214,364	35.5	54,521	27,906	104.9	764,058	186,458	32.3	6.7	93.3
1860	604,215	391,623	184.2	26,615	18,950	247.2	577,600	372,673	181.9	4.4	95.6
1850	212,592	—	—	7,665	—	—	204,927	—	—	3.6	96.4

SOURCE: U.S. Censuses.
NOTE: — means data not available.

to be, in David Goldfield's words, the regionalists' key concern — "the nature and timing of regional formation and growth."[9]

Goldfield has accordingly proposed that historians take a "geohistorical approach," which would include "not only economic interaction but cultural, political, demographic and technological variables as well." Each variable is itself a complex entity, as his definition of culture indicates. For Goldfield, the historian should pay particular attention to the "dynamism of human interaction" to explain how and why certain cities (and regions) grow in the ways that they do; among other things, the impact of entrepreneurial skill and the area's receptivity to innovation are important cultural concepts, because these characteristics help determine the timing of a region's expansion, as well as the extent and nature of its future economic interactions. This analytical framework also permits consideration of the strategic importance that governments of all levels assume in shaping a region's economic capabilities, the impact of demographic changes on regional employment opportunities, trade routes and growth potential, and, finally, a recognition of the profound social, economic, and political alterations that technological innovations — for example, the railroad — can usher in. Taken together, these elements create a dynamic model of urbanization that, significantly, grants an active role to the very human beings who formulated (and endured) the rise of urban America.[10]

It is this multifaceted regional perspective that we will employ to sketch out the broad outlines of the formative period of Texas' urbanization. And we do mean sketch, for a chapter cannot fully explore the many and varied elements that make up a full-fledged regional analysis. We shall therefore limit our discussion both by time and content. What follows is a speculative analysis of the rise of urban Texas — especially its three major cities, Dallas, Houston, and San Antonio — beginning in the mid-nineteenth century and concluding in the years immediately following WW II.

We have divided this chronology into three parts. The critical first stage in Texas' urbanization occurred between 1836 and the late 1880s. It was then that the three emerging urban communities to a large extent operated independently of one another, an independence that would diminish with the laying down of a statewide railroad network during the late nineteenth century. The second stage emerged at precisely this point, when each of these cities began to compete directly with the others for regional supremacy. This competition fundamentally reshuffled the state's urban hierarchy by the 1920s. The third stage emerged during the 1930s, especially during World War II, when Dallas, Houston, and San Antonio in different ways sought to capitalize on (and extend) their resource bases, which were critical for the accelerated growth and development of Sunbelt Texas.

Within this time frame, we especially focus on one of the central factors in these three cities' development: the entrepreneurial elite. By examining its actions we not only can establish the means by which these inde-

pendent polities merged their economic futures, but we also can explore
the influence that politics, demography, and technology exerted on that
merger.

The sheer size of the state of Texas ensured that the evolving urban hierarchy of the nineteenth century would be especially complex. There was
sufficient room, in a very literal sense, for the development of several subregional, initially independent, urban centers. Major cities, such as Dallas,
Houston, and San Antonio, had distinctive local economic bases, which
were not initially in conflict with one another. San Antonio served the South
Texas subregion; Dallas–Fort Worth, the north-central agricultural area;
Houston-Galveston, the eastern cotton- and lumber-producing area. Each
of these major urban centers spent the early years of its development
capitalizing on nearby opportunities in relative isolation from the others.
Those opportunities were sufficiently impressive to generate rapid population growth, which was, however, of a remarkably similar magnitude for
each center, as the census data reveal.

By the 1890s, none of these cities had achieved dominance over the entire state. These early years were nonetheless critical to the future development of the regional urban hierarchy. Local elites with characteristics peculiar to their own circumstances emerged in each of the major cities. Their
ability to compete with one another for regional leadership would be cir-
cumscribed by the personal background and experience of each elite community and by the ways in which their initial experiences in city building
had shaped their vision of their particular community's future development.

The cultural matrix of the three towns is fundamentally different. The
business communities of Dallas and Houston historically have had more
aggressive attitudes toward growth than has San Antonio. Part of the explanation for this lies in the social origins of each of the nineteeth-century
merchant groups. As Kenneth Wheeler points out, most of the merchants
in Houston came from the Mid-Atlantic and New England regions, where
the culture of entrepreneurial innovation and urban development was well
defined. The Allen brothers of Houston are a perfect example of how this
urban culture's perceptions are applied to a *de novo* situation. Shortly after
the Battle of San Jacinto, these brothers from New York searched East
Texas for possible sites for a city. Their understanding of the relationship
between the function and location of cities led them to select the site of
modern Houston, "at the most interior point of year-round navigation in
Texas." Location was not destiny, however: Houston continued to grow
precisely because its mercantile elite was skilled in the ways and means
of urban development.[11]

Nothing better illustrates the merchants' aggressive attitudes and behavior
than Houston's railroad construction program. They acted quickly to
develop a transportation system that would control and expand the city's

developing hinterland. Beginning with the Houston Tap in 1856, Houstonians built a rail system that bound the hinterland to the local economy. Rail lines southeast toward Galveston, southwest toward Columbia, west to Alleyton, northwest to Millican, and east to Beaumont linked the area's population and resources to Houston's economy by 1861; of the 450 miles of track laid in Texas before the Civil War, 80 percent led to Houston. As these various links were completed, Houston's entrepreneurs reaped the benefits. The volume of cotton arriving in the city increased dramatically, as did that of other raw materials, such as lumber and hides. This aggressive rail-building program thus laid the foundations for individual fortunes and significant local capital accumulations for further urban investments.[12]

This entrepreneurial aggressiveness continued unabated after the Civil War. The city's elite instigated a public meeting in 1866 at which Houstonians approved a coherent blueprint for the city's future development. Part of this blueprint required additional railroad building, especially an extension of the Houston and Texas Central to Dallas. Completion of that line gave Houston a connection with a transcontinental route (the Southern Pacific) and tied the two most dynamic urban economies in the region together for the first time.[13]

Dallas displayed the same aggressive entrepreneurial attitude that guided Houston's development. Its most important business leaders seem to have moved to the city from the Upper South and Middle West, regions that had been developed as extensions of the urban-oriented, innovative northeastern culture. This connection was literally played out in John S. Armstrong's life. The father of this early Dallas booster had been a Mississippi riverboat pilot. Armstrong therefore grew to maturity surrounded by practical examples of the nation's urban market economy. He demonstrated how well he had learned his lessons by successfully applying himself to the development of a large wholesale grocery empire in the 1880s.

Others were similarly oriented. Col. John C. McCoy had played a key role in the development of Kansas City and John Nealy Bryan, officially Dallas's first settler, had been a town promoter in Arkansas. Like the Allen brothers in Houston, Bryan and McCoy came to Texas to raise cities, not cattle. Bryan's life history offers an intriguing look at the entrepreneurial spirit at work in Dallas. According to legend, Bryan came to the site on the Trinity River vowing to turn it into a great city. Instead, he became the town's first eccentric, failed to capitalize on the early Dallas boom, and died a drunk. Hardly the picture of entrepreneurial innovation. But, in fact, he was an innovator and knew what steps to take to stimulate urban expansion. In 1866, for example, he presided over a public meeting in which the fledgling business community laid out its goals for future development, especially railroad connections to eastern markets, indicating that both Bryan and the more successful Dallas merchants had a cohesive sense of how to promote their community.[14]

Nowhere is this more clear than in the extremely aggressive manner in which men such as William Gaston acquired Dallas's first railroad connections. In 1871, for instance, Gaston was instrumental in raising money and donating land to lure the Houston and Texas Central Railroad, which initially had intended to bypass Dallas eight miles to the east. The Texas and Pacific Railroad, an intercontinental line, also intended to bypass Dallas fifty miles to the south, but again local business leaders displayed their aggressiveness and guile. Gaston and his colleagues convinced their state representative to attach a rider to an unrelated bill that stipulated that the T&P must pass within one mile of Browder Springs, a community near Dallas. This required a major shift in the railroad's planned construction line and understandably enraged the directors. They were pacified, however, by a two hundred thousand dollar Dallas bond issue and five thousand dollars in cash, which were put at the railroad's disposal. The Dallas business community's political savvy, swift and concerted action, and use of cash resources testify to its sophisticated understanding of the means to (and profits to be won from) urban development.[15]

San Antonio is another story altogether, for its has displayed a remarkable lack of entrepreneurial aggressiveness. The social origins of the prominent members of its mercantile community in the nineteenth century helped set the context for this behavior. These men were Irish and German, and they usually migrated to South Texas directly from Europe or from the lower southern states; they therefore did not have connections to the northeastern urban culture of innovation, as did their peers in Houston and Dallas, nor did they engage in vigorous town promotion. Instead, the city's location tended to dominate its citizens' economic behavior and its prospects for development, as its numerous military establishments suggest. The U.S. Army chose San Antonio because of its strategic location, from which it could readily supply its western garrisons. The local merchants did not exert pressure on their political representatives to bring the army to the town, nor did its presence require private promotional schemes; there was no need for local business people to invest their profits in town building, since the army, after 1845, did that for them.[16]

Indeed, this reliance on external sources of capital and initiative inhibited the development of an indigeneous promotional spirit. San Antonio has no parallel to the Dallas and Houston community commitment to local development; there was no public meeting immediately following the Civil War, for instance, like the ones in which those communities' leaders outlined the course of future growth. In fact, San Antonio's major merchants exhibited a striking indifference to that engine of nineteenth-century city building, the railroad. Little wonder, then, that San Antonio was the last of these three major metropolitan areas to be hooked into the national railroad and commercial network during the nineteenth century.[17]

The San Antonio merchants' economic orientation provides some clues as to why they seemed so sluggish compared with their peers in Houston and Dallas. Many of the prominent German merchants engaged in extensive trade with the U.S. Army, acting as middlemen between the German farming communities in Central Texas and the army quartermasters in San Antonio. The Irish, on the other hand, looked south of the border for their economic opportunities. Men like John Twohig and B. M. McCarthy established agencies in the Rio Grande Valley and carried on an often illegal trade with Mexico. Neither supplying the army nor trading with Mexico encouraged these merchants to become involved in local town-building activities. While the military was admittedly an important element in the San Antonio economy, it did not stimulate rapid urbanization. The garrisons were too small to generate the level of demands that would permit the accumulation of large sums of investment capital.[18]

The same situation was true for the Irish-dominated trade with Mexico, a trade that was by no means promising. The colonial Mexican economy, for example, was beset by two main obstacles to sustained growth — inadequate transportation facilities and an inefficient economic organization. These obstacles were not overcome after independence in 1821 because of the half-century or more of internal social and political turmoil and the international warfare that followed. These problems were reflected in the nation's per capita income figure, which, according to John Coatsworth, began to fall after independence and did not stop sliding until after 1860. Only in the Porfiriato (1877–1910) did the economy stabilize and income levels rise, and at that the per capita income was still approximately one-tenth the U.S. figures.[19]

None of this boded well for the commercial fortunes (and futures) of the Irish commercial agents in San Antonio; Mexico certainly was not the kind of market that would lead suppliers to expand their inventories or to extend their investments. Even when the Mexican economy began to recover and grow at an annual rate of 2.3 percent in the late nineteenth century, San Antonio merchants could not take advantage of that growth. The very goods that San Antonio initially exported to Mexico — cotton and hides — were now the mainstays of northern Mexico's brisk export trade to the United States.[20]

San Antonio's trade with Mexico, then, did not permit extensive capital accumulation. Kenneth Wheeler's analysis of the property holdings of San Antonio merchants in the 1860 census makes this point very clear. Prior to the Civil War, no merchant "controlled property worth as much as two hundred thousand dollars." At the same time, some of Houston's "merchant princes," who benefited from a rich hinterland and direct access to the national commercial network, controlled more than three times that amount of property. William Marsh Rice's fortune was worth $750,000 in 1860, William J. Hutchins weighed in with $700,000, and the net worth of four other men was considerably more than $250,000. The accumulation of property, in short, is a quick measure of mercantile skill and aggressiveness, and San Antonio's merchants failed in comparison with counterparts in Houston and Dallas.[21]

That failure by itself did not determine San Antonio's position relative to Houston and Dallas. There were other elements involved, including the productive capacity of its rural hinterland, the political culture (and climate) within which its merchants operated, and the technological advances the community was willing (and able) to embrace. Yet San Antonio's population continued to keep pace with its competitors because of the largely independent and underdeveloped nature of its subregion, which enabled it to remain temporarily unchallenged as the agricultural service center of South Texas. But this growth and primacy masked the long-term effects of the city-building options that local entrepreneurs chose. And these choices, when linked to the business community's nonaggressiveness, made San Antonio less competitive when the race for regional dominance emerged full blown in the early twentieth century.

As the twentieth century began, the nature and consequences of urban growth in Texas changed. Previously, the underdeveloped state economy had permitted subregional urban development to flourish. Each of the major cities had had plenty to occupy itself in its immediate hinterland, and growth had fed off entrepreneurial activities that aimed at strengthening each city's hold over its surrounding territory. Railroad construction had facilitated subregional growth by linking each city's hinterland more closely to it, but the completion of that building program also marked the beginning of a new phase of urban progress in which competition for regional dominance became the key theme.

Superficially, Dallas, Houston, and San Antonio seemed to their respective entrepreneurs to be well situated to achieve regional dominance. But the very physical setting of Houston and Dallas posed a problem. Each had to contend with a nearby (and aggressive) rival — Galveston and Fort Worth, respectively — before either could realistically consider reaching for statewide control. San Antonio's problem was of another sort: it had no twin city, no nearby rival. Given this, there was no guarantee that any of these communities could establish permanent superiority within the state's urban hierarchy. In these fluid circumstances, where anything seemed possible, the successes and failures that local entrepreneurs had previously experienced would now play a crucial role in determining the outcome of the race for regional dominance, for, in spite of the fluidity of the general situation, one major factor that governed the process of urban growth was firmly in place. Each city now had a clearly recognizable economic elite composed of those who had survived the vagaries of founding businesses in new urban environments. Their collective experience represented local wisdom about the appropriate ways to promote growth.

Appropriateness would be a critical measure of new initiatives. Growth propositions which had conceptual links to previously successful ideas would attract greater favor than those which did not. Thus "collective wisdom" would both stimulate and discourage particular strategies for further expansion of each local economy. In addition, that wisdom would affect the ways in which entrepreneurs perceived and acted on new opportunities. If, for instance, taking significant risks to achieve important objectives was considered "normal" by entrepreneurs in one city but not in another, they would be apt to display a more aggressive approach to new developments than would their more conservative rivals. Thus, individual differences in the collective wisdom of each city's entrepreneurial group would, in combination with actual circumstances, shape the distinctive growth patterns of Dallas, Houston, and San Antonio as each city struggled for regional dominance.

The importance and impact of collective wisdom is perhaps nowhere more apparent than in San Antonio. It had achieved its prosperity as a service center to an agricultural hinterland through minimal effort on the part of its local business leaders. Underlying the standard rhetoric about inevitable growth was a profound complacency based on the historical lesson that progress need not occur at the cost of effort. Individual businesspeople certainly worked hard enough, but they did not engage in any concerted group activities to promote local development. They simply benefited from the extraordinary opportunities that stemmed from the structural changes the railroad's arrival wrought on the local economy after 1877.

At the outset of the twentieth century, then, local wisdom in San Antonio denied any important place to collective effort or risk taking. Individualism reigned supreme, reflected in the fact that the city had no Chamber of Commerce until 1910, and the organization that emerged in that year was not, in fact, representative of the entire business community. Instead, it was the creation and preserve of a minority of local entrepreneurs who did have a commitment to collective effort, but who could not command the attention, let alone the support, of their compatriots.

These were not the best of circumstances in which to compete for regional dominance. Yet some San Antonians tried. They did so in a time-honored, often effective, way by seeking to exploit new technologies to promote urban growth. Two businessmen, Luther Clegg and William Tuttle, both important members of the newly organized Chamber of Commerce, recognized that San Antonio needed a powerful new approach to growth if it was to compete successfully with Houston and Dallas. Both men had some acquaintance with technological issues, since Clegg owned a large printing business and Tuttle was the general manager of San Antonio's transportation and utilities corporation.[22]

Tuttle and Clegg seized on the airplane as the weapon that would offset the advantages San Antonio's rivals were developing after 1900. Houston was rapidly becoming a major port, and the discovery of the East Texas oil fields, beginning in 1901, promised to transform the Bayou City into a boomtown. Dallas was about to capitalize on its success as a banking center to finance, and siphon the profits from, oil exploration and agricultural development in West Texas. Isolated from these ventures by its location, San Antonio desperately needed a development tool that had the potential to match the economic power of ports and oil wells, but that did not derive from serendipitous geographic location. Aircraft technology and manufacturing were not tied to geography. The high mobility of this industry meant its development depended on whether local entrepreneurs would willingly assume the risk involved in investing in such a speculative venture.

Clegg and Tuttle approached the problem of capturing this technology for San Antonio indirectly. Their campaign to bring aviation to town combined propaganda with a ploy to exploit the city's now-traditional association with the U.S. Army. Capitalizing on local as well as national fascination with the airplane, beginning in 1910, they arranged flying demonstrations by notable aviators. While striving to build public interest in airplanes, the two men also worked with army officers stationed at Fort Sam Houston who advocated the military uses of airplanes. Presumably, these officers would be interested in helping establish local manufacturing plants that would build planes they could fly, and the plane owners would have contracts for military craft that would in effect subsidize the construction and development costs inherent in the new technology.

This campaign almost worked. By 1915 a local flying club jointly sponsored by the army and the chamber had created an organizational basis for cooperation between the civilian and military advocates of airpower. At least one manufacturer had inquired about establishing a plant in San Antonio. The war in Europe was forcefully demonstrating the practical military uses of aircraft, and the U.S. government had become acutely aware of the need for massive investments in all aspects of the armed forces.

These favorable portents did not, however, come to fruition. America's entry into World War I should have precipitated some commitments to aircraft production locally, but it did not. The reasons for this failure remain obscure. One key factor, however, seems to have been the absence of widespread interest among local business people in aircraft technology's potential role in stimulating growth. Clegg and Tuttle, despite nearly continuous effort, had not succeeded in establishing a broad coalition to support their own commitment to this new technology. When both men found their attention diverted to other activities — Tuttle enlisted in the army and served in France while Clegg became absorbed in locating land for new army bases around the city — their entire initiative collapsed because there was no one else willing or able to assume the leadership of their campaign.

Why only two men or, at best, a tiny handful of their friends, should understand the potential of airplanes as a new technology capable of promoting urban growth is an intriguing problem. But Clegg and Tuttle were attempting to do something that was beyond the comprehension of their associates. First and foremost, they were not trying to establish a new business venture for *themselves;* instead, they sought to create a new industry for their *city.* Nothing in the collective wisdom of San Antonio's entrepreneurs had taught them the importance of cooperative action for a common good. Local business people were quite willing to condone individual initiatives that benefited the individual; they were not, however, prepared to take risks as a group, because, in their experience, growth had occurred without assuming risks or employing collective effort.

Events after the war only underscored the lack of interest in group support of common objectives. By the early twenties, the Rio Grande Valley had become a major truck farming area with critical problems. The valley had only one rail connection to its national markets, and that was through Houston. Burgeoning productivity and inadequate transportation caused long shipping delays, large losses from spoilage, and hard feelings about Houston's dominance over the area. Representatives from the valley approached San Antonio's Chamber of Commerce for help. They needed another railroad out of the valley and were willing to transfer their business to San Antonio if a new line could be built.[23]

This was a situation that San Antonio's entrepreneurs could hardly ignore. Furthermore, wholesale agriculture and livestock activities formed the core of the city's economy. There should have been sufficient incentive and experience to prompt a determined effort to capture this valuable market for the local economy, but nothing happened. The chamber attempted to stimulate interest in this opportunity by sponsoring tours of the valley. Almost no one participated. A rail line did begin to inch its way south, but it was beset by financial difficulties stemming from a lack of support in San Antonio. The line remained unfinished through the decade, and the pleas for help from the valley gradually stopped.

San Antonio was unable to employ cooperative group effort to deal with the problems of competing with its rivals for regional dominance. That this was so disturbed some San Antonians, who, as the 1930 census approached, recognized that their city's population and economic growth had not kept pace with those of Houston and Dallas. In a desperate effort to avoid the negative connotations of the forthcoming statistical survey, some politicians proposed that the city annex large portions of Bexar County to inflate its population figures. But even this quick fix failed to secure community favor, and the decennial census revealed the inescapable fact: San Antonio, the largest city in Texas in 1910, was doomed to a distant third place in the emerging urban hierarchy less than a generation later.[24]

In sharp contrast to San Antonio, cooperative effort among Dallas's business people had been the norm since the city's founding. By the beginning of the twentieth century, Dallas had joined the ranks of such cities as Denver and Los Angeles in demonstrating that viable urban centers could be made to exist through uncommon concerted determination in places where ordinary common sense ought to have prevailed. But Dallas's drive for regional dominance was complicated, paradoxically, by an excess of aggressive boosterism — not its own, but that of its sister city, Fort Worth, located a mere thirty-five miles to the west.

Fort Worth began as one of the several army outposts created to guard the Texas frontier in the 1840s. Like Dallas, it struggled for many years to establish itself as a viable city. And as in Dallas, that struggle created an extraordinarily ambitious, aggressive group of local boosters who refused to acknowledge that geography was destiny. Their ambition, skill, and determination, combined with their city's location, effectively split Dallas's "natural" hinterland in two. During the late nineteenth century, Dallas's market area essentially developed in East Central Texas; Fort Worth's evolved in West Central Texas.[25]

By 1900 it was by no means clear that Dallas would inevitably subdue Fort Worth's challenge. Indeed, events quickly demonstrated that Fort Worth's business people were extremely competent competitors. Both cities experienced spectacular growth during the next decade, and even though Fort Worth remained the smaller of the two cities in 1910, its rate of growth, in fact, exceeded Dallas's by 58 percent. Aggressive boosterism at a time of rapid, general population growth in North Texas therefore characterized both cities, and each reaped significant benefits without being able to overpower its neighbor.[26] Dallas did, of course, finally dominate its rival. In retrospect, it appears that Dallas's businesspeople won this race by adopting a more sophisticated approach to economic development than their adversaries had.[27]

As the twentieth century began, both cities were essentially agricultural processing centers. Dallas was more committed to cotton and its by-products (for example, cottonseed oil); Fort Worth concentrated on the cattle industry and wheat. This general similarity in economic activity, however, obscured some significant, though incipient, differences in fundamental strategies. Shortly after 1900, Fort Worth's community leaders in effect announced the essential focus that would shape the city's growth until World War II. They mounted a determined and successful campaign to make Fort Worth a nationally important meat-packing center. Both Armour and Swift built major processing facilites in 1902 and 1903, which employed about five thousand people by 1914. "Cowtown" had at last created its unequivocal destiny. By 1929, Fort Worth was the state's main center of meat packing, an industry that was outranked by only petroleum refining in terms of total product value.[28]

In the meantime, Dallas's businesspeople pursued a more diversified strategy. The city strengthened its role as a cotton center. In the years after World War I, it became the largest inland cotton market in the nation. But finance and manufacturing became increasingly important to the local economy. Industrial development began as a spinoff from Dallas's involvement in cotton when, during the 1880s, local entrepreneurs started making gin machinery. Over the next twenty years, the city evolved into the second-largest center for manufacturing farm machinery in the world.[29]

Simultaneously, local financiers busied themselves with establishing a flourishing insurance and banking sector. Beginning with Praetorian Mutual Life Company in 1898, Dallas's business people went on to found such major companies as Southwestern Life (1903) and Southland Life (1908). In the meantime, the bankers were not idle. Backed by the Chamber of Commerce, they promoted an ambitious interurban rail network radiating north and south out of Dallas. As the lines progressed, representatives from the chamber made weekly excursions to every town now connected to Dallas to encourage economic ties to their city. Such aggressive marketing paid off. By 1906, Dallas was the state's most important banking center. This campaign to make Dallas a financial powerhouse culminated in 1914, when the city won an intense competition with five rivals (including Fort Worth) to become the headquarters for the Eleventh District of the Federal Reserve.[30]

As the world war approached, Dallas found itself with a diverse economic base that complemented, and would soon overshadow, its commitments to cotton. The city could offer prospective businesspeople a large pool of skilled workers and significant local financial assistance for their ventures. Unlike Fort Worth, Dallas had the capacity to deal successfully with a wide range of development possibilities. One example of this flexibility occurred in automobile manufacturing.

Late in 1909, Henry Ford established a sales and service center in Dallas. There is no explanation for his choice of Dallas over Fort Worth, but his decision hardly made any dramatic difference in the local economy, since the center employed only two men. But this operation grew rapidly, and Dallas quickly became an important market for Ford cars. Dallas next became a candidate for an assembly plant as industrial decentralization began in the auto industry. Although it is a matter of speculation at this point, the availability of a skilled labor force and the willingness of local bankers to provide funding probably helped Ford make his decision to build the city's first assembly line in 1913. Within a year, that plant was insufficient to handle demand, and a new factory replaced it. In 1925, a still larger plant was constructed. By the end of the twenties, Dallas had become a major auto manufacturing center.[31]

The Ford Motor Company's commitment to build in Dallas was symbolic of a general trend. During the twenties, Dallas became a significant industrial center, at least by southern standards. The number of manufacturing jobs doubled during the decade. Local boosters sought to solidify this boon by formally incorporating industrial development into their strategic planning. In 1928, the city's financial leaders organized Industrial Dallas, Inc., and raised five hundred thousand dollars to fund a four-year campaign to attract even more business. They did quite well. Entrepreneurs established a thousand companies in Dallas during this campaign.[32]

Diversification proved to be the key to Dallas's triumph over Fort Worth. Meat packing had two inherent limitations in generating economic development. First, the work force was essentially static. Fort Worth's single largest enterprise simply did not create many more jobs after the initial hirings. Second, the industry's product value was deceptive. Although the total value of the product seemed impressive, several other industries outranked it in the value added by manufacturing. Meat processing therefore did not generate nearly as much income as other industries might have for the local economy. In round figures, the total value of Dallas's manufacturing output was $168 million in 1929; Fort Worth's was $131 million. The value added by manufacturing, however, was $65 million for Dallas, $33 million for Fort Worth. These differences translated into growth disparities and victory for Dallas over its neighbor. In the twenty years following 1910, Dallas's population grew to exceed Fort Worth's by nearly one hundred thousand, and Dallas became the second-largest city in the state.[33]

Like Dallas, Houston had to contend with a powerful urban rival — Galveston — for much of the nineteenth century. And the Houston business elite countered Galveston's expansionist designs in much the same way that Dallas had met the challenge of Fort Worth — with an intensely cooperative effort. Time and again its civic leaders called public meetings to build a consensus around a particular agenda — the building of a deep water channel or the floating of bonds to finance a wide range of public services. Each was touted similarly: economic growth, the rhetoric ran, was a vital first step toward increased political power and social improvement. That commercial interests set the agenda around which popular support was then rallied was also part of the pattern; Houstonians were accustomed to wielding public monies to advance private gain.

The success that such a strategy brought reinforced the collective wisdom that such a strategy was indeed an appropriate response to the challenges of economic growth and urban rivalry. It also gave life to an ever-expanding boosterism that many visitors to the Bayou City found comical. "After you listen to the talk of these pioneer veterans for awhile," one noted wryly, "you begin to feel that the creation of the world, the arrangement of the solar system and all subsequent events, including the discovery of America, were provisions of an all-wise Providence, arranged with a direct view of the commercial interests of Houston."[34]

This confidence, of course, was exaggerated. By 1900, Galveston seemed on the verge of surpassing its rival to the north. But in that year Houstonians had the last laugh, for providence — in tragic and miraculous ways — seemed to have intervened in the affairs of the city. Two extraordinary events occurred between September, 1900, and January, 1901, which not only forever settled the rivalry between Galveston and Houston in the latter's favor, but also gave Houston a new economic resource that set the stage for its rise to regional (and national) prominence.[35]

In September, 1900, a powerful hurricane churned across the Gulf of Mexico, generating a six-foot tidal wave before it. Storm and wave smashed across Galveston Island, killing six thousand people and destroying thirty million dollars' worth of property. The consequences were as many as they were devastating. Although its docks were rebuilt, Galveston never regained the commerce that had once made it a major entrepôt; its economic decline was matched by a sharp reduction in the island community's population. Moreover, its vulnerability to storms only reinforced Houston's once-improbable claim that a deep water port fifty miles to the interior was essential to the Texas Gulf economy. This claim gained unexpected confirmation when in early 1901 the tremendous Spindletop oil field was brought in, followed by other major discoveries of black gold in East Texas and the coastal plain in succeeding years. Quirks of nature thus laid the foundation for Houston's economic primacy.[36]

But that primacy was not inevitable. Instead, it grew out of concerted efforts on the part of Houston's economic and political leadership to capitalize on sudden shifts in events, as a close examination of the development of the Houston Ship Channel indicates.

There is no logical (or natural) reason why Houston should have become one of the busiest seaports in the nation. That it has become so is due in large measure to the intercity rivalry between Galveston and Houston. In the 1890s, for example, Galveston secured six million dollars in federal monies to build jetties that in turn raised the level of water in its channel to twenty-five feet by 1896; Galveston was now a deep water port, and railroads in Houston began to consider building spurs to the island, lines that would have drained commerce and power southeastward. Within a year, Houston had obtained congressional approval for a survey for its own twenty-five-foot channel from Main Street along Buffalo Bayou through Galveston Bay to the Gulf. It also managed a political coup: its freshman congressman, Tom Ball, was assigned to the Rivers and Harbors Committee, which oversaw the financing of such projects. Working from within, Ball was able to keep the idea of a deep water channel afloat, and immediately after the hurricane battered Galveston, he secured a million-dollar appropriation for the Houston channel. Good luck and political skill had helped advance Houston's cause.[37]

Luck and political acumen were required in even greater measure when in 1908 the project stalled. At that point, Horace Baldwin Rice proved a worthy heir of his uncle William Marsh Rice, a man whose commercial instincts and organizational abilities had helped drive Houston's growth in the mid-nineteenth century. As mayor of Houston in 1908, Rice called a public meeting in which he proposed that the city take over the channel project. To that end, the community received the approval of the state legislature to establish a navigational district that could issue bonds. Rice and members of the Houston Business League then traveled to Washington, where they proposed to match federal funds for the channel, a unique cost-sharing plan that Congress was only too happy to accept. That source of funding secured, the commercial and political leaders of Houston sought to convince a reluctant citizenry to float $1.25 million in bonds to meet the city's share of the construction costs. Although successful in this regard, another hitch developed: few bought the bonds. Here again the civic elite stepped in. Under the direction of financier Jesse H. Jones, the major banks, whose presidents had been active in the deep water port movement, agreed to purchase any outstanding bonds, and the financial crisis was solved.[38]

The port movement was a political gamble and an immense financial risk, but it is no surprise that the city's entrepreneurial elite reacted in the ways that it did; after all, they had a long history of embarking on speculative ventures and of coordinating public and private interests to ensure economic growth and diversification. And the dividends in this case were handsome indeed. By 1914, Houston had a deep water channel to the sea; by 1920, it had surpassed Galveston in terms of tonnage and value of cargo carried; and ten years later it was the nation's third-busiest port.[39]

The importance of this channel to Houston's economic development cannot be overstated. It established the Bayou City as a significant distribution point, across whose wharves imports and exports passed. It did not remain at this level long, however. With the rapid discovery and development of the oil fields to the east, the city's economy was converted once again, this time into an industrial one, a conversion that (again) was not preordained. As Harold Platt has argued, this new level of economic activity was due to the "abilities of [Houston's] business leaders to recognize the far-reaching implications of Spindletop for the cities of the region." Drawing on eastern speculative capital, these leaders laid down the pipelines through which the oil flowed to the new refineries and the tankers waiting in the ship channel, a flow that perforce quickened during the boom in automobile production and sales during the 1920s. The profits from these ventures enabled Houston not only to far outstrip Galveston but to extend its dominance statewide, as the 1930 census revealed: in that year: Houston became the largest city in Texas.[40]

By 1930, the urban hierarchy that has since characterized Texas was set. Houston had surpassed Dallas and San Antonio in terms of population and economic power. The reasons for the continuation of this rank order for more than fifty years could also be glimpsed at that time. During the second stage of urbanization, the economies of Houston and Dallas were transformed from agrarian marketplaces to increasingly sophisticated manufacturing, industrial, and financial centers, a transformation that San Antonio did not undergo. Moreover, the economies of the two leading cities continued to expand for another (and important) reason: they were driven by the very forces that would drive the larger national economy throughout most of the twentieth century—oil, natural gas and petrochemicals, airplane and automobile manufacturing.

These industries enabled Houston and Dallas to generate such a high level of economic activity during the third stage of urbanization, dating from the late 1930s to the early 1960s, that they could create a multiplier effect: each lured new industries and spun off from old ones; each amassed larger amounts of capital to reinvest; each expanded its pool of skilled labor and management. Houston and Dallas had become, in Harvey Molotch's terms, "growth machines."[41]

The role of entrepreneurs in this new context changed in subtle and significant ways. During the first two stages, their task had been to create an urban infrastructure that was at once innovative and potent, one that fundamentally altered the city's economic base in ways that made its physical location of minor economic importance; the Houston Ship Channel and the arrival of the Federal Reserve Bank in Dallas served each city in this way. Once the entrepreneurs had set these structures in place, however, their task became one of exploiting these newfound advantages. This, too, required extensive human action and intervention, but it was on a different order from that of previous years.[42]

The building of Houston's petrochemical industry, especially the synthetic-rubber plants, during World War II is a case in point. Prior to the war, there were no synthetic-rubber plants in Houston or anywhere else in the United States; natural rubber had to be imported from Brazil or the Malay Peninsula, and neither area produced enough to meet the needs of the American war economy. This issue became critical when Malaysia was absorbed into the Japanese empire early in the war. But where in the United States would this new industry be established? Houston was a logical site for a number of reasons: it had the natural resources and refining capacity; it had the transportation and pipeline network necessary to move the various chemicals; and it had the skilled personnel to organize and operate the new industry. All of these advantages were drawn into place because of the ship channel. But logic alone did not determine why Houston became one of the leading centers of the petrochemical industry. Instead, the city's political influence was crucial.

Jesse H. Jones was the key player in this regard. Long a commercial and financial leader in the Bayou City, Jones served concurrently as the secretary of commerce and as head of the Reconstruction Finance Corporation during the war. As such, he was deeply involved in the development of a synthetic rubber industry in spite of President Roosevelt's initial hesitancy. And Houston benefited directly from Jones's actions. Federal monies were channeled to the city and its hinterland for the construction of a vast array of chemical plants and refineries, which then received large government contracts to produce synthetic rubber and other war matériel. By the late 1940s, the total investment in the Houston area neared one billion dollars.[43]

The impact of these funds on the Houston economy was profound. The petrochemical industry created thousands of jobs, the city's population grew markedly, and these people and the companies for which they worked pumped billions of dollars into the regional economy. But it is important to note that this infusion of money and population depended on an earlier transformation of Houston's economic structure. "We have the basic industries here," the Chamber of Commerce noted in 1957, "because we have the port," an observation that both acknowledged the precedent-setting nature of the ship channel and testified to the willingness (and ability) of the city's commercial and industrial elite to build on that precedent. How appropriate that Jesse Jones was intimately involved in both processes.[44]

The tradition of aggressive entrepreneurial activity and of collective risk taking that Jones (and Horace Baldwin Rice before him) represented emerged anew in the late 1950s as Houston sought to become the site of NASA's Manned Space Center (MSC). Indeed, the entrepreneurs' understanding of how to stimulate economic growth, now embodied in a collective wisdom tested over a century, was the prime reason why Houston became "Space City U.S.A." And once again this wisdom fused economic and locational advantages with intense political pressure; the latter highlighted the former, without which Houston's chances for landing the MSC would have been significantly diminished.[45]

Vice-President Lyndon Johnson and Albert Thomas, a Houston congressman, applied the most direct pressure on NASA in Washington following John F. Kennedy's election in 1960. Johnson served as chairman of the National Aeronautics and Space Council, a post from which he lobbied extensively on behalf of his state's largest city. Thomas was also strategically placed as chairman of the House Independent Offices Appropriations Committee, which was responsible for NASA's budget. He, too, proved "a veritable one-man lobby for his home city." His lobbying received the strong support of two other congressmen, Olin Teague (College Station) and Robert Casey (Houston), who served on the House Space Committee.[46]

The maneuverings of these Texas politicians in Washington dovetailed with those in Houston itself. Here, the interlocking relationship between Humble Oil Company, Rice University, and Brown and Root, a powerful Houston engineering firm, helped further set the stage for securing the MSC. One of the requirements that NASA set for the site, for example, was a thousand-acre parcel on which to build its new facility. Humble Oil donated the required acreage to Rice University, with the explicit understanding that it would be donated in turn to the MSC. George Brown, of Brown and Root, chaired the Rice Board of Trustees at the time (and was a close friend of Johnson's), and Kenneth Pitzer, then president of Rice, accepted the agreement. They then used their considerable political clout to use the land gift as bait. Houston, in short, may have had the industrial base and port facilities that NASA desired, but its elite made certain that these advantages were cast in the brightest of lights.[47]

They were, of course, rewarded for their efforts. Rice University received federal grants to underwrite graduate study in space science, Brown and Root obtained a $1.5 million contract to design portions of NASA's new home in Clear Lake, and Humble Oil developed the fifteen thousand acres it controlled around the MSC, developments in which many of NASA's work force were housed.[48]

More impressive still were the larger economic dividends that accrued from the Manned Space Center. In mid-1963, just two years after NASA decided to move to Houston, the agency spent $1 million a month in the city; one year later its salaries alone came to $3.2 million a month. These figures provide a clue to the amount of spin-off income that would be spent on housing construction and sales and must be added to the millions lavished on the development of related aerospace, computer, and electronic companies that fed off and built on NASA's presence in the Bayou City. Only then can one begin to understand why some believed that the MSC helped Houston move "inexorably across the bridge of mid-century into the inordinate frontiers of a new Time — a Time when man could leave the planet of his birth and reach out, beyond, into the distant splendor of the stars themselves." NASA's presence may well have been of stellar proportions, but it had a final set of down-to-earth consequences. Houston's economy was diversified, its regional hegemony tightened, and its national presence and power solidified.[49]

Dallas, too, sought to diversify its economy. And although that diversification enabled it to gain primacy over Fort Worth in 1930, it did not end their urban rivalry. Indeed, businesspeople in the two cities continued their intense competition, since both groups were accustomed to making possible the impossible. But there was now a critical difference. Dallas's more diverse economy produced a larger amount of capital than Fort Worth's, a situation that gave Dallas's businesspeople more flexibility and opportunities for city building than their rivals had.

Two developments in the 1930s demonstrated how Dallas entrepreneurs employed their capital advantage to solidify their position as Texas' second city. First, they solved their oil problem. Houston had risen to its preeminent status by encouraging petroleum-related industrial development. Never loath to learn from a good example, Dallas businesspeople looked for an opportunity to develop this resource in the local economy. They had one problem, however: Dallas County was one of the few in Texas without any nearby oil fields. On the other hand, Dallas had never had any significant local natural resources, and the city by now had a long tradition of ignoring such minor deficiencies. Local entrepreneurs, therefore, solved the oil problem in their standard fashion: lacking a resource, they simply bought it. In November, 1930, a group of Dallas businesspeople, led by H. L. Hunt, purchased one of the major East Texas oil fields from "Dad" Joiner, a famous wildcatter.[50]

Although in retrospect this purchase seems an eminently safe investment, at the time there was no guarantee that this particular field would be a continuing success. Doubts about the field's productivity had, in fact, prompted Joiner to sell. The purchase indicated the perennial willingness of Dallas's investors to take significant risks in city building. And in this case the gamble paid off handsomely. Petroleum became an important local industry as Dallas became a financial and legal center for oil, and local business leaders expanded on the opportunity by establishing spin-offs in oil well equipment, machinery manufacturing, and distribution companies.[51]

The other significant economic event of the 1930s had more symbolic than immediately practical applications. In 1936, Texas would celebrate its centennial, and fierce competition arose among the state's various cities to capture the exposition. Houston had a strong claim, since the San Jacinto battleground was close by. San Antonio had perhaps an even better claim as the site of the state's most famous shrine to Texas liberty, the Alamo. Dallas had not even existed in 1836. Naturally, Dallas won the competition. It did so through the same time-honored device that had characterized its growth: if you don't have it, buy it. Armed with $3.5 million that the Chamber of Commerce raised, a delegation of Dallasites descended on the state legislators in Austin and persuaded them to designate their city as the site of the centennial exposition. Not only did they capture an economic generator, but they bought some history in the process.[52]

The centennial in effect confirmed Dallas as a major competitor in the race for regional dominance. It was an enormously effective advertisement for the city's power, which was emphasized by the absurdity of holding such an event far from the hallowed halls of Texas liberty.

Although an amazing demonstration of aggressive boosterism, the lessons of the campaign to obtain the centennial were in some ways even more important than the event itself. Banker R. L. Thornton, who had been the principal influence behind most Dallas entrepreneurial ventures since the late 1920s, led the campaign. He found the effort frustrating because it involved coordinating and placating so many individuals and interests in the local business community. As in any booster group, public unity obscured internal divisions that at times impeded effective decision making. In response to this problem, Thornton sought to centralize control over Dallas's economic development. With the assistance of a few other major boosters, he created the Dallas Citizens' Council in 1937. Initially limited to a hundred members who controlled Dallas's most important businesses, the council essentially assumed control of the city's urban development.[53]

Centralized, rapid decision making quickly became an important tool in Dallas's continued growth. In the late 1930s, for example, both Dallas and Fort Worth sought to acquire aircraft manufacturing plants. By 1939, the federal government, under President Roosevelt's prodding, was beginning to invest heavily in defense industries. Part of Roosevelt's program involved a massive increase in the nation's ability to produce warplanes. Furthermore, the government was willing to subsidize aircraft production, and Congress created the Defense Plant Corporation, as part of the Reconstruction Finance Corporation Act of 1940, to build new manufacturing facilities. With the prospect of large federal subsidies and contracts on the horizon, aircraft manufacturers began casting about for suitable sites.

Since new aircraft factories could locate essentially anywhere, aggressive boosters all over the country had an extraordinary opportunity to capture a major industry for their localities. In reality, however, Texas had some significant advantages over its potential rivals. Jesse Jones, Houston's preeminent booster, was chair of the directors of the Reconstruction Finance Corporation (RFC), under whose aegis the Defense Plant Corporation (DPC) functioned; and the DPC, which spent nearly eight billion dollars between 1941 and 1945, had two Texans on its board, M. Tilford Jones (Houston) and Thomas W. Griffiths (Dallas). Although there is no direct evidence that these men conspired to channel funds to their home state, DPC funding had a distinctive pattern. Texas received funding for ninety-two projects to the tune of nearly $650 million, the fourth-largest share of DPC funds, after Michigan, Ohio, and Illinois. But what is particularly striking is that Texas is the only one of these four that could not be classified as an industrial state before the war. With these funds, it quickly joined the industrial ranks. Its boosters had clearly been busy.[54]

They were no less busy on the local level. There was, it seems, a kind of division of the spoils. Houston obtained an impressive array of petroleum-related industries; North Texas secured an equally impressive collection of airplane manufacturing plants. Dallas, after intense lobbying of the RFC directed by the Dallas Chamber of Commerce, landed North American Aviation, whose 855,000 square feet of floor space made it the "largest industrial room in the world" at the time. Embarrassed by its riches, Dallas then did the unthinkable: its civic and commercial elite supported Fort Worth in its successful bid to obtain Convair! The Citizens Council and the Dallas Chamber of Commerce also cooperated with Jesse Jones and the RFC to obtain a significant new industry whose labor needs became the basis for Dallas's population boom during the 1940s. (Fort Worth's population also increased rapidly, but not nearly enough to challenge Dallas's position as the state's second-largest city.)[55]

Following the end of World War II, aircraft manufacturing became the new core of the Dallas economy. Even though some of the larger manufacturers either closed or drastically curtailed their operations after 1945, others replaced them as the evolving Cold War created an unusual demand for investment in the nation's defense industries. Entrepreneurs seeking plant space and a highly skilled labor force found both in quantity in Dallas. Temco, Chance Vought, and Bell all established large plant operations in the late 1940s. Related industries also evolved rapidly in a classic spin-off pattern: by the early fifties, Dallas was home to companies manufacturing radar equipment, aircraft engine fuel, aircraft parts, and communications equipment. Little more than a century after its founding, Dallas had emerged as a central force in the nation's industrial economy.[56]

San Antonio could make no such claim. As a survey of its economic base in the late 1940s and early 1950s reveals, the city's function had changed little since the beginning of the century. Essentially, it had remained an agricultural service center. It provided basic livestock processing — stockyards and slaughterhouses — and a leather finishing industry (boots and saddles). It served as well as a marketing and transshipping point for these and other agricultural goods and as a distribution center for farm implements and machines manufactured elsewhere. Not surprisingly, its two major industries — the breweries and pecan shelling — were agriculture-based, and neither generated extensive investment capital nor created spin-off growth of any substance.[57]

This set of economic facts must be placed in the larger political context. Unlike Dallas and Houston, San Antonio had a profoundly divided booster community. The River City's business and political elite was incapable of creating a common economic policy for the city, one that might have diversified and strengthened its economy, because of the collective wisdom concerning the proper relationship between business and government. In Houston and Dallas, the two elements had long been fused. In San Antonio the tradition was the reverse: since the late nineteenth century, its business people had been antagonistic to government as a viable partner in economic development. Only with the establishment of the Good Government League in the 1950s would a sense of collaboration emerge, a collaboration that had been a political fact of life in Dallas and Houston for more than half a century.[58]

As this overview of pre-Sunbelt Texas urbanization indicates, entrepreneurial skill and receptivity to innovation are critical cultural variables in the character and timing of urban development. This runs counter, of course, to the argument that geography is destiny. But the irony of the history of Texas' three major cities is that the least successful of them in terms of fashioning a coherent growth strategy — San Antonio — is the only one with a clear geographical raison d'être. Neither Houston nor Dallas (or Galveston or Fort Worth) has any strong geographical reason for being located where it is.[59]

If geography is not destiny, the key to sustained, even vigorous, economic growth lies in the aggressive determination of these cities' founders (and succeeding generations) to create major urban centers despite the logic of place. This aggressiveness was intensified in Dallas and Houston because of the presence of other aggressive elites in what, in effect, were twin cities. This intensity was heightened further by the very absence of any significant geographical advantage. Thus a situation was created in which the city that lost to its neighbor would suffer disproportionately. Galveston's rapid population loss following the hurricane, the rise of Houston, and the increasing gap between the population statistics for Dallas and Fort Worth testify to the impact that economic growth (and decline) can have. And without any pronounced geographical advantage, neither city could offset its rival's continued growth. In the end, all of this gave rise to an almost perversely competitive situation, typified in the refusal of Amon Carter, a Fort Worth booster, even to buy lunch in Dallas for fear that such would help his competitor's economy. In this context, geographic destiny mattered not at all.[60]

The Texas urban experience, then, not only illuminates important theoretical issues in urban history but suggests as well that a more balanced assessment of the state's evolution is necessary. Its urban communities played a clear role in determining its economic and political structures from the very beginning. It is just as clear, however, that to achieve that balance will require more research. Only then will we fully understand and appreciate the theoretical implications and historical context of the rise of urban Texas.

Part II.

Politics and Development

2. Frugal and Sparing:
Interest Groups, Politics, and
City Building in San Antonio, 1870–85

David R. Johnson

Boosters and boosterism generally enjoy good repute among urban historians. True, boosters' exuberant rhetoric and excessive claims seem quaint, their faith in inevitable growth appears naïve to a more sophisticated era, and their enthusiasm for quick results often leaves a problematic legacy of hasty construction and poorly planned (or nonexistent) development. But their exuberance, faith, and enthusiasm encourage local pride, unify diverse social groups in a common goal, and foster a public-spirited business community. Boosterism has been, in short, an important element in the city-building process.

Groups capable of influencing local development did not spring miraculously from the founding of every city. Instead, they evolved from the elements of location, population mixture, values, and luck peculiar to specific cities. The precise nature, ability, and success of any city's booster community depends on a process of blending diverse local interest groups into a coherent whole. Since the exact combination of elements, and the ways they interacted, differed from place to place, the composition of booster communities, and their goals, displayed considerable diversity. They all wanted their city to prosper, but how it would prosper, and who would decide what constituted prosperity, varied significantly from place to place and from region to region.[1]

The peculiarities of early city building may help explain why, for example, boosters in San Antonio evolved a vision of development in which an exceptionally dominant business community displayed a remarkable complacency toward economic opportunity, a hostility to local government as a useful tool in development, and a particularly narrow interpretation of what constituted prosperity.

San Antonio in 1870 was a city trying to overcome a series of disappointments and travails. Although the oldest of the state's major cities, it enjoyed no important initial advantages from that distinction. The city owed its location to the supply and communication needs of settlements that the Spanish established in East Texas during the early eighteenth century. But those settlements never developed sufficiently to create a stable hinterland for San Antonio.

The town achieved its greatest prosperity prior to 1836, when Louisiana, temporarily under Spanish control after 1762, became a major market for Texas cattle and horses. San Antonio's population increased to roughly twenty-five hundred by the early nineteenth century in response to the needs of the South Texas ranching economy. The loss of that market after 1803, combined with the political instability engendered by first the Mexican and then the Texas revolutions, caused economic stagnation and population decline until the late 1840s.

San Antonio was too far west to benefit particularly from the influx of American settlers into eastern Texas. Galveston and Houston, both established shortly after Texas independence, moved quickly to capture those settlers for their own hinterlands. San Antonio remained remote from the mainstream of settlement until the mid-1840s. It was also hindered by a lack of a significant merchant group, a shortage of local capital, and the presence of a large, poor population of Mexicans whom Americans treated with a mixture of suspicion and disdain.[2]

Economic conditions began to improve with the outbreak of the Mexican War (1846). San Antonio's strategic position made it an important army base. After the war, the army stayed to protect settlers moving into Central Texas, and the town became a convenient supply depot for all the outposts. Simultaneously, large numbers of German immigrants began settling in the area around San Antonio. Some merchants now contracted with the army to furnish food and other sundries, which they purchased from the outlying German communities; others developed trade with those settlements for various imported goods. These economic activities helped spur modest growth, as the town's population reached thirty-five hundred by 1850.[3]

During the next two decades, San Antonio enjoyed significant growth. The surrounding German farming communities produced surpluses for export to other areas, ranching revived, and the town's location along one of the major highways to California encouraged development. During the Civil War, San Antonio's inland location enhanced its importance temporarily. Secure from any federal army, San Antonio supplied the Confederacy with meat and canned goods and shipped large quantities of cotton to Mexico. Although the rate of growth slowed appreciably during the war, San Antonio had still achieved a respectable population of just over twelve thousand by 1870.[4]

Yet all was not well with the community. The war had been costly in ways that were difficult to measure, but that would unavoidably affect the future course of development. First, it shattered the emerging booster coalition of businessmen and politicians. Some Unionists fled while local vigilantes terrorized others, creating memories that would be hard to suppress following the war. The war also seems to have suspended the orderly evolution of some community institutions. Church construction, for example, simply stopped, apparently because the tensions arising from the war crippled fund raising. Important ethnic groups, such as the German Catholics and Lutherans and the American Episcopalians and Presbyterians, lost an important focal point of community life and the city suffered a setback in the development of a coherent internal social structure. In addition, the war halted the most important development project initiated by the local boosters prior to 1860, the construction of a rail connection with the coast. The demise of this project perpetuated the principal disadvantages of the city — its inadequate transportation and communication facilities. Finally, the war left San Antonio bankrupt. Capital once again became scarce, and neither the city nor the business community had the resources to engage in developmental activities.[5]

Social geography further complicated the economic problems facing the city. Local topography had determined the initial pattern of settlement in the Spanish period. Two major waterways, San Pedro Creek and the San Antonio River, originated north and northeast of the city, respectively, and flowed south on roughly parallel lines. The Spanish had established the town on the west side of the river, between the two streams. Mission San Antonio de Valero (the Alamo) was across the river, on the east side. These dispositions influenced the evolution of housing patterns until the 1850s. San Antonio's Mexican population settled west of the river, as did most of the earliest American immigrants. Just before the Civil War the west side was therefore the more developed and, in some ways, the more prestigious area of town. Prominent merchants and politicians lived on the west side; the city's first major recreational area, San Pedro Park, was located at the source of the creek; the first omnibus line ran from the downtown out to the park; and most of the early important developers initially invested in west side land.[6]

This settlement pattern began to change as large numbers of Germans and more Americans arrived, accompanied by smaller but significant groups of English, Irish, French, and Poles. East side development began in earnest. Irish immigrants gravitated to an area immediately north of the Alamo, drawn by the prospect of jobs at the U.S. Army Supply Depot on Alamo Plaza. The Germans chose to settle along the Acequia Madre, a major north-south irrigation ditch, which bisected the entire east side. Other groups also favored east side locations, though the Americans and French tended to distribute themselves fairly evenly around the city. Blacks, whose numbers increased 230 percent during the 1860s, divided themselves evenly between the east and west sides, living in tight clusters among the white population.[7]

Important divisions within the city, rooted in ethnic settlement choices, emerged from the development of the east side. Two-thirds of the Germans, who were now the second-largest group in the city, lived on the east side; three-fourths of the Mexicans, who had dropped to third place among ethnic groups, lived on the west side. Generally speaking, the Germans were

Table 2.1

Ethnic Distribution of Heads of Household by Ward, San Antonio

Country of Birth	Westside Wards				Eastside Wards				Total	
	1		2		3		4			
	No.	%	No.	%	No.	%	No.	%	No.	%
United States	22	(26.1)	19	(22.6)	20	(23.8)	23	(27.3)	84	(99.8)
Germany	11	(14.6)	14	(18.6)	25	(33.3)	25	(33.3)	75	(99.8)
Mexico	22	(40.7)	19	(35.1)	6	(11.1)	7	(12.9)	54	(99.8)
France	3	(33.3)	2	(22.2)	1	(11.1)	3	(33.3)	9	(99.9)
Ireland	1	(14.2)	2	(28.5)	4	(57.1)	0	(0.0)	7	(99.8)
England	0	(0.0)	1	(33.3)	0	(0.0)	2	(66.6)	3	(99.9)
Poland	0	(0.0)	0	(0.0)	1	(50.0)	1	(50.0)	2	(100.0)
Other	1	(10.0)	4	(40.0)	2	(20.0)	3	(30.0)	10	(100.0)
Unknown	0	(0.0)	1	(50.0)	0	(0.0)	1	(50.0)	2	(100.0)
TOTAL	60		62		59		65		246	

SOURCE: Ten percent random sample of heads of household, Population Schedules of the Ninth Census, roll 1575, v. 2: Bell and Bexar Counties. The figure for native-born Americans includes blacks.

probably the most successful ethnic group; the Mexicans and blacks were the least successful. Contrasting levels of entrepreneurial skill, wealth, organizational ability, and, ultimately, political power combined with social geography to make the Germans the dominant element in the city and the east side the more prestigious area in which to live. Any effort to reunite San Antonio's booster coalition, reestablish its development priorities, and rejoin the race for urban dominance in Texas had to take into account the implications of the Germans' geographical distribution and economic position in the community.

In these circumstances, a booster campaign might seem precisely what San Antonio needed. By focusing on the theme of civic progress, local elites could generate a public-spirited enthusiasm that would obscure ethnic, economic, and geographical divisions and unite the community in a common goal. This apparently is precisely what Houston did immediately following the Civil War.[8] Yet it did not happen in San Antonio. Instead, San Antonians fought among themselves for several years over the nature of their community and who would control it. When a coalition of interests finally emerged to dominate local affairs in 1875, ethnic values and ambitions, and Reconstruction politics, combined to shape a very different community ethic characterized by a remarkable absence of public spirit and by intense conservatism.

The search for a booster ethic that most San Antonians could embrace began in November, 1867, when the military governor of Texas dismissed the elected city council and replaced it with Republican appointees. For the next five years, the Republicans tried vainly to establish dominance over San Antonio's political and economic development. In the process, they propounded a series of ideas and concrete programs that provoked opposition from various quarters. Eventually, the diverse elements of the Republicans' opposition recognized their common interests and combined.

At the outset of this process, however, neither the Republicans nor their opponents were particularly well organized. The Republicans faced the formidable tasks of building a viable political party and gaining community acceptance; the opposition, particularly the Democrats, had to find ways to frustrate the Republicans without being able to defeat them at the polls (no elections would be held until 1872).

Reliable Republicans were rare in San Antonio. A few devoted party men, such as A. W. Kempton, arrived soon after the war. Kempton's personal history is obscure, although he served in the Union Army, rising to the rank of captain. He was an extreme partisan and a firm believer in Negro rights. James P. Newcomb and Edward Degener represented two other sources of Republicanism in San Antonio. A native Texan, Newcomb held outspoken Union views that had made him persona non grata in 1861. He spent the war in California, where he acquired Radical Republican beliefs. Returning to San Antonio, Newcomb became a major figure in the local and state party. Degener emigrated to San Antonio from Germany. A Unionist like Newcomb, he lost two sons in a famous massacre perpetrated by local Confederate troops during the war. Personal tragedy, and a commitment to Negro suffrage and universal public education, made Degener a partisan Republican.[9]

Local Republican leaders like Newcomb and Degener probably expected a great deal of support from San Antonio's German community. Superficially, that seemed a reasonable expectation. Like many other cities, San Antonio had returned a large minority vote against secession. Local lore held that German voters had been primarily responsible for that vote. Then, too, a vociferous group of Forty-Eighters had briefly attracted attention for their antislavery views, and other Germans supported women's rights.

But such behavior did not necessarily mean that the Germans would automatically vote Republican. Unionist sentiment, for example, was not necessarily any stronger among Germans in Bexar County than among other ethnic groups. Prominent German community leaders, such as Edward Braden, Gustav Frasch, and John H. Kampmann, all of whom were born in Germany, served in the Confederate Army. Kampmann even raised his own company. Most Germans were hardly abolitionists, nor were they particularly interested in civil rights for blacks. Events would demonstrate that San Antonio's Germans were primarily interested in advancing their own economic and political power, regardless of partisan considerations. In short, the Republicans' hold over these voters depended on whether the party's programs and policies conformed to German perceptions of their own best interests.[10]

Realistically, though, the Republicans had no practical alternative to tying their fortunes to the German community. Every appeal to native-born American or Mexican voters and community leaders failed. In an attempt, for example, to attract capable men into the party, the Republicans swallowed their partisan pride and appointed Democrats and former Confederates to office. But these appointees, either through prior design or because of pressure from colleagues, promptly resigned. While frustrating the Republicans' recruiting efforts, these resignations also served to paralyze local government. Lacking a quorum at council meetings, the Republicans could not enact important legislation. [11]

In these circumstances, it is not surprising that the Germans dominated local government during the so-called Republican era in local politics. After numerous attempts to create a balanced city council, the Republicans settled for a situation in which all the aldermen came from the east side. Five of the eight were native-born Germans, giving them the major role in deciding policy issues. [12]

The German's ability to dominate local affairs considerably complicated Republican efforts to implement the party's program of economic development for San Antonio. American Republicans like Newcomb, J. S. Lockwood, and Samuel G. Newton wanted to stimulate the local economy by reviving a railroad project for San Antonio, building a streetcar system, and establishing a Board of Trade. None of these projects succeeded. Memories of previous problems with railroads, combined with an ongoing, bitter lawsuit against the city over payment of bonds on the defunct road, apparently made it impossible to stimulate any interest in this project. Streetcars would have facilitated neighborhood development and increased land values, but the corporation that Newcomb established to build the system needed council approval to begin operations. The council never even debated authorization. The Board of Trade, founded by three important Republicans in 1872, did not require council blessing, but it did need the business community's support. None was forthcoming. [13]

Economic development did not cease simply because the Republicans could not implement their agenda. German businessmen rapidly transformed Commerce Street, the city's major commercial artery, into their private preserve. The council quickly granted requests for improvements along Commerce, supervised construction, and upheld property owners' claims against the city whenever potential losses from street realignments occurred. [14]

In addition, the council acted promptly to deal with situations involving the German community's other economic interests. Many German merchants, for example, maintained profitable relations with the U.S. Army's Quartermaster Depot. When the local military commander threatened to move the depot to New Braunfels in 1868, a council delegation immediately promised to provide better facilities for the post. This initiated a seven-year search for a new base site, which culminated in the creation of Fort

Sam Houston—located, as it happened, on the far east side of town.[15]

Finally, the council proved anxious to please the Agricultural Association of Western Texas. This organization, which began operations in 1868, consisted overwhelmingly of German and southern white (primarily Democratic) merchants who intended to coordinate and control the development of the city's rich agricultural and livestock resources in its hinterland. When the association petitioned to use San Pedro Park as the site for its annual fairs, the council not only granted the petition, it voted to pay for improvements to the park that would facilitate the association's activities.[16]

The local Republican party thus consisted of two unequal parts: a small group of non-Germans and a much larger number of elite German businessmen who controlled city government and implemented their own agenda. This was an inherently unstable situation. When the minority group made the fatal mistake of injecting ideological issues into local politics and proceeded to threaten German control of local government as well, the precarious coalition disintegrated. A new coalition emerged, one that was more balanced and representative of key interest groups and therefore more stable.

It is unclear from the available evidence why the non-German Republican minority introduced ideological issues into local politics. James Newcomb's personality may have been critical. Newcomb was an impassioned man who consistently espoused extreme views.[17] Furthermore, as secretary of state in the Radical administration of Gov. Edmund Davis, he had the power to implement his ideas. The precipitating event was a new city charter for San Antonio in 1870. Newcomb apparently wrote it; only three or four close political asociates saw the draft; and the legislature passed it without scrutiny or debate.[18]

Most provisions of the new charter embodied fairly standard clauses regarding typical urban housekeeping functions. There were exceptions, however. First, the charter eliminated elections for a number of citywide offices and gave the council power to appoint them instead. Newcomb doubled the tax rate (to one percent on a dollar of assessed value); he created a separate Public School Board with taxing authority; he gave the mayor and the council enormous power to supervise elections, including the power to declare an entire ward's vote invalid in certain circumstances; and he authorized the council to regulate public morality, especially with regard to gambling, dancing, and drinking. He envisioned, in short, a much more energetic and intrusive form of government with an enhanced revenue base to fund its expanded powers.[19]

The new charter aroused immediate opposition rooted in a profoundly different perspective on the role and scope of government in urban life. Many Germans and southern Democrats suddenly found that they had a great deal in common. Public education, for example, had never been a high priority for southerners. San Antonio's Germans had maintained their own school since 1858, and had no desire to send their children any-where else. Local German Catholics were particularly adamant on this point.[20]

Government regulation of public morality also stirred opposition. San Antonio's Episcopalians and Presbyterians, who were predominantly south-erners, could join Irish and German Catholics and German Lutherans in a minimalist approach to political meddling in moral issues.[21] Higher taxes angered the business community, which consisted overwhelmingly of south-erners and Germans.[22] Finally, the arbitrary imposition of a charter that increased the power of the local authorities deeply offended conservative beliefs in democratic processes and minimal government.[23]

Opposition to the new charter was not long in coming, once its con-tents became known in the late summer of 1870. In mid-September, the rabidly Democratic *San Antonio Herald* issued an editorial appeal to local citizens "to rid themselves of the incubus of an enormous taxation, which will paralyze their energies, depopulate our fair city, and pauperize them-selves and families" by supporting repeal of the charter.[24] A day later the *Herald* announced a meeting to adopt resolutions denouncing the charter. Phrasing its announcement in strictly ideological terms, the paper urged attendance by "all those who believe that the people of a republican gov-ernment should have something to say in the adoption of a city charter that imposes city officials upon them without their votes of consent, and who are authorized to tax them to such an extent that many of them may see their goods and chattels, land and tenements sold from under them, and their families starve for bread."[25]

Not surprisingly, the results of the meeting mirrored the *Herald*'s sen-timents. A Resolutions Committee presented a series of objections, ob-viously prepared in advance, that denounced the charter. These resolutions, which the meeting adopted without significant debate, asserted that a new charter was unnecessary and condemned the secrecy surrounding its adop-tion as "contrary to a due sense of propriety, and in violation of the rights of a free people governed by a Republican form of Government." Further-more, the charter granted powers that, "if exercised, oppress, harass, and injuriously affect the material prosperity of our people,—the system of taxa-tion therein provided for approaching the standard of confiscation."[26]

This meeting marked a major turning point in local politics. Prior to 1870 San Antonio's southern community had cooperated with the Ger-mans in economic development through their mutual participation as di-rectors of the Agricultural Association and local insurance companies. Now they united against the charter, with the Germans assuming the major burden in organizing the opposition. Of the twenty-seven men who exer-cised leadership roles in the meeting, fifteen were German, and a majority of them were prominent businessmen. The other twelve participants, while coming from a variety of ethnic backgrounds, were either important businessmen or leading Democratic politicians.[27] Newcomb's charter had precipitated a new alliance in local politics and had, in the process, given southern Democrats the ability to influence council policies even though they did not hold office.

Over the next two years the German-Democratic alliance managed the city's affairs, paying little attention to the fact that the Republicans officially controlled local government. Following a presentation of the anti-charter meeting's resolutions, the council promised to ignore the most obnoxious provisions of that document.[28] The alliance was also able to undermine one of the Newcomb charter's key reforms when the state legislature agreed in 1871 to eliminate the Board of Education and return control over the public schools to the council (which ignored the schools for the next four years).[29]

Republican conceptions of public morality also came under attack. In February, 1871, Mayor W. C. A. Thielepape fired city marshal A. W. Kempton, one of the few real Republicans in the administration. The new marshal, a southern Democrat, had made no effort to prevent the reopening of the gambling houses that Kempton had closed—a pointed reminder, if any was needed by this time, that Republican views enjoyed little support.[30]

Kempton's dismissal provoked a confrontation between Newcomb Republicans and the city. Governor Davis refused to recognize Mayor Thielepape's authority to fire Kempton; the mayor refused to keep Kempton as marshal. The controversy simmered through the summer, reaching a crisis in September. Newcomb wrote a letter to the council challenging its right to appoint city officers. The council retorted with a letter signed by every alderman and the mayor defending its prerogatives. Governor Davis stepped into the fray by issuing a marshal's commission to Kempton. When the council balked at this, Davis requested the resignations of the entire city administration.[31] Davis's action provoked a German threat to abandon the Republican party. August Siemering, editor of the *San Antonio Express* and the *Freie Presse* and a major spokesman for San Antonio's Germans, warned Newcomb that "this city is still a Republican community and will support the Governor and the Administration, if the Governor will let us settle our little local affairs. If not, we must do the best we can. But I see breakers ahead."[32]

Fearful of losing German voters, Davis temporarily backed off, but Newcomb continued to look for ways to reassert Republican authority in the city. He compiled more evidence of German duplicity in the months following the September confrontation. Local correspondents kept up a steady stream of complaints against Thielepape's administration, pointing to a "truckling spirit," which pandered to the interests of Germans and Rebels to the detriment of true Republicans.[33]

Finally, in March, 1872, a temporary political contretemps provided a convenient excuse to purge the administration. The council had approved the purchase of some valuable land at the source of the San Antonio River from George Brackenridge, an extremely powerful local banker. Brackenridge had demanded an extortionate price, and the council's action caused an uproar. Governor Davis intervened once again, replacing Thielepape and almost all the aldermen. The new administration retained a strong contingent of businessmen, but there were only three Germans on a council that now had a more reliably Republican character.[34]

Newcomb's victory was short-lived. After five years of rule by fiat, the state government had finally authorized local elections for fall, 1872. With the elections at hand, the German-Democratic alliance began organizing its return to power. During August and September, it established Democratic/Liberal Republican Clubs in every ward.[35] In mid-October their city convention nominated François Giraud for mayor and George S. Deats for recorder. Giraud, a civil engineer from Charleston, South Carolina, and Deats, a craftsman from Louisiana, represented the southern interest group in the German-Democratic coalition. At least four of the eight alderman candidates were Germans, with the others representing the various ethnic and economic groups among local southerners and Democrats.[36] Shortly after this convention, prominent Germans called a separate meeting of their community. Raising the banner of nonpartisanship, they announced that "as true and sound republicans" they would support only those candidates who possessed "unquestionable honesty and general business capacity." This meeting then endorsed the Democratic/Liberal Republican ticket, with just enough exceptions among alderman candidates to demonstrate the independent nature of the coalition.[37]

The regular Republican and Democratic parties made feeble attempts to present separate slates for this election. But their candidate selections indicated the futility of their efforts. The Democrats endorsed Giraud, Deats, and four of the Democratic/Liberal Republican alderman candidates. Partisan pride may have prevented a similar capitulation among the Republicans. They slated only two Democratic/Republicans on their ticket and nominated Samuel G. Newton for mayor. Since Newton had been Governor Davis's choice to replace Thielepape the previous March, his nomination indicates an extraordinary insensitivity to the undercurrents of local politics. The Republicans were apparently convinced that the average German voter would refuse to support his community leaders in the election.[38]

Not surprisingly, the Democratic/Liberal Republicans swept the elections, losing only one alderman contest, and that to an independent German candidate in the Fourth Ward.[39] This election effectively ended any hopes the Republicans had to become a major party in San Antonio. Hereafter, local Republicans would be reduced to scurrying about in search of temporary alliances with various disaffected groups, none of whom would have sufficient electoral support to create a viable basis for a Republican resurgence. And this defeat also marked the end of any role Republican concepts of urban development might have played in the future of the city.

The November, 1872, election nevertheless continued the contest between partisan and coalition politics for control of San Antonio's development. With the Republicans reduced to impotence, Giraud's administration supervised a transitional period in which the regular Democratic party fought the German-southern business elite for dominance. This struggle lasted for the next two years, culminating in the triumph of coalition politics.

For the moment, however, the agendas of the two groups coincided fairly closely. Both supported charter reform, a resolution of the city's fiscal problems, and some systematic approach to urban improvements.[40] Charter reform, as the issue that had roiled the waters of local politics for two years, had the highest priority. Shortly after the November election, the new council authorized appointment of a citizens' committee to draft amendments to the Newcomb charter. Working through the following spring, this committee finally proposed changes reflecting local interpretations of general republican beliefs in fiscal restraint, the nature of public service, and accountability. The city was restrained from borrowing *any* money without a referendum; aldermen were to serve without pay, since the office was one of "trust and honor only"; and there would be four aldermen per ward, with elections for two of them to be held every other year.[41]

To the chagrin of its supporters, the committee's amendments died in political turmoil in Austin. Unfortunately, the precise reasons for this defeat have not survived. But there is some evidence that the defeat occurred because of tensions between the factions supporting the Democratic/Liberal Republican coalition. The committee, in an interesting move, had recommended contracting San Antonio's city limits. Several powerful landowners had exerted pressure to redefine the boundary to place their properties outside the city, and hence beyond the reach of the city's taxing authority. All the property involved lay on the west side of town; all the landowners (with one exception) lived on the west side. The amendment redefining the city's boundaries, in other words, reflected the continuing struggle between the east and west sides of town for precedence, with west side developers seeking personal advantage from charter reform.[42]

Although this was hardly a unique phenomenon in urban politics, it proved fatal to this reform effort. The legislature rejected the amendments. When the news reached San Antonio, local reaction apparently focused on the role the boundary line played in the rejection, possibly exacerbating east-west political relations in the process.[43] The reformers resubmitted the amendments, but the Senate, in a departure from standard practice, rewrote them. Even that did not avail, however. The negotiations and rewriting consumed so much time that the amended charter reached the governor too late for his signature, the legislature having adjourned. Or so he claimed. Edmund Davis was still governor, and he may have used a technicality to strike back at the San Antonians who had caused him and his party so much grief.[44]

This defeat delayed charter reform until 1874. Learning from their previous mistakes, the council avoided any overtly controversial proposals and excluded private citizens from the deliberations. A committee of one alderman from each ward plus the city attorney prepared a series of amendments that proposed three aldermen for each ward (with one elected annually); made most citywide offices elective rather than appointive; established a limit on the city's bonding capacity (with concomitant provisions for sinking funds and special tax assessments to create such funds); and addressed various minor housekeeping functions. These changes became effective following a local referendum in December, 1874.[45]

As the Democratic/Liberal Republican coalition struggled with charter reform, it also wrestled with the city's fiscal problems. The council's financial policies and practices since the Civil War had been chaotically contradictory. At the close of the war, the city found itself essentially bankrupt because all its assets had been invested in Confederate bonds. The council's efforts to rectify the situation had encountered a variety of obstacles. Businessmen frequently protested the size of the annual license tax, which was supposed to be a major source of revenue. Other taxpayers simply refused to pay their assessments, which created a sizable list of delinquents by 1875.[46] But the council also contributed to the problem. Despite uncertain revenues, the aldermen displayed a casual attitude toward expenditures. They authorized projects that curried favor with business (such as localized street and drainage improvements), assumed the debts of the fire companies, and, most amazing, in one case compensated a businessman for a fire loss amounting to five thousand dollars. When revenues failed to equal expenses, the aldermen simply authorized the mayor to borrow enough from local bankers to meet current obligations, usually at 12 percent interest.[47]

This cavalier attitude on the part of delinquent taxpayers and aldermen created a large debt by 1872, although precisely how large no one could say. Undeterred by the lack of accurate information, the Giraud administration released a statement on the city's financial condition soon after assuming office. Since the statement dealt only with receipts and expenditures during Samuel Newton's brief mayoral term, it appears to have been an attempt to discredit Republican policies and, at the same time, to create a rationale for greater fiscal restraint in the new government.[48]

Discrediting the previous administration proved easier than mastering the city's budget. The council had to cope with the consequences of the accumulated debt at the same time that it attempted to restrain spending. In these circumstances, it needed strong leadership and agreement among the members about priorities.

The east side German community apparently intended to provide the leadership in Giraud's administration, using the council's Finance, Ways and Means Committee as its base of power. Because it proposed bond referenda, reviewed the costs of improvements, and supervised city accounts, Finance was the most powerful committee in the council. Following the uproar over Newcomb's charter in 1870, Mayor Thielepape had split the membership of this committee equally between the west side's heavily Democratic Ward One and the east side's German-Republican Ward Three. Since Giraud's administration was simply a formalized continuation of the previously unofficial cooperation between the Germans and the Democrats, it would have been reasonable for both to continue sharing power on the Finance Committee. But it was not to be. As a disgruntled Republican remarked to Newcomb, "The Dutch . . . can not be depended on unless they have their own way entirely."[49] It would appear that at least part of the Germans' price for their participation in Giraud's coalition was the Finance Committee. He appointed only east side Germans to the committee in January, 1873, giving them the dominant voice in any attempts to impose fiscal restraint on the council. Although there is no direct evidence of the Democrats' reaction to this coup, it was not a division of the spoils likely to elicit favorable comment from them, especially considering the committee's previous composition.[50]

With Finance firmly under their control, the Germans quickly assumed a leading role in establishing an agenda for the administration. On the same day that Giraud made his committee appointments, alderman Alex Michel, now on the Finance Committee, sponsored a resolution directing the Improvements Committee to report a general plan for public improvements. This resolution, whether deliberately or not, effectively upstaged alderman Joseph Sweeney, a Democrat from Ward One, who proposed a special committee to report on a general system of waterworks and irrigation, a necessary, but much narrower, priority. Sweeney's proposal passed; Michel then offered his resolution, making Sweeney's idea superfluous when it also passed. The coalition's partners do not seem to have been consulting one another very effectively.[51]

Ordinarily, committees acted on council resolutions within a month. In this case, however, the Improvements Committee did not submit a response for six months, an unheard-of delay. Since Giraud had carefully balanced this committee to represent the geographical and political elements of his coalition, the long delay implies that the committee had difficulty reaching a consensus. Part of the difficulty may have derived from the unique task before the committee, since this was the first attempt to establish a planning document for urban improvements. But the delay also implies a struggle between the competing agendas of the coalition's partners.

The committee assigned the highest priorities to improving transportation and communication within the city; it allotted second place to flood control and drainage; and it recommended the creation of a water supply system. Specific "wish lists" balanced development projects for the east and west sides. Thus the committee suggested that each section of town should have a major north-south thoroughfare, and that the principal east-west streets should be macadamized. Drainage problems on both sides of the river received equal attention. Predictably, the committee endorsed a program to pave streets in the business district. On the other hand, there was a hint of the stress involved in balancing demands in the committee's support of flood control measures for both areas of town. The west side suffered far more from flooding, but the committee endorsed a large project for the east side as well. And the east side won a clear victory in the recommendations on the placement of bridges. The committee suggested two: one across the river on the north side, to connect the east side to the city's stone quarries to reduce construction costs; the other across the river on the far south side, to facilitate communication between the First and Fourth wards. If actually built, the northern bridge would be an important stimulus to east side development. Finally, the committee split on the issue of a waterworks, saying that a private company could provide the service, although "it would probably be more advantageous to the City to own the works."[52]

Despite the delay, and the hints of problems of balancing sectional interests, this blueprint was an important new step in the evolution of a nonpartisan German-southern business coalition that combined a concern for economy in government with an interest in planned development. As a statement of intentions, its specific recommendations were less important than the fact that such a plan existed. Local politicians and businessmen had not had such an organized conception of government's role in development since the aborted Republican program. With its provision that particular parts of the plan would not be implemented until funding became available, it allayed the concern over an aggressive taxation policy, which had played such a key role in the Republicans' demise. This plan, in sum, defined the initial parameters of the emerging booster coalition's ambition.

The council's unanimous adoption of the plan in July, 1873, however, marked the end, not the beginning, of coherent policy making during the Giraud administration. Parochialism and financial problems effectively blocked implementation. The aldermen seemed unable to resist authorizing highly localized improvement projects. Even before the council received the plan, the east side aldermen managed to obtain approval for street improvements in their area. Since the city had no funds to pay for these projects, the council continued its past practice of issuing bonds to the contractors, adding to the city's growing debt for the sake of sectional advantage. This incident hardly inspired restraint among west side aldermen.[53]

In these circumstances the Finance Committee's efforts to create a semblance of order in the city's finances suffered innumerable setbacks. Even simple accounting procedures were lacking. The committee achieved an important reform in September, 1873, when the council approved an ordinance dividing the city budget into two separate categories (special and general funds) for the first time.[54] At least the committee now had a fund reserved for paying the interest and principal on the debt. But after July, the council blithely ignored its own plan, adding to the debt with notes and bonds to "pay" for local projects. Furthermore, tax delinquency remained a major problem, and the shortage of cash forced the council to borrow money just to meet payments on notes and bonds that fell due periodically. Hoping to gain control over the debt problem, the Finance Committee finally obtained council approval in June, 1874, to issue sixty thousand dollars in thirty-year bonds, using the proceeds to redeem all the city's notes and short-term bonds.[55] Further financial reform had to wait for a change in administration.

As the January, 1875, elections approached, the Democratic/Liberal Republican coalition unraveled. The reasons for this remain obscure, since the individuals involved were not prone to offer public or private reasons for events. Yet the split became obvious by their actions. For the first time since 1867, the Democrats eschewed coalition with the east side Germans and presented a complete slate of candidates on strictly party lines.

The Democrats did not completely ignore the Germans, however. Gustav Friesleben, city surveyor since 1857, received the nomination for that position again. Friesleben, however, lived in the Second Ward and was closely associated with west side developers. Furthermore, twice as many citywide office nominations went to west siders as to east siders. The Democrats did nominate two east side Germans for aldermen in their respective wards. But the other four aldermanic nominations on the east side went to non-Germans. If we extrapolate from this pattern of nominations, the Democrats appeared determined to reassert partisanship in local politics and west side dominance in the perennial conflict between the city's two sections.[56]

The demise of the Democratic/Liberal Republican coalition provided an opportunity, however, for the various elements of the city's booster community to coalesce behind their own candidates and programs. Meeting in early January, the Bexar County Republican Committee voted to turn itself into a "nonpartisan" citizens' organization to nominate an Independent ticket.[57]

Party affiliations mattered less to the Independents than a commitment to a particular vision of community development. Virginian James H. French, the Independent candidate for mayor, was a Democrat from the west side who had actively supported the Confederacy; Tennesseean Theophilius G. Anderson, candidate for recorder, lived on the east side and belonged to one of the few Radical Republican families in town; Julius Hoyer, the German-born candidate for collector from the east side, had served in city government throughout the Civil War.[58] The remainder of the Independent ticket had equally diverse backgrounds. As a group, these candidates belonged, as did the Democrats, to the local elite. But the Independents did offer the voters a slate that was more representative of the various economic, political, and ethnic interest groups throughout the city than did the Democrats. Although the Herald promptly branded the Independents a Radical Republican front, subsequent events would make it clear that this was the last stage in the evolution of a booster coalition pursuing the goals of fiscal restraint and orderly development in a nonpartisan framework.[59]

The election was not an outright triumph for the Independents. Democrats won three of nine city offices and seven of twelve alderman positions. French edged out W. R. Knox to become mayor, winning by only 122 votes out of 1,926 cast.[60] If anything, the election demonstrated the persistence of the east-west split in the city and the importance of a balanced ticket to overcome sectional divisiveness. Democrats could count on overwhelming support in the First Ward; Independents thoroughly dominated the Third Ward. The other two wards wavered in their preferences, perhaps responding as much to a candidate's personal popularity as to his political affiliation. In this election, the Democrats did well in both wards, especially in the alderman races, but the vote totals were very close and certainly offered no grounds for complacency (see table 2.2).

When the government convened following the elections, then, the Democrats held nominal control of the council while the Independents dominated the citywide offices. These results reflected the differing strengths of the two parties. Both represented essentially conservative attitudes toward government and development. The Democrats, however, were relatively more parochial and hence less interested in general programs of community evolution, whereas the Independents had a broader perspective and expected government to cooperate with business to develop the city. As the new government commenced operations, the key issue was which variety of conservatism would dominate public affairs.

A direct confrontation between the Democratic majority and Mayor French settled that crucial question less than a month later. The Democrats, headed by Trevanion T. Teel, immediately challenged French's right to recommend patronage appointments to various offices. Teel insisted that the mayor had to submit the names of everyone who applied; French insisted that he would only submit those he deemed qualified. Asserting their majority, the Democrats passed an ordinance limiting French's appointive powers. French vetoed it, pointing out that the charter defined his authority in these matters. Teel's Democrats retaliated by defeating the first nominations French submitted.[61]

Table 2.2
Percentage of Vote Received by Winning Candidates, San Antonio, 1875

		West Side Wards		East Side Wards	
Office	Party	1	2	3	4
Mayor	I	29.16	47.87	68.13	59.16
Collector	I	33.05	51.93	67.83	67.84
Recorder	I	33.61	52.80	72.90	64.59
Treasurer	I	30.83	51.16	70.90	61.50
Marshal	I	30.89	49.22	64.57	49.26
Physician	I	33.61	48.52	71.30	63.44
Attorney	D	75.56	66.99	39.20	52.11
Street commissioner	D	73.74	59.53	45.34	42.10
Alderman					
Place 1	D	72.45			
Place 2	D		65.73		
Place 3	I			84.34	
Place 4	D				55.13

SOURCE: Calculated from election returns, Council Minutes, Journal D, January 15, 1875.

NOTE: The alderman returns are calculated for each party's slate in each ward; although the Democrats carried three of four wards, two of their candidates would desert the party to support French on the council.

But then Democratic opposition suddenly crumbled. The reasons for this collapse remain unclear, but the Democrats' parochialism may have been their undoing. French nominated Teel's brother for the important post of west side market master, for example. Ethnic antagonisms may also have obscured party loyalty, as the Germans, regardless of formal affiliation, voted for or against candidates depending on their nativity.[62] Whatever the cause, French emerged the victor. And so did nonpartisanship. Throughout the remainder of French's long tenure as mayor (until 1885), party affiliations had no decisive role either in appointments or in policy matters.

Having survived the most important challenge to his authority and to his approach to governing, French turned his attention to implementing the agenda of the booster coalition. There would be some changes in detail, but the basic blueprint derived from the 1873 plan. And just as the goals remained the same, so did the problems. The council still lacked a sense of fiscal responsibility; the city was still short of money; the debt continued to increase; improvements still occurred piecemeal.

French became the first politician to confront the disparity between booster aspirations and council behavior directly. Compared to his predecessors, he was an unusually active mayor who clearly intended to impose his will on city government and urban development. He did not always succeed, in part because of his own flaws, but also because the particular variety of boosterism that sustained his coalition for ten years placed limits on its expectations regarding the ways San Antonio should develop.

Throughout his tenure as mayor, French attempted to lead by defining the council's basic agenda and, by using his veto power, to keep the council from straying too far from his objectives. Annual messages, heretofore an occasional event, became a fixture that French used to establish priorities and suggest solutions to fundamental problems. He began by grappling with the perennial problems of servicing the debt and financing public improvements. In April, 1875, French surveyed these topics in a message that revealed the basic ideological assumptions of the booster coalition as well as the coalition's commitment to procedural regularity and fiscal restraint.

French announced that the city's debt amounted to nearly eighty thousand dollars (not including thirty thousand dollars in bonds the council had issued to pay for local contracting work). More than half that sum was due in 1875. The mayor suggested that the council could meet its obligations either by issuing bonds or by raising taxes. Having presented the options, French expressed his preference. Noting that a tax assessment would fall exclusively on property holders, he argued that "business or trade is interested more particularly in good government, and the protection which such necessarily affords; therefore, [it] is and ought to be required to pay its full share of the expenses pertaining to its proper administration, and it would seem both unwise and unjust to ask that it contribute also to the permanent improvement of the city." Furthermore, French asserted that "an increase of revenue [which would occur through a tax to pay the debt] would lead to extravagance, and once this tax is levied, it would be found very difficult to dispense with it."[63] In sum, French was expressing the view that the general public should assume the cost of public improvements and that tax increases, even for specific purposes, should be avoided because government was inherently incapable of restraint. These ideological assumptions would pervade his entire tenure as mayor.

Having made clear his general preferences, French endorsed a bond issue, but he also recommended that the council adopt more rigorous budgeting techniques. Specifically, he suggested that the council estimate the annual cost of each item in the budget, appropriate that amount, and prohibit transfers of funds from one account to another. In an important victory for fiscal planning and restraint, the council approved French's recommendations by an overwhelming eleven to one vote.[64]

French kept a tight rein on the council's freewheeling spending tendencies thereafter. The Finance Committee was his principal ally. As in Giraud's administration, the east side dominated that committee, holding four of its five seats. (Three of the aldermen represented the Third Ward, the booster coalition's most important source of support.)[65] The crucial confrontation between past spending habits and French's program of restraint occurred in July. Ignoring, as usual, the city charter, which required special assessments of property owners to pay for public improvements, the council passed an ordinance authorizing a number of street projects. French vetoed the ordinance, using the occasion to criticize the council's entire approach to improvements: "If the Charter which requires that a due proportion of the cost of any such improvements shall be paid by the parties benefited, is to be ignored entirely, the grading and macadamizing of Streets will continue to be controlled by favoritism, and made too often without regard to the financial condition of the City or to the interests of its citizens." A motion to override the veto lost when the council failed to muster the necessary two-thirds vote. Four aldermen supported French; all were members of the Finance Committee. After the motion to override lost, alderman William Prescott, of the Finance Committee, moved that all street improvements be halted for the fiscal year. His motion passed with two-thirds of the votes in favor coming from the Finance Committee.[66] Threatened with this moratorium, the council capitulated. Within a month, it passed an improvement package that included a special assessment for the first time, establishing another standard practice regarding city development.[67]

Standardization indeed became another major theme of French's first year in office. Previous administrations had paid little attention to basic procedural matters; French did so with a vengeance. The council adopted procedures for passing ordinances, rules governing its meetings, regulations dealing with official misconduct, and ordinances defining the duties of several city officials.[68]

In the meantime, the council also addressed other important issues relating to urban development. The city offered a contract to build a waterworks to a New York company. After some months' delay, the company declined because it disliked the terms of the agreement. This rejection delayed construction of a waterworks for two more years, but when a local company finally built this utility, the booster coalition had implemented a key element of the 1873 plan.[69] With the waterworks project temporarily suspended, the council granted a franchise to construct a street railway system to August Belknap, a New Yorker who had recently moved to San Antonio. Although the first line did not begin operating until 1878, the council had at least initiated another important stimulant to local development.[70]

French had an extraordinary first year in office. No previous council had done so much to standardize government operations and restrain expenses. By the end of the year, the budget was under control, the debt had actually declined by nearly a third, and there was a surplus in the city treasury.[71] Much remained to be done, though, and it is unfortunate for the city that 1875 marked the high point of French's tenure as mayor rather than the beginning of a major effort among local boosters to promote further community progress. Such an effort never materialized because of the peculiar characteristics of the coalition that had made French's election possible.

The coalition that supported French and the Independents tended to draw its membership from the more successful German and southern American merchants, proprietors, and professionals in San Antonio. In the 1875 election, for example, 52 percent of the Independents, but only 38 percent of the Democrats, were merchants or proprietors. I could not determine the occupations of almost a quarter of the Independents, compared to over 40 percent of the Democrats — suggesting that the Democrats were less prominent men. The Independent ticket, with its careful balance of the east and west sections of the city, compared to the Democrats' bias toward the west side, again indicates that the Independents had created a coalition united by a shared vision of how the city should develop.[72]

But that vision now became a problem for San Antonio. The coalition supported administrative and budgetary reform, planning of a sort, and some types of development projects. However, the coalition did not intend that this program should encourage an activist local government, and, perhaps more astonishing, these boosters did not envision themselves as assuming an active role in urban development either. Committed to their own self-aggrandizement, they had, with few exceptions, no particular interest in contributing to the well-being of the entire community.

Nothing better illustrates the lack of public spirit among this booster elite than the issues of San Antonio's first railroad and taxes for public improvements. Rail connections with the coast and the north had long been San Antonio's most conspicuous deficiency. Without a railroad, the city could not hope to compete with its regional rivals for population and urban power. Local businessmen, however, had little interest in such matters. Following the abortive effort to build a line before the Civil War, they simply abandoned further efforts, leaving the task to any outsider who cared to try. Content with military contracts and their trade with local ranchers and farmers, businessmen, with few exceptions, steadfastly refused to interest themselves in a railroad project. Of the 115 men who were most active in local economic and political affairs, only 7 played any role in bringing the first railroad to town in 1877, and the nature of their contribution is instructive. None purchased stock in the road or served as company officers. Instead, they sent emissaries to assure the Bostonians that San Antonio indeed desired a railroad. When the road came within thirty miles of town, the Boston syndicate demanded that San Antonio at least contribute something to its completion. Only then did a few businessmen organize a public meeting to endorse a bond referendum for the railroad. In sum, local businesspeople displayed a stunning indifference to promoting the most important source of growth the city would acquire in the nineteenth century.[73]

These same businessmen, however, exhibited a far more aggressive attitude toward taxation. French himself expressed the coalition's basic approach to taxes in his financial message to the council in 1876. Stressing the need to be "frugal and sparing," he declared that "situated as we are it becomes our bounden duty to use every effort to keep down and even reduce taxation."[74] Low taxes remained his passion for the duration of his service as mayor, and he did succeed in reducing the tax rate by 25 percent in 1878.[75] In contrast to the discredited Republican program, the booster coalition now in charge of local government intended to keep annual taxes as low as possible, shifting the burden for public improvements onto future generations through bond issues.

Unfortunately, this policy did not work as well in practice as the coalition expected. Most of the problem derived from members' own unrelenting demand for tax relief. Despite French's continuous campaign to restrain expenses, pay off the city debt, and reduce taxes, many members of the coalition remained unsatisfied. Their dissatisfaction created a serious political crisis, undermined the city's credit, and crippled the council's ability to use bonds to pay for improvements.

The crisis apparently originated in the booster coalition's combined fears of a resurgent Democratic party and the potential effects of the national depression on San Antonio in late 1878 (ironically, within a month of French's tax reduction). In late November, a group of fifty-four businessmen organized the Taxpayers' Association to deal with these problems.[76] Like the Independent coalition, the Taxpayers' Association drew its members from every ward in the city. A survey of the residential pattern of the association indicates, though, that the Third and First wards led this revolt. Eighteen members of the association lived in the Third Ward, sixteen in the First. Residents of the Fourth Ward displayed the least enthusiasm for the association, contributing only seven members. (Ward Two contributed thirteen; I could not identify the residences of two members.[77] The city's key economic and political activists provided the leadership, with twenty-four of them joining the association and dominating its decisions.[78]

By mid-December, the association had defined its goals, announcing demands for a reduction in salaries for city officials and a charter amendment to restrict bonding capacity to ten thousand dollars a year. Most astonishing, the association announced that it would campaign to reduce the city limits. This last idea demonstrated an extraordinary passion for economy in government. San Antonio's struggle to keep pace with the growth being generated by the railroad would be resolved by the simple expedient of ignoring it.[79] Intending to implement these goals by capturing control of city government, the association endorsed a ticket to oppose French in the upcoming election.[80]

The association suffered a crushing defeat at the polls in January, 1879. None of its candidates won. But the victory of French's coalition, which now seemed to have embraced several Democrats, concealed an important shift in voting patterns. The First and Third wards reversed their previous allegiances. Until 1879, the Third Ward had been a bastion of strength for the Independent coalition. The coalition again carried the Third comfortably, but suffered a dramatic drop in the percentage of the vote it attracted. French, for example, had won the Third with 68 percent of the vote in 1875, and 73 percent in 1877; this time he drew only 53 percent. The First Ward, stubbornly Democratic until now, shifted dramatically into the Independent column. French had never received more than 30 percent of the vote; in 1879 he won 65 percent of the ballots cast. Similar voting shifts occurred for the other candidates on French's ticket. Furthermore, these changes were permanent. In subsequent elections, the Independents' greatest victory margins came in the First Ward, while the Third became increasingly unreliable, signaling a discontent with the Independent coalition that created difficulties over public policy during the remainder of French's years as mayor. Even in defeat the Taxpayers' Association had had a significant impact on local politics.[81]

Unable to oust French, the association switched tactics. A delegation asked to consult with the council regarding city affairs. French headed a special committee for this purpose, and although no record of their discussions has survived, the association apparently managed to neutralize any potential council opposition to its plans to lobby in the state legislature for charter amendments.[82] The association must have received a friendly reception at Austin, because in April the legislature approved charter amendments that reduced the number of elected city officials from nine to four, gave the council power to appoint the other five, and restricted the city's bonding capacity to ten thousand dollars a year. (It is unclear what happened to the association's demand for a reduction in the city's boundaries.)[83]

These amendments represented a resounding victory for the association. Previously, its members had essentially been only one interest group within the Independent coalition and had had to negotiate with the other elements in the council to achieve their goals. Their successful lobbying in the state legislature now gave priority to their views on local government. Economy descended with a vengeance.

Within a year the city's finances were in shambles, and public improvements ground to a halt. Hard times had provoked a fourfold increase in the amount of tax delinquencies, requiring the council to borrow just to pay expenses. The restriction on bonding capacity undermined the city's credit, as the financial markets displayed an unwillingness to lend money under these circumstances. After two years of surpluses, the budget showed a deficit, a problem that became typical after 1880.[84]

Not surprisingly, French abandoned his annual practice of defining priorities in public improvements, claiming instead that there were no improvements of pressing importance. Perhaps venting his frustration, he did, however, warn the council that

San Antonio cannot afford to be a laggard in the race of progress. She has been sleeping for more than a hundred years, and to cities, like individuals, opportunities seldom come more than once. The idea of making our city attractive to strangers by beautifying our parks, improving our streets and sidewalks, furnishing to our people those conveniences which modern society demands, not as luxuries merely, but as the very essentials to comfort and health, is one that is gradually impressing itself upon our people."

Having delivered his lecture on the necessity of improvements, French concluded with an announcement that he did not intend to seek reelection in 1881, an indication of his bitterness over the consequences of the Taxpayers' Association's success in the legislature.[85]

French's threat to step aside could not conceal, indeed it reflected, the fact that the interest group favoring economy had triumphed over the faction supporting planning and public improvements in the Independent coalition. Strapped for revenue, rigidly confined in its bonding capacity, city government ceased to play a significant role in urban development while French remained mayor. Now a subordinate instead of an equal partner in the coalition, the group interested in developing the city's infrastructure could occasionally obtain council consent for referenda on bond issues to fund ambitious plans for street improvements, sewers, and drainage projects. Without the support of their economy-minded partners, however, they could not obtain voter approval of these plans.[86]

Responding to popular opinion, and to the views of the now-dominant partner in the Independent coalition, the council usually refused to authorize even minimal improvements unless the property owners affected would agree beforehand to a special assessment. The initiative for improvements thus passed to private citizens, who steadfastly refused to agree to any assessments. One irate property owner even challenged the city's right to make such levies in a court case that was not decided in the city's favor until 1884.[87] In the meantime, the lawsuit made the council even more cautious in its approach to improvements.

Most San Antonians apparently did not mind unpaved streets, massive mud holes, unlighted avenues, and numerous other inconveniences. They welcomed growth, but did nothing to promote it or to provide for it. French, in one of his most acerbic moods, defined the essential qualities of the local booster mentality. Returning once again to his concern about the relationship between continued growth and improvements, he ventured the opinion that, "if we are to continue to grow in population, and become a prosperous city, those so materially interested in its growth and prosperity must realize, ere it is too late, the necessity for making some sacrifices." He warned against the prevailing habit of "relying upon the enterprise and energy of others" and predicted that without some local initiative the current prosperity would recede, leaving the city "to the fate that has overtaken so many cities in the past, struggling on in the slough of despond, but still proclaiming to the world the natural advantages of San Antonio."[88]

Complacency, an indifference to economic opportunity, nonpartisanship, and a commitment to economy in public affairs had become the prevailing characteristics of San Antonio's booster community.[89] The long struggle to define priorities and determine the role of government in local development had ended. Although there would be occasional departures from these attitudes, they constituted the fundamental consensus among San Antonians as to the proper attitudes toward growth and the uses of government well into the twentieth century.

This consensus emerged just as the city was entering the most sustained period of growth and prosperity in its history. Growth validated the wisdom of the booster consensus: there was no need to change fundamental assumptions, because the city was destined for greatness. Furthermore, the type of growth that occurred did not alter the essential character of San Antonio's economy. The city continued to be a service center supplying the needs of an agricultural-ranching hinterland. Although regional and national developments probably dictated San Antonio's economic functions at this time, the city's continued focus on service activities helped reinforce the particular assumptions and values that had already evolved into a coherent vision of San Antonio's destiny. The relatively simple economic structure associated with service functions precluded the emergence of a more complex economy and social structure. In the absence of social and political complications that characterized more complex urban economies, San Antonio's booster community did not have to confront contrary visions of local development.[90]

In these circumstances San Antonio's businessmen played a more prominent role in social and political affairs than was true in multifunctional cities. Elsewhere, businessmen had to compete for control of public policies with a wider range of interest groups. San Antonio's business community had to deal with some potentially divisive local issues, such as the insistence of the Germans on a very large role in local affairs. But a fortunate congruence of ideological perspectives eventually overcame this particular problem. Southern-born Americans discovered that San Antonio's German population generally shared their views on the role of government in local development. Such shared perspectives made nonpartisanship a natural mechanism to unite the two groups, perhaps not accidentally resolving the east-west split in the city. Nonpartisanship as a tool to win control of, and then dominate, government further reinforced the preeminence of business by undermining the role of political parties as independent actors in the process of guiding local development. In the absence of serious competition, local businessmen therefore assumed command of the city's destiny.

Their dominance, however, created potentially serious problems regarding San Antonio's future development. When growth faltered, as it did after 1910, the booster community had no effective response, because the assumptions underlying its consensus were incapable of generating responses appropriate to adversity. Handicapped by their own version of development, they could only await another round of outside intervention to resuscitate growth, which obviated the necessity of reexamining their fundamental assumptions.

3. Boss Tweed and V. O. Key in Texas

Amy Bridges

A Reformer is one who sets forth cheerfully toward sure defeat.
— RICHARD S. CHILDS

In its city politics as in everything else, Texas is part Old South and part Sunbelt-Southwest. In *Southern Politics* (1949), V. O. Key described the political life of the former Confederate states, noting that the most important characteristic of the Old South was that it was solidly and exclusively Democratic. The absence of party competition led to fluid if not chaotic factionalism, highly personalized politics, and bizarre coalitions. In this setting, it was difficult for voters to relate candidacy to platform and, even when they could, it was almost impossible to throw the rascals out. The raison d'être of this system was the exclusion of blacks from the electorate; the consequence — belying the presence of populist rhetoric — was a conservative regime in which elections could not serve popular purposes.[1] Like the rest of the South, Texas and its cities were bastions of Democratic fidelity, the white primary, the poll tax, populist rhetoric, and conservative policy.

The cities of Texas also shared a pattern of political development common to the urban Southwest. Just as the big cities of the Northeast and Midwest have commonly been governed by political machines, and the cities of the South by Bourbon Coalitions (affluent whites and blacks), the cities of the Southwest have boasted a distinctive style of local politics. It is in the Southwest that the municipal reform movement had its greatest triumphs in the Progressive era. Since that time, citywide elections, nonpartisanship, and commission and council-manager governments have been the rule not only for small cities (as in other regions), but also for big cities. If elsewhere municipal reformers have been confined to smaller cities or condemned to valiant but futile opposition, in the urban Southwest good government advocates have ruled for generations.

The course of reform governance in the urban Southwest may be broken into three periods: from the turn of the century to World War II, from World War II to 1976, and from 1976 to the present. It is fair to say that the cities of the Southwest were politically founded in the Progressive era. Between the turn of the century and the First World War, Houston, Fort Worth, Austin, Dallas, Oklahoma City, Tulsa, Phoenix, San Diego, San Jose, and Albuquerque first incorporated, enacted new city charters, or were given new city charters by their state legislatures. Like the best-known case of municipal reform, Galveston, nearly all of these cities adopted commission and, later, city manager charters (or some combination).

Reform charters created an environment that made political organization building difficult and so promoted political disorder. The result, just as in the one-party politics of V. O. Key's South, was a bewildering array of factions and personalities, transient alliances, and picturesque demagogues. These last, like the men of *Southern Politics,* offered populist symbols in a repressive environment. At the same time, there continued to be opportunities for petty corruption, for collusion among city officials and real estate or utility interests, for the political use of municipal employment, and for courting the disadvantaged. So, like Boss Tweed, the occasional politician of insight might triumph over institutional adversity. (Tweed, after all, was never mayor of New York City, although he was surely its reigning politician.) By the trust other politicians might put in his good word, Tweed constructed a "ring"; by the thoroughness of his use of municipal employment, he built an organization; by his solicitousness for the outcast, he organized intense popular support. In varying proportions, then, from city to city, politics in the Sunbelt looked before World War II as if Boss Tweed and V. O. Key had gone west.

The cities of the Southwest were refounded in the years immediately following the Second World War. Between 1945 and 1955, San Antonio, Houston, Albuquerque, San Jose, Phoenix, and Dallas adopted new reform charters or witnessed other significant regime changes. These new regimes served as the basis for most textbook accounts of municipal reform. In Phoenix, the Charter Government Commission, in Albuquerque, the Albuquerque Citizens' Committee, in San Antonio, the Good Government League, in San Jose, the Progress Committee, and elsewhere in the Southwest similar organizations dominated local government for two or three decades. Small, efficient, and largely concerned with orderly growth, these governments were popular among middle-class and affluent voters. Nonpartisanship, citywide elections, and more directly exclusionary rules minimized the representation of other potential constituents and kept their dissatisfactions from becoming effective political demands. These governments actively recruited industry and investment from elsewhere in the country, aggressively annexed suburban territories, and unabashedly pursued growth as their first priority.

Both the structure and the priorities of those governments provoked political opposition. Opponents of growth voted down bond proposals and argued that small was better. Civil rights advocates demanded greater representation for people of color, different growth priorities, and redistribution to provide schooling and services more equitably. In 1976, the U.S. Department of Justice declared that San Antonio's annexation of suburban areas was in fact a discriminatory effort aimed at keeping Anglo voters a majority in the electorate. The department required that San Antonio change to a district system of representation. That change ushered in the third era of politics in the Southwest, one of greater representation of people of color and changed governmental priorities as a result.

While the reform governance of the postwar era and the civil rights revolution of the last ten years have received some scholarly attention, the early years of municipal reform in the Southwest have been, for the most part, neglected.[2] And it is with those years in Texas, when municipal reformers had triumphed de jure but not de facto, that this chapter is concerned.

In the Progressive era, cities across the nation embraced municipal reform. Galveston's adoption of commission government was the first recognized success, giving Texas a special place in Progressive lore. The leaders of Texas' cities were eager, moreover, in the pursuit of Progressive goals. The League of Texas Municipalities held meetings and published a journal, *Texas Municipalities,* to spread the gospel of reform. *Texas Municipalities* and the annual convention of the league served as forums for discussion of issues like utility regulation, growth strategies, sanitation, and the appropriate division of labor between the Chamber of Commerce and City Hall (the former to "create sentiment" and the latter to "execute the plan as a result of the sentiment").

Galveston, because it was one of the first and because of the spectacular circumstances in which reform was adopted and implemented there, influenced both Progressive thinking and the choices of other southwestern cities. After Galveston was devastated by a hurricane in 1900, prominent citizens on the Deep Water Committee drafted a plan for a new and businesslike administration. Under the auspices of the commission government they created, these men rebuilt the city into a port. The achievements of Galveston's commission government were trumpeted at the National Municipal League meetings in 1906, in *Harper's Weekly, McClure's,* and elsewhere. As Bradley Rice puts it, "Galveston's contribution to municipal reform . . . temporarily became the core of urban progressivism."[3] Galveston having shown which way the wind was blowing, cities across the Southwest to the Pacific followed the path it had set, adopting similar charters.

The rapid adoption of reform government across the Southwest and in smaller cities elsewhere has been explained in a number of ways. For some time, of course, there existed a well-financed movement promoting municipal reform. Samuel Hays, James Weinstein, and I have argued that this movement was pioneered, organized, and funded by business leaders whose goals were centralizing administration, limiting their tax burden, rationalizing land use, and controlling municipal finance. Over time, a corps of professionals—planners, engineers, political science professors, journalists, and newspaper editors—emerged as a kind of reform intelligentsia, writing model charters, advocating reform governance, chronicling its prog-

ress, and developing professional knowledge of good administrative practice. Municipal reform found broader support among ordinary citizens for
the goals of efficient methods, lower taxes, and an end to corruption. In
the older cities of the Midwest and the East, anti-immigrant sentiment also
played a role in constructing reform sentiment.[4]

In addition to the sustained efforts of urban elites and the impact of
Galveston's success, regional factors play a role in explaining the spread
of reform. For the older cities of the Northeast and Midwest, it is usually
argued that entrenched machine organizations, to which immigrant electorates were fiercely loyal, succeeded in staving off the assaults of well-heeled
reformers. It follows that in the Southwest an electorate more homogeneous,
more conservative, and more probusiness provided an environment that
was hostile to machine building but that enabled municipal reform to
flourish.[5] Similarly, it has been argued that the realignment of 1896, not
well rooted in the West, meant that strong parties failed to emerge there,
resulting in a greater "regional receptivity to reform" in the Progressive
years.[6] Political culture and the national party system, then, reinforced one
another to produce in the Southwest a region of cities almost exclusively
governed by reformers.

A third explanation, like the second, focuses on the place of the Southwest in the national political economy. In an excellent and suggestive study
of charter reform in Houston, Harold Platt argues that those business
leaders who wished to integrate Houston more closely into the national
economy were the greatest advocates of municipal reform. In Houston and
elsewhere, moreover, reformers were met with accusations that they were
funded by, or tied to, eastern financial interests. In the absence of further
investigation, one does not know if these accusations were merely recur-
sions to populist rhetoric or had some basis in contemporary fact. The
municipal government preferences of eastern bankers are, however, beyond
doubting, and it may be that the small but hopeful cities of the Southwest
were particularly vulnerable to pressure from those who they hoped would
invest in their industry, their transportation systems, and their municipal
services.[7]

Even in the Sunbelt, however, reform government was a contentious
proposition. Galveston itself provides good evidence of this. The Galveston Plan was a portent of things to come not only as a case of successful
reform, but also for the kinds of opposition it aroused. Some who opposed the Galveston Plan voiced apprehension about "rich man's government." In fact, the men of the Deep Water Committee did own a controlling interest in the city's banks and corporations and in much of the city's
real estate as well. More emphatically, the plan was opposed as undemocratic. As proposed — and as implemented at first — the commissioners in
Galveston's new government were appointed by the governor. This provoked one politician to claim that the plan "disfranchises free citizens of

Texas, destroys the right of local self-government, violates the Constitution of the States, holds in derision the Declaration of Independence, [and] tramples underfoot the fundamental principles of a free republic." More succinctly, the plan was denounced as "receivership in disguise."[8]

Even when commissioners were elected, commission government was opposed as unrepresentative, because ward representation was replaced with citywide elections. For example, in Albuquerque the *Morning Journal* argued that under the mayor-council system, the working person could "go to his alderman and secure anything in reason for his ward," while under the proposed commission plan, worker and neighborhood would not be represented. For this and other reasons, the *Journal* opposed the commission plan, fearing domination by the "silk stocking" Fourth Ward. Similarly, Hispanic politicians cautioned their constitutents that the influence of Spanish-speaking voters would likely decline under commission government.[9]

Opposition to city manager government was more vitriolic. Like opponents of commission government, opponents of city manager plans feared "big business in the saddle" and, with more emphasis, the undemocratic character of an appointed executive. In Austin, city manager government was called "kaiserism";[10] in San Diego, the manager was called a "Czar";[11] in Houston, the prospective manager was likened to Hitler and the plan called the "German Plan." One Houston attorney insisted that "the city manager form of government is an infant species of dictatorship," while a local pastor urged the people of Houston not to "vote away their right to vote."[12]

In the face of this sort of opposition, reformers turned to state legislatures to secure reform charters. Both Galveston's commission plan and, four years later, a similar charter for Houston, were awarded by the Texas legislature. In the case of Galveston, the governor made clear that without the new charter no aid would be forthcoming from the state administration.[13] Similarly, California's cities were required to be nonpartisan, and Oklahoma's cities were awarded charters by the state government shortly after Oklahoma joined the Union.[14]

Moreover, where localities did pass judgment on reform charters, electorates were quite small. Everywhere, as the cities of the Sunbelt were founded, suffrage was radically restricted. Texas provides the most straightforward example. The poll tax, enacted in 1903, slashed the number of registered voters in Houston from 76 percent of the potential electorate to 32 percent.[15] California enacted a literacy test in 1896, and Arizona and Oklahoma entered the Union with a literacy requirement for suffrage,[16] requirements that one suspects particularly disenfranchised the Spanish-speaking and the poor.

In sum, reform government in the Southwest was not the simple product of political culture and consensus (as little is, of course, in politics).

There was a constituency for reform, but there was also strong opposition. There were, moreover, many whose opinions were not solicited, since they were excluded from political life. This being the case, it should not surprise us that reformers did not succeed at institutionalizing municipal reform.

The business leaders who organized reform government, the citizens who supported it, and the intellectuals who propagandized for it shared a vision of what it should look like. In this vision, the abolition of ward representation and parties broke the link between particularistic citizen demands and municipal government. The reduction of the role of the mayor to merely ceremonial — where the office continued to exist at all — did away with opportunities for demagoguery. City managers, appointed rather than elected, were to be "removed as far as possible from the immediate effects of public opinion."[17] Municipal employees were to be hired on merit not because of political persuasion. City councils were to be the architects of broad policies, while city managers planned coherently, administered professionally, provided city councils with a range of efficient options for realizing their policies, and were consistently frugal. Confident that the creation of new institutional arrangements would bring all else to pass, reformers campaigned for new charters, saw them enacted, and retired from politics.

At least in Texas, the immediate effects of reform in the first decade of the century were dramatic. The abolition of ward representation and restricted suffrage, taken together, changed the composition of city councils. In Galveston, at-large election of councilmen after 1895 "effectively ended Negro participation in Galveston's city government" and returned three men who carried the city but not the ward in which they resided.[18]

More profoundly, new charters altered the balance of political power. Before 1900 in both Galveston and Houston, citywide labor organizations were influential and important in city politics. Moreover, these white organizations were allied with black labor organizations.[19] Even a generation after reform government was established, labor had not reestablished such a political role. Citywide elections also changed both representation and rewards. In Houston it was claimed that at-large elections not only resulted in different officials than wards would have elected, but also skewed policy outcomes. Testifying before the Houston Charter Commission in 1938, one commissioner argued that, while residents on the south side of town supplied four-fifths of the city's tax revenue, a like amount or more of the city's expenditures were lavished on the neighborhoods of the north and east.[20]

Reform charters did, as reformers intended, make the construction of a centralized and dominating political machine nearly impossible. Nonpartisanship created an environment in which unity among politicians was very difficult to achieve; in Texas, one-party politics had the same effect. In both the commission form and later, under city manager charters, the tendency to disorganization and factionalism was extremely strong. Across the Southwest, a profusion of transient alliances, factions, and "rings" governed with little consistency and few notable politicians. In Phoenix, "a curious combination of big city bossism and Old West frontierism" characterized city government for decades.[21] In San Diego, "each election was a free-for-all, with independent candidates enlisting as much personal support as possible."[22] In Albuquerque, "the uproar and confusion of factionalism engulfed" the early years of the city manager plan.[23] Hastily constructed alliances were offered to citizens as the "independent ticket," the "People's ticket," the "citizens' ticket," the "charter ticket," the "progressive ticket," the "nonpartisan ticket," or, on a more boosterish note, tickets like "Greater Albuquerque," "Forward Dallas," "Onward Austin," and so on.

The commission form of government was, in addition, subject to quite straightforward politicization. In the pure commission form, citizens elected, citywide, the heads of city departments. Citizens in Austin, for example, elected five commissioners who headed the Departments of Parks and Public Property, Streets and Improvements, Police and Public Safety, Finance, and Public Affairs, the head of the last also serving as mayor.[24]

Commissioners inevitably became closely associated with their service-providing bureaucracy. Services provided won friends among citizens and among the firms most closely concerned with departmental work. Employment opportunities provided the material for construction of personal machines. This was the situation in Dallas, for example, which had nonpartisan commission government from 1907 to 1931. In the genteel language of a proreform observer, "It was common practice for [each commissioner] to depend for political support on his departmental subordinates." Similarly, he went on, the commissioner was bound to court the favor of "those pressure groups that had a direct interest, usually a selfish one, in his work."[25] In Houston, commissioners became so closely associated with the services they administered that even when the city abandoned this form of commission government, councilmen persisted in playing their old roles. As one explained to the Houston Charter Commission in 1938, if citizens continued to expect council members to help them with their utility or paving or sewer problems, the hapless politician could only — as a responsible public servant — respond. That this built his personal following among the people was simply the side effect, an unintended consequence, of his desire to do good.[26]

San Antonio exhibited just such a pathological institutionalization of commission government. Created in 1914, the commission rapidly passed from control by reformers and their allies to control by professional politicians. Many of these had long been active in San Antonio politics; indeed, they were part of the very political organization reformers wanted to replace. Without civil service regulation, the skillful use of patronage enabled the commissioners to build an unbeatable machine. By 1930, this government's inability to provide adequate infrastructure or services to the growing city provoked dissatisfaction. Intermittent reform insurgencies interrupted ring domination on occasion, but San Antonio's reformers did not successfully organize for sustained political work—and a city manager charter—until after World War II.[27]

Failing to halt the collusion of city officials and interest groups, the courting of constituent interests, or patronage employment, the commission form also failed to provide for centralization or leadership, encouraging instead entrepreneurialism among the commissioners.[28] There was conflict among commissioners for budget shares and over the boundaries of departments. Worse, elections hardly secured competent administrators, since voters were not able to judge managerial ability. At best, collusion among commissioners might create a "ring" that governed coherently; more often, competing cliques and individuals worked to keep themselves in office.[29] In Denver these and other problems converted the city's businessmen from procommission reformers to advocates of the old strong mayor form in just three years. The *Denver Times* summarized their judgment: "The return of [the boss] may mean 'one man' power, but that is better than no-man power."[30] Elsewhere, commission government was longer-lived, but gave rise to the same dissatisfactions and a search for an alternative.

The alternative and common successor to commission government was the city manager plan.[31] City manager government, if not subject to the same forms of politicization as commission government, was nevertheless equally difficult to institutionalize. City councils were loath to give up the prerogatives to which they were accustomed, and war with managers was the common result. Phoenix, for example, had thirty-one managers in thirty-five years,[32] and Oklahoma City had fifteen managers in thirty-nine years.[33] In Albuquerque, the city council insisted on interfering with municipal administration. At times, council members' resistance to manager government was manifested by their refusal to search for a qualified manager, appointing instead local men who might not be qualified but who could be expected to be cooperative. On other occasions, the council did appoint qualified men, who quickly quit in disgust.[34] Similarly, San Diego had four city managers in three years. There, too, the city council showed little disposition to bring the charter to life, alienating those managers who hoped to take their executive responsibilities seriously. As the *San Diego Union* commented, the City Council functioned as "a group of co-equal and rival city managers, each eager to have a finger in every pie."[35]

This political disarray created opportunities for able politicians. Moreover, while it was possible early in the century to restrict the electorate radically, over time the local electorate became both larger and more diverse. This, too, presented possibilities to skillful political leaders. In San Jose, the "Bigley Machine" governed for nearly a decade and a half; in Austin, Andrew Zilker coordinated governance despite a series of charter changes, and Tom Miller served as mayor into the postwar era. In Dallas, briefly, J. Waddy Tate provided leadership under the commission form. In Albuquerque, Clyde Tingley dominated commission government from 1923 to 1946 (except for 1934–38, when he was governor). Most impressively, in Houston, Oscar Holcombe dominated city government for three decades, despite charters that created environments hostile to centralization.

These men presented a populist image of themselves as friends to organized labor and people of color. All were openly opposed to commission and then manager government. None were ignorant of the political uses of municipal employment, and each of the Sunbelt centralizers used federal resources generated in the New Deal years to build personal and political support. Holcombe, Miller, and Tingley ensured their dominance of city politics by pursuing growth strategies that courted not only the kind of small business owner always dependent on city government (like tavern owners) but also the sort of far-seeing (and wealthier) business leader whose economic stake was in planning, real estate, and growth.

Oscar Holcombe was far and away the most successful urban politician in prewar Texas. He dominated his city for nearly three decades by organizing massive popular support and conducting administrations efficient enough to stave off, for a generation, another round of reforming zeal. Holcombe first served as mayor in 1921 and left that office for the last time in 1957, having served as mayor for twenty-two of the intervening thirty-six years. This period embraced massive political changes in both nation and state, and several charter changes in Houston. Houston had a commission form of government until 1942, when it adopted the city manager form. Holcombe was relentless in his opposition to the manager charter. Echoing labor's claims that the city manager form was undemocratic, Holcombe campaigned in 1946 that "Tammany Hall has never had a more subservient and obedient 'puppet government' than this inner circle of the Charter Committee machine has inflicted on Houston during the last four years." The hand-picked candidates of the Charter Committee, he continued, "will . . . owe their allegiance, not to you, the people, but to their . . . master minds, the inner circle of the Charter Committee political machine."[36] Elected mayor in 1947, Holcombe declared that he had received "a mandate . . . to no longer be governed by all of the cumbersome and impractical limitations and restrictions of the city manager system" and pledged to ignore the charter to the extent he legally could. Houston, Holcombe insisted, was too large to be governed "by the city manager part time remote control system."[37]

Holcombe had strong ties to organized labor and to the black community, and on at least one occasion won the endorsement of the city's Spanish-language press.[38] In the 1920s, Holcombe had endorsements from a long list of unions.[39] His opposition to city manager government allied him with organized labor for the next two decades. Holcombe was also solicitous of the black community, supporting the United Negro College Fund and promoting Texas State University for Negroes. Blacks were also included in Holcombe's efforts to provide services for Houston. In his 1946 campaign, Holcombe boasted that he had built or obtained as gifts to the city Jefferson Davis Hospital, Tuberculosis Hospital, the Children's Tubercular Hospital, and Houston Negro.[40] The next year, Holcombe testified before Congress in favor of expanded funding for public housing to solve the "daily growing . . . problem — our slums and the great number of people forced to live in them."[41]

Holcombe was also a skillful booster of Houston, traveling to St. Louis and Rocky Mountain cities to promote Houston's virtues as a port. More, he was a pioneer in appointing a planning commission for Houston as early as the 1920s. His campaigns consistently stressed public improvements to accommodate growth: roads, bridges, water plants, a new farmers' market, sewers, expanded fire protection. In this vein, Holcombe was as comfortable with reform rhetoric as any member of the Charter Committee, claiming in one reelection campaign, "By your votes you . . . employed me as manager of this great business institution; now comes the time for the biannual meeting of the stockholders of the corporation of Houston."[42] Nevertheless, the form should not be mistaken for the substance. Holcombe carefully surveyed municipal employees, offering pledge cards (with union labels!) which they might "just sign and return."[43]

In Austin, Andrew Zilker, and later Tom Miller, played roles comparable to Holcombe's. If Holcombe was a political fox and progrowth centralizer, Zilker was a self-made man who shared his wealth with the community and directed its politics from behind the scenes. Austin changed from mayor-council government to commission government in 1909, and adopted city manager provisions between 1924 and 1926. Zilker exercised influence in all three regimes. He held office under the first, was important to the Yett administration (1919–26) in the second, and organized the election of a protégé as mayor during the third. Like Holcombe, Zilker opposed municipal reform and allied himself with those antagonistic to it.[44]

Under the mayor-council government, Zilker's own ward, and political stronghold, was the Tenth. One anecdotal index of popular attachment to the old mayor-council government and Zilker's political forces is that the Recreation Department's boys' club was still called the "Tenth Ward Club" twenty years after the Tenth Ward was done away with. More generally, "ward and neighborhood patriotism" persisted well beyond the time when they corresponded to real political boundaries.[45]

Like Zilker, Tom Miller came from a lower-class family (and also from a neighborhood that felt unrepresented under the manager plan).[46] Miller was both prolabor and pro–New Deal, strengthening ties to the union movement.[47] Both Zilker and Miller solicited the support of Austin's black community.[48] The contrast between the political elitism of the first city manager and the populism of Miller, Zilker, and their allies could hardly be more pronounced. "Shocked by the [politicians'] practice of speaking at Negro churches," the manager "resentfully" compared their electoral support for Miller and his political friends "with that of the rats to the Pied Piper."[49]

Miller first campaigned for the city council in 1933. In that year, reformers ran a "City Ticket" and the opposition a "People's Ticket." The City Ticket campaigned in radio speeches, although City Ticket candidates themselves did not address the public. Rather, City Ticket supporters and sponsors urged the electorate to vote for City Ticket candidates. By contrast, the People's Ticket began its campaign with mass meetings at which candidates spoke to the public (later, People's Ticket candidates also made radio addresses). Miller argued in his own behalf that his home was built by union labor and that the workers in his employ were paid well. After the People's Ticket won, Miller was elected mayor by the City Council.

Under the charter, the mayor had "no regular administrative duties," nor did the mayor have a veto. Instead, official obligations were ceremonial. Nevertheless, Miller was clearly the center and driving force of the government. He served as mayor until 1949, and again from 1955 to 1961. His good relations with the city manager, his prominent association with powerful Democrats like Roosevelt and Lyndon Johnson, and the excellent ratings on Austin's bonds were symptomatic of his able reconciliation of the demands of reform tenets, economic growth, and popular support.[50]

While Miller had important characteristics in common with other centralizing politicians in the Southwest, Austin during Miller's mayoralty realized reform government to a greater extent than did Houston. It might be said that Houston and those cities that suffered from disorder and factionalism created — from a reformer's point of view — pathological institutionalizations of reform politics. By contrast, Austin, by accommodating those social forces reformers usually antagonized, created a government that came closer to reformers' hopes. Over the subsequent decade, there was political learning on both sides. On the one hand, politicians reconciled themselves to a political system with fewer opportunities for patronage appointments, gaining in exchange command of a government with a much larger budget for municipal improvements. On the other, the city's most ardent reformers and boosters learned to broaden their appeal. For example, to secure a majority for a large bond issue, reformers promised (and delivered) streets and sewers to Austin's black neighborhoods.[51] Moreover, once Miller and the City Council worked out a settled division of labor with the city manager, business leaders, and reformers were content to return from campaigning to private pursuits and allow politicians to govern, secure that "their interests [were] not threatened."[52]

In all of this Austin was the exception, at least for the moment. It was, perhaps, however, an indicator of things to come, for if Sunbelt reformers were defeated, they were neither cheerful nor secure that their interests were safe. In the 1940s, there was another round of reform campaigning and charter revision. So it may be said that, in the years immediately following the Second World War, the cities of the Sunbelt were refounded, and the reign of Boss Tweed and V. O. Key brought to an end. That, of course, is another story.

This preliminary account of the first two generations of reform government in Texas and, by extension, in the Southwest, adds some regional balance to our knowledge of city politics and provides a portrait of early reform governance.

Reform charters came into existence across the Southwest not because of cultural disposition or political consensus, but under circumstances that gave reformers the political advantage. For historical reasons, the party system of 1896 was not (outside of Texas) strongly rooted in the region, which eliminated the strongest barrier to reform, party organization. In Texas, one-party politics accomplished that which weak party organization accomplished elsewhere. Moreover, features common to the political systems of the southwestern states — restricted suffrage and state intervention in local government — facilitated reform victories. Finally, it is possible that the small but ambitious cities of the Southwest were particularly vulnerable to the political wishes of the eastern institutions whose capital was so dearly needed for growth. Thus the establishment of reform governments reflected the regional political economy more strongly than it did popular political sentiment.

Those who fought for municipal reform desired orderly growth and efficient administration. To those ends, they sought to loosen, if not to sever, the ties of politicians to popular groups and to institute businesslike management practices. Broadly speaking, since reform government was not the clear choice of the majority, and since reform charters inadequately provided for representation, reform was institutionalized in ways heavily dependent on "extraconstitutional" devices to organize consent and popular support. This was so even in Austin; where reformers came closest to realizing their goals. There reformers and politicians eventually accommodated one another, as well as those popular groups antagonistic to reform government.

Reform charters disorganized politicians without effectively inhibiting their most grievous practices. Thus the most frequent pattern of reform politics in the Southwest was an array of factions, personal followings, and hastily assembled and equally short-lived alliances. While some politicians (for example, the commissioner who headed a department) attempted to build strong client followings, on the whole, such governments could be neither responsive nor efficient. It is this most common pattern of politics under reform charters that replicates significant features of V. O. Key's South.

Key himself argued that "technically the description of the politics of the [one-party] south amounts to the problem of analyzing the political struggle under a system of nonpartisan elections."[53] The strongest evidence that this is so is found in the commonalities between the one-party reform cities of Texas (where nonpartisanship would have endangered the white primary and, so, profoundly threatened the balance of political forces) and the nonpartisan politics of cities elsewhere in the Southwest. The factionalism promoted by both systems made voter choice difficult and throwing the rascals out nearly impossible.[54]

Another pattern of reform politics was possible when a politician of particular ability transcended the institutional barriers to centralization, managed government coherently, and organized popular support. These were the Boss Tweeds of the Sunbelt. Tweed created order out of New York's political disorder in the 1860s. On the one hand, he worked in the city and the state legislature to amend the city's charter in ways that strengthened home rule and centralized control. On the other, Tweed arranged for government donations to denominational schools, orphanages, hospitals, and the like. Of this money, nearly three-quarters went to Catholic institutions at a time of widespread anti-Catholic feeling.[55]

Like Tweed, Sunbelt centralizers formed strong alliances with other politicians, put government employees to good organizational use, and styled themselves the benefactors of laboring people and those of low status. If the benefits awarded those constituencies were small, they were important in the regional political context. Moreover, Sunbelt centralizers benefited from those institutional arrangements meant to distance politician from constituency. The antidemocratic features of reform charters gave politicians latitude in the concessions they granted, while the legal environment of the region was hostile to disadvantaged constituencies. Sunbelt Tweeds built personal support from political concession and, unlike the Boss himself, did not share voter loyalty with a party.

Sunbelt centralizers had a contemporary counterpart in Kansas City's Tom Pendergast. Pendergast constructed a formidable machine, despite Kansas City's city manager charter. In 1938, when would-be reformers met as the Houston Charter Commission to draft charter changes (which were not successful), Pendergast was the subject of some discussion. One member of the commission had this to say about him:

> I respect a good politician. I respect Tom Pendergast. I would accept his word as quickly as I would accept the word of anyone . . . This is the part they

played. They control the popular vote. . . . Mr. Pendergast is wise enough that he and his organization will retain their power. They must give Kansas City good government. . . . It is a pleasure to go to Kansas City and to see the constitution of the streets and see the good judgment and taste that has been exercised in their public buildings. It is a pleasure to read of the structures which have been built making it one of the most attractive cities to live in in this country. That has come from the city manager form of government.[56]

If that reformer was right, Pendergast governed because he and his colleagues accepted a division of labor between themselves and the city manager. The politicians organized consent while the city manager saw to it that the city's infrastructure kept pace with growth (and, one presumes, that the city was fiscally sound). It may be that those in Houston and elsewhere who valued growth came to value the services of politicians who could "control the popular vote" and who themselves put growth at the top of municipal government's agenda. Surely this was at the heart of the compromise reached in Austin.

These, then, were the patterns of local politics in the prewar Sunbelt. But questions remain about these local political regimes. First, having sketched the broad lines of compromise between politicians and reformers, it must still be asked, Who got what? Second, how may differences between southwestern cities account for differences in their political styles? Third, how may the development of local politics in the Southwest be more closely and systematically linked to the region's relation to national politics and economics? Finally, what was it about these regimes that provoked a new generation of reformers to refound the cities of the Southwest after the Second World War? Even without answers to these questions, this discussion of politics in the cities of the prewar Sunbelt has provided an account of the triumph of municipal reform there, of what reformers wrought, and of what came to be despite them.

Part III.

Gender and Race

4. Women, Religion, and Reform in Galveston, 1880–1920

Elizabeth Hayes Turner

In 1915 Mary Ritter Beard, in her pathbreaking *Woman's Work in Municipalities,* detailed the enormous contributions women had made to Progressive era reform in the nation's cities and towns. She quipped a bit one-sidedly that "thousands of men may loaf around clubs without ever showing the slightest concern about the great battle for decent living conditions . . . in our cities, but it is a rare woman's club that long remains indifferent to such momentous matters." As if to echo the praise of women's organized efforts and also to demonstrate that theirs was a progressive spirit, the editors of the *Galveston Tribune* devoted an entire section of their 1915 special edition to the city's three most important women's associations with a headline that read: "Women's Organizations in Galveston Are in Flourishing Condition."[1]

The first of the three women's groups to receive approval of publisher and public was the Women's Health Protective Association (WHPA), founded in 1901 in the wake of the 1900 hurricane. The *Tribune* stated that the WHPA had "labored earnestly, and successfully, for the improvement of sanitary conditions and beautification of the city." Then with a note of wariness, the paper congratulated the women of the city for forming a suffrage society in 1912. "There's nothing frantic or fanatical about the Galveston Equal Suffrage Association," the editors reassured the citizens, "it believes in education of the people on this question and presents arguments for the cause in a dignified . . . manner." "With progress a key note of the times . . . the suffragists will not be discouraged by any temporary defeats, they say, . . . but will keep right on with their vigorous campaign for equal rights."[2]

The third association featured was the Young Women's Christian Association (YWCA), begun only months earlier, in December, 1914. Remarking on this group's instant success, the paper noted that "the association is in handsome quarters, has a general secretary, an assistant secretary, a travelers' aid bureau at the union station, a cafeteria, [and] a gymnasium almost ready."[3]

It would be difficult to miss the point that the white women of the city had created collectively not just a club but a facility with services solely for the city's women and girls. With goals that reached from advancing civic and political reform to attending to the needs of the female population in the city, these three associations represented to the citizens of Galveston the flower of women's social-progressive idealism.[4]

Both Mary Beard and the editors of the *Galveston Tribune* had concentrated exclusively on social problems and on urban women organizing to combat and to resolve them in keeping with progressive ideals. It is a highly informative lesson on the political activities of the unenfranchised, but it does not tell us much about the community of women who stood behind the associations. Today, historians are asking how white southern women entered into reforming activities in the Progressive era. Which churches and church societies served as forums for women's social activism? Did links exist between women's congregational societies and progressive reform groups? What agents, agencies, or events helped women organize? Who were these women and what experiences did they bring with them? How did women's reforming activities shape their attitudes toward other women and especially toward their expanding role in the public workplace? Perhaps most important to this chapter, after these questions have been explored, is to adumbrate the evolution in Galveston of a "women's community," an informal alliance of politically and socially active white women who motivated and sustained women's progressive activism. By focusing on this community, on the increasingly democratic nature of the three most important Progressive era associations of women as featured in the *Galveston Tribune,* and on the urban environment from which they evolved, patterns of involvement will begin to emerge that may help to shape our understanding of the southern women's Progressive movement.

Historians have long reasoned that the origins of southern women's reform in the Progressive era stemmed from the "women's organizations of the Protestant churches." Anne F. Scott discovered that by 1900 "the public life of virtually every Southern woman . . . began in a church society"; the result, she writes, was that women "essentially invented the welfare state." Accordingly, women's church societies of the 1870s and 1880s served as predecessors to the voluntary associations established by women for the purpose of social reform in the 1890s and the first two decades of the twentieth century. Taking this concept a bit further in their studies of specific church and semireligious associations, Scott and Jean E. Friedman assign considerable importance to the links between evangelical foreign and home mission societies, the Women's Christian Temperance Union (WCTU), and the southern women's suffrage movement. They depict women as moving from the protected enclosures of Baptist and Methodist churches to the more worldly realm of public Prohibition. Recognizing the difficulty of enacting reform by moral suasion and the unlikelihood of prohibition legislation passing without the vote, the WCTU endorsed women's suffrage as early as 1879. A number of WCTU members joined the ranks of the suffragists secure in the goal of perfecting the community and guarding the home. A lock-step model emerges of southern women issuing forth from evangelical societies to join the WCTU and then marching toward membership in their states' equal suffrage associations.[5]

This structural model helps to explain how women from a conservative South were able to foster social reform movements that addressed the problems of intemperance, child labor, prison reform, early childhood education, and the white slave traffic without abandoning an evangelical heritage. It has the advantage of providing an ideological explanation for the coexistence of such diverse elements as foreign mission, Prohibition, and suffrage societies. Through direct conversion experiences, belief in the perfectability of humanity, and hope of legal adoption of domestic values, evangelical women were encouraged to follow the path already outlined toward reform. This model may very well help describe women's reform activities at the state level, or in communities where Methodists and Baptists predominated, or where the WCTU was organized early and grew vigorously, but the South is not monolithic, and the model does not account for the origins of women's reform movements in some of its urban areas.[6]

To confirm or reject the hypothetical model that southern female reformers were the product of prior experience in evangelical organizations, studies detailing the influences that encouraged Progressive era social change need to be undertaken. Biographies of southern suffragists have given us specific information about individual female reformers.[7] And there have been several histories that chronicle change for women within church denominations.[8] But what are needed to understand the origins of reform led by women in the South are community-level studies of women's organizations, both religious and secular, that may have fostered or promoted reforming impulses. This chapter calls for that kind of research while presenting some preliminary findings of such a study of one southern community.

Recently, urban historians have not only recognized the importance of urban centers to the South's regional distinctiveness, but they have also pointed to significant differences among southern cities in their rates of growth, cultural values, and social organization. Don Harrison Doyle argues that New South railway centers such as Atlanta and Nashville attracted younger men into civic-commercial leadership. These differed from the more relaxed, liquor-imbibing businessmen found in the seaport cities of Charleston and Mobile. In the interior cities, social status was dependent on achievement, but in the older seaport cities, elite status belonged to an entrenched upper class.[9] Doyle does not take religion into account in his study, but a comparison of denominational preference in these four cities clearly presents a pattern consistent with his claims of difference in social organization between younger interior cities and older seaport cities. Atlanta, Nashville, and also Louisville, Memphis, Montgomery, Houston, and Dallas had greater numbers of Protestant communicants in the evangelical denominations than did the seaport cities of Charleston, Mobile, New Orleans, or Galveston (see tables 4.1 and 4.2).

The inland cities seemed to allow greater upward social mobility; newcomers who ventured into wholesale produce, dry goods, lumber, iron, textile, and other manufacturing trades were given opportunities to rise to positions of commercial and civic leadership.[10] Undoubtedly, many of these young men and their wives belonged to the less-prestigious but faster-growing Baptist and Methodist churches. Despite the fact that in 1916, 92.4 percent of Baptists and 89.8 percent of Methodists still resided in the countryside, in cities that sprang up out of the farming hinterlands, Baptists and Methodists flourished.[11]

In each of the seaboard cities in 1906, the largest percentage of Protestants were Episcopalians, followed in three cities by Lutherans and members of the Methodist Episcopal Church (North). In all but Mobile, Baptists and members of the Methodist Episcopal Church (South) were the least prevalent. Seaboard cities had higher percentages of Catholics, Germans, and other immigrant groups than did the interior cities (Kentucky and Texas excepted). A more tolerant attitude toward drinking prevailed in cities where seamen found recreation and, on another level, where

Table 4.1

Protestant Denominations by Inland City, 1906

Denomination	Atlanta (%)	Nashville (%)	Louisville (%)	Memphis (%)	Montgomery (%)	Houston (%)	Dallas (%)
Baptist	19.5	11.6	16.8	8.6	9.4	9.1	17.7
M.E.C.S.	21.4	22.1	8.9	17.6	12.4	19.9	19.4
Dis. Ch.		10.8	8.4	4.2	2.5	4.9	9.8
Pres. U.S.	7.5	8.5	6.3	9.9	5.1	8.4	7.0
Epis.	4.3	4.1	5.9	7.1	4.4	8.3	5.6
G.E.			15.2			3.1	
TOTAL Protestant population	53,644	37,908	60,680	31,623	21,502	15,860	22,917
TOTAL Catholic population	5,079	5,865	85,170	5,270	3,006	13,743	9,284

SOURCE: U.S. Bureau of the Census, *Religious Bodies: 1906*. Pt. 1: *Summary and General Tables* (Washington, D.C., 1910), pp. 410–94.

NOTES: Totals include black congregants; with the exception of the Episcopal Church, white communicants only are included in percentages. Protestant totals include members above age twelve; Catholic totals include members above age nine.

Baptist = Baptist–Southern Convention

M.E.C.S. = Methodist Episcopal Church, South

Dis. Ch. = Disciples of Christ and Churches of Christ

Pres. U.S. = Presbyterian Church of the U.S.

Epis. = Protestant Episcopal Church

G.E. = German Evangelical Synod of North America

Table 4.2

Protestant Denominations by Port City, 1906

Denomination	Charleston (%)	Mobile (%)	New Orleans (%)	Galveston (%)
Baptist	5.1	7.1	2.6	9.7
M.E.C.S.	7.5	12.0	6.3	11.3
Pres. U.S.	4.5	6.6	9.9	7.2
M.E.C.	12.7		9.0	12.3
Lutheran	8.7(a)		13.6(b)	13.7(c)
Epis.	14.3	12.7	14.0	23.2
TOTAL Protestant population	20,030	19,451	36,875	5,504
TOTAL Catholic population	7,602	13,579	148,579	14,872

SOURCE: U.S. Bureau of the Census, *Religious Bodies: 1906.* Pt. 1: *Summary and General Tables* (Washington, D.C., 1910), pp. 410–94.

NOTES: Totals include black congregants; with the exception of the Episcopal Church, white communicants only are included in percentages. Protestant totals include members above age twelve; Catholic totals include members above age nine.

Baptist = Baptists–Southern Convention

M.E.C.S. = Methodist Episcopal Church, South

Pres. U.S. = Presbyterian Church of the U.S.

M.E.C. = Methodist Episcopal Church, North

Lutheran = (a) United Synod of the Evangelical Lutheran Church in the South; (b) Evangelical Lutheran Synodical Conference of America and Evangelical Joint Lutheran Synod of Ohio and Other States; (c) General Council of the Evangelical Lutheran Church in North America and Evangelical Lutheran Synod of Iowa and Other States

Epis. = Protestant Episcopal Church

the habits of Europeans were easily assimilated.[12] Moreover, status belonged to the more firmly entrenched social elites, who were primarily of the nonevangelical denominations; in Protestant circles, this usually meant Episcopalian.

This discussion of New South cities, male elites, and denominational preference is relevant to the study of southern urban women reformers, most of whom were wives, daughters, and sisters of men wielding commercial or political power. Before 1900, in those interior cities and towns where Baptists and Methodists predominated and their members achieved upper-middle and upper-class status, women of the evangelical missionary societies and the WCTU were accorded positions of leadership within secular voluntary associations. But in Galveston, and possibly in the other seaport cities, evangelical women were seldom afforded elite status and therefore did not generally participate in the leadership of the reform organizations. Studies of the religious origins of women's reform movements in the South must therefore take into consideration not only denominational predominance in cities but also geographic and economic factors, class structure, and opportunities for upward social mobility.

Focusing on a trans-Mississippi seaport has certain advantages not afforded by a study of the older seaboard cities. First, Texas offers fertile territory for the study of reform, particularly since the state produced Populist, Prohibitionist, and Progressive movements and concluded a successful women's suffrage campaign. Second, Galveston by 1880 had become the state's largest city, but its population of only twenty-two thousand makes it a manageable site for study. It was also a dynamic city and, unlike Charleston and Mobile, did not decay between 1865 and 1900. In 1890, Galveston's citizens secured $7.5 million in federal aid for the construction of a deep water port; by 1900, Galveston was shipping 64 percent of the Texas cotton crop to world markets.

Before the hurricane of September, 1900, the city had grown to nearly thirty-eight thousand, but in 1910, Galveston was no longer the largest city in Texas. Unlike interior cities such as Dallas and Fort Worth, Galveston's richly diversified population included a majority of Catholics, most of whom were German and Irish immigrants or their descendants. Of the city's Protestants, Episcopalians were the most numerous. Most of the socially elite families were either Episcopalians (for example, Sealy, Hutchings, League, and Rosenberg), Presbyterians (Trueheart, Austin), or Jews (Kempner, Lasker, Lovenberg, Kopperl, and Blum). In 1906, 44.1 percent of Protestants belonged to the more liturgical Episcopal, Presbyterian, and Lutheran churches. Baptists, Methodists, and members of other evangelical denominations made up only 34 percent of Protestants, but among them could be found the Ballingers and the Moodys. Because Galveston in the eighteen eighties and nineties combined the dynamic elements of a young, rising New South city with the denominational and class structure of an older port city, it provides an opportunity to test and evaluate the origins of progressive women reformers whose attitudes were not informed or shaped by the evangelical churches.[13]

To understand better the intricate network of the origins of the women's movement in Galveston, I have examined the records of three broad types of organization, including those of the women's societies of seven white Protestant churches and one Jewish congregation; four white benevolent institutions managed by women and founded in the 1880s and 1890s; and four white women's reform organizations of the post-1900 period.[14] An analysis of the goals, activities, and leadership of each organization reveals several patterns. First, women's church and synagogue societies of the 1870s and 1880s varied in their goals and purposes, some serving only their own congregations, others serving the foreign mission field, and still others directing their energies toward the community principally in the form of relief for the poor. Second, the majority of women who became officers of the benevolent institutions emerged from churches where the women's societies had fed, clothed, and housed the city's worthy poor (that is, those who had not succumbed to vices such as drink or prostitution). And third, the leaders of the women's organizations founded to help rebuild the city after the disaster of 1900 drew the majority of their officers from the boards of "lady managers" of the benevolent institutions. The percentage of suffrage leaders who were associated with congregations generally, and with predecessor women's organizations specifically, drops slightly in 1912 (mostly because of age difference), but a link did exist between the women's church societies that provided relief for the poor, women's benevolent institutions, and women's reform and suffrage organizations of the Progressive era. [15]

This study also reveals that evangelical women's mission societies and the WCTU played virtually no role in the creation of a coterie of volunteer progressive female reformers in Galveston. The WCTU never enjoyed the popularity in Galveston that it did in interior Texas cities, in part because there were fewer members of evangelical denominations in Galveston, and because in this port city, saloons, as well as immigrants' drinking customs, were tolerated and too profitable to oppose. Moreover, Methodists and Baptists, who were largely of the middle and lower-middle classes, provided most of the membership of the WCTU, giving that organization a middle-class but not an elite status.

Reform in Galveston was engendered by elite women who responded to the urban conditions peculiar to that city in the 1880s and 1890s. These conditions set the stage for local women's reform movements, not agendas created by national women's organizations such as the WCTU. The foundations of the women's reform movement rested on those congregational women's societies that had actively pursued community relief for twenty years and their successor organizations, designed to care for the city's dependents, that is, orphans, widows, and children of the factory district. Some historians call this a branch of the social gospel movement and attempt to link women's interests in community charity to the social gospelers' "crusade for justice and righteousness in all areas of the common life." [16] Others, most notably Samuel S. Hill, have concluded that southern churches did not involve themselves in the social gospel movement, except for their strong advocacy of Prohibition.

Galveston, however, was atypical of the South as a whole; urban problems pushed quickly to the fore after the Civil War and were met not by members of the major southern evangelical denominations but by Episcopal women, who predominated in the leadership of Galveston's congregational relief societies and benevolent institutions. Did Galveston's Episcopal women receive stimuli from their northern sisters, who, as Mary Donovan has shown, acted with purposeful conviction concerning the problems of the urban poor as early as the mid-nineteenth century? The answer must be a qualified yes, based on circumstantial rather than direct evidence. But like their northern coreligionists, Galveston's churchwomen were inspired more by conditions at their doorstep and by the call of local rectors to remember their duty to the poor than by the pronouncements of distant theologians of the social gospel. Moreover, as Episcopalians tended to be wealthier and more prominent in business and civic affairs, noblesse oblige was central to the creation of a reforming elite. Activist elite women also came from families that had long practiced philanthropy and were interested in social issues; evidence of family support for their social involvement can be seen in the numbers of men who became associate members of the Women's Health Protective Association and the Galveston Equal Suffrage Association.[17]

Although religious and class affiliations are not the only features that identify women activists before 1900, they serve as a starting place for a discussion of women's involvement in community life. Between 1875 and 1890, women from virtually all of the churches and synagogues formed congregational societies that raised money for their own churches, supported missionaries, or cared for the dependents within their own congregations. But Trinity Episcopal Church, the most successful Protestant church in Galveston both before and after the Civil War, was one of the earliest to form a women's society to aid the city's poor.[18]

Its involvement in city relief work began in the wake of a hurricane in September, 1875, that left the homeless in need of food, shelter, and clothing. Trinity Church Guild organized the relief effort, divided the city into districts with a committee in charge of each, and employed both men and women in the direct distribution of aid. This effort taught participating women an important organizing technique; they eventually adopted for themselves the name Trinity Guild and decided to meet weekly for the dispensing of regular, systematic charity to the city's poor. This was the first organization in the city to reach beyond the walls of the church to aid community members regardless of ethnicity, race, or denomination. By 1880, Trinity Guild had "relieved not less than 260 indigent families, given away 483 garments to the worthy poor, supplied work to sewing women, and furnished many suffering and needy with fuel and shoes, also material for work."[19]

In 1880, a second group of women chartered the Ladies Aid Society of the First Presbyterian Church (LASFPC) and wrote that they intended "to help aid and encourage charitable work according to their judgment."[20] The forces of feminine benevolence stemmed not only from witnessing scenes of distressing poverty but also from individual religious convictions. The ladies of the First Presbyterian Church shared these sentiments when they recorded that their pastor, Dr. William Scott, "asked a blessing upon our labors for the coming year . . . that we in ministering to the needy and suffering might through our sympathy with them be brought into closer kinship with Him whose earthly life was passed amid scenes of sorrow and suffering, thereby leading both us and them to a higher spiritual life." Hence, out of a sense of moral stewardship rather than a desire to exert religious authority over individual sinners, Presbyterian and Episcopal women broadened their charity to include those unaffiliated with their denominations and even the unchurched.[21]

It was timely for the women to regard the worthy poor as objects of their religious and humanitarian sensibilities, for by 1885, the city desperately needed more relief agencies. A great fire in that year devastated the business section, creating requests for aid beyond the norm. Even in the best of times, there were no provisions in the city ordinances for indigents, just the usual vagrancy laws calling for arrest and fine for persons "likely to become chargeable to the city as paupers."[22] With the demise of the Freedmen's Bureau in 1868, care of the impoverished under Texas law fell to the county commissioners, who benefited only those who had been residents of Texas one year and of Galveston County for six months. Short-term residents, recent arrivals, or those whom the county court did not find "so indigent, so infirm, sick, or disabled as to become an object of public care and support," were ineligible for county relief. Most who sought aid were not interested in public support, for the county could offer them only a humiliating existence outside the city on the county poor farm.[23]

Those who petitioned the two women's societies for aid generally were persons with no connection to any other benevolent associations in the city. Supplicants included stranded travelers, disabled working-class men and women, abandoned women with children, sick mothers with small children, factory girls, and indigent, friendless widows—the "worthy poor" for whom no existing private agencies existed. Although the women endeavored to relieve the distress of all worthy petitioners, in fact the largest group to receive aid were women (over 80 percent between 1890 and 1901). Less than 20 percent were men, and approximately 12 percent of the total recipients were black. Of all society's needy, women had the fewest connections to private charity. In a city where nearly every woman's economic station bordered on dependency, middle- and upper-class women reached across class barriers to aid working-class women. Thus these two women's church societies served not just as superficial charitable organizations but as essential safety nets for the city's unattached and unconnected.[24]

Women were helped in ways other than with direct relief. Episcopal and Presbyterian women held teas for factory girls and nursing students, subsidized training for working women, set up "industrial schools" to teach domestic skills, and supported poor women who chose to divorce runaway husbands.[25] These community-oriented women activists, rather than ignoring the reality of the city, embraced it, crossing class and, occasionally, race lines. But they remained basically within the domestic realm, taking their sense of woman's moral authority from within the home and pressing it into service for the community.

The women's church societies served a critical need as proto-welfare agencies in an underinstitutionalized period of the city's history, but the societies chose not to establish asylums for the city's dependents. Instead, representatives from the various church and temple societies formed an interfaith force by applying the energies of the city's most affluent women to the task of institution building. Drawing on their experience with congregational societies, elite women between 1878 and 1894 founded four benevolent institutions that were administered by boards of lady managers. Two orphanages, the Island City Protestant-Israelitish Orphans' Home (1880, later the Galveston Orphans' Home), and the Home for Homeless Children (1894, later the Lasker Home for Children); a home for aged women, the Old Woman's Home (1888, later the Letitia Rosenberg Home for Women); and the state's first free kindergarten, the Johanna Runge Free Kindergarten (1893), were added to the already existing St. Mary's Catholic orphanage and the county poor farm. Of some thirty-one officers of the oldest of these, the Galveston Orphans' Home, serving between 1880 and 1900, 52 percent were Episcopalian; 19 percent, Presbyterian; 16 percent, Jewish; 10 percent, Baptist; and 3 percent, Methodist. Moreover, 45 percent of the officers were members of the two community-oriented women's church societies, Trinity Guild and the Ladies Aid Society of the First Presbyterian Church.[26]

The boards of lady managers of the four new benevolent institutions became self-perpetuating; new members were recruited by the presiding managers. To become a board member, a woman had to be actively engaged in church or temple work or belong to an elite family that had long practiced philanthropy. Boards of female managers constituted a female hierarchy, a religious voluntary elite where status was as important as piety. The members' responsibilities as caretakers of orphans, aged women, and children from the factory district were commensurate with their stature within the community, and though they may have used the boards for their own social purposes, there is no doubt that they also advanced their roles as semipublic servants while allowing broader application of women's domestic values.

The 1890s brought to Galveston a welter of women's organizations — hereditary-patriotic societies, social clubs, fraternal auxiliaries, literary clubs, and even short-lived chapters of the WCTU and the Texas Equal Suffrage Association.[27] Out of all of these associations, only those societies and boards that recognized the problems of poor working-class men and women (brought to Galveston by the promise of jobs) and that attempted to ameliorate their suffering were likely to prepare women to become agents for social change in the Progressive period. It was primarily the boards of lady managers of these institutions that educated women for civic leadership in the decades that followed and that presaged the advent of a progressive women's community. Despite all of this preparation in developing a women's leadership network, it still took a cataclysmic event, the hurricane of 1900, to provide both a need and a great opportunity for founding the city's foremost progressive women's reform organization.

This storm created the very worst kind of social disorder. As it swept from the Gulf of Mexico across Galveston Island with winds over one hundred miles per hour, it brought fifteen-to-thirty-foot waves crashing in on the city's southeast neighborhoods. When the structures closest to the sea collapsed from the force of gale and tide, they became battering rams against the houses to the north of them. Structure upon structure fell and piled up in a semicircle surrounding the business and more affluent sections of the city. The storm left in its wake a mountain of debris containing the remains of houses, household furnishings, dead animals, and approximately six thousand sodden human corpses. Survivors sought their dead wherever they could find them, burying them in shallow graves in any available plot of ground. Disposal of the unclaimed was left to the hastily devised Committee of Public Safety. At first, the committee tried interment, but the ground was too saturated for mass graves. Removal and burial at sea was attempted, but the bodies washed ashore. In the September heat, corpses quickly reached a state of putrefaction before the workers could remove them from the tangled mounds of debris. Finally, at the insistence of the city's medical community, the committee burned the corpses in great funeral pyres across the once-thriving port city.[28]

This appalling lack of decorum in the consignment of fellow citizens to their eternal resting places weighed on the consciences of survivors, especially the women, who, following southern tradition, had cared for the graves of their relatives.[29] By December, the fires no longer burned, and in March, 1901, sixty-six women survivors, veteran organizers from the women's congregational societies and benevolent institutions, gathered to establish the Women's Health Protective Association (WHPA).[30] The WHPA's most immediate task was to aid in the removal of debris and then to transfer bodies from makeshift graves to a cemetery on the west end of the island, where a marker provided by the women paid tribute to the storm's victims.[31] Without much fanfare, the first Progressive era women's organization emerged from the mud and devastation of the battered community.

One other very significant event occurred with the formation of the WHPA. Unlike the boards of lady managers of the benevolent institutions, which had been exclusive and self-perpetuating, the WHPA was open to all white adult women in the community and the officers were elected by the members. In the midst of crisis, the first democratic, citywide women's association had been created. It heralded the formation of a progressive women's community in Galveston.[32]

The notion of a women's community is both old and new. The recognition that women in the nineteenth century belonged to a separate sphere is now accepted wisdom. The origins of the sphere, the manner in which women responded to their separation, the extent to which this sphere created a women's culture, and the differentials within it based on class are still being explored and debated by feminist theorists. Historians agree, however, that the ideals of the separate sphere operated well into the twentieth century, perpetuating a kind of cultural lag with respect to the changing economic and social status of women.[33]

This sphere was alive and well in Galveston in 1900 as evidenced by the forty-one managing boards, societies, clubs, and associations of women. Most women belonged to more than one association, or were elected to more than one board; virtually all belonged to a church or synagogue. Growing out of the separate sphere yet grounded in its tenets of ennobled womanhood, a network of women interested and active in urban affairs became visible both to the community and to other women. Judging from the numbers of women engaged in club or association work, the pull must have been magnetic and presaged a time when all of this womanpower could be brought together for a combined purpose. A women's community committed to Progressive ideals, experienced in the complexities of organizational work, and open to women of different classes and religious backgrounds evolved between 1901 and 1920 as women collectively faced the immense problem of urban reconstruction.[34]

The coalescing of women from various clubs, boards, and auxiliaries began slowly in 1901 with the founding of the WHPA, which during the next nineteen years became one of the city's largest civic reform organizations. In 1916, the WHPA reported five hundred members. Eventually the members organized the replanting of the island following the grade raising. (The surface of the island was raised several feet by pumping millions of cubic yards of sand from the sea and, although it partially eliminated the danger of flooding, it killed most of the existing grass and shrubs.)[35] When the grade raising was completed in 1911, WHPA members, armed with public approval, experience in managing large projects, and continuing interest in the welfare of the community, shifted the organization's emphasis from beautification to public health and sanitation.

Before 1913, the WHPA applied pressure to city government by petition, by consultation with individual commissioners, and by public criticism. But in February, 1913, in concert with the Galveston Commercial Association, the WHPA asked Dr. J. P. Simonds, head of the Laboratory of Preventive Medicine of the University of Texas Department of Medicine in Galveston, to conduct a sanitary survey. Plans "to make Galveston the cleanest city in Texas [were] to be built on a scientific foundation." The survey concluded that the unsanitary condition of the city's dairies was to blame for the high bacteria levels found in the milk, which led to infant intestinal disorders, dehydration, and even death. To lower child mortality and to improve public health, cleaner dairies, markets, and restaurants were deemed essential. Now the women had a cudgel with which to coerce commissioners to enforce existing pure milk and pure food laws.[36]

Others in the community began to clamor for action. The editor of the *Galveston Daily Herald* proposed that the city Board of Commissioners appoint a WHPA member "with full pay" to inspect the city alleys, streets, and yards. The advent of the sanitary survey prompted the *Herald* to lambaste city health officer C. W. Trueheart: "the trouble is that the health department is headed by an old fossil and that his assistants are relics of the stone age. . . . Appoint some woman on the police force and we will guarantee that she will see that these unsightly, these unsanitary places disappear." Despite calls for their elevation to city officialdom, the women had to continue lobbying for reform. Promises were extracted from city commissioners for reports on the conditions of dairies, but the results showed little improvement since the publication of the sanitation survey. Of the forty-seven dairies subjected to inspection, twenty-one exceeded the standard one hundred thousand bacteria per cubic centimeter; three showed over one million bacteria. And this in the middle of winter![37]

WHPA members sent their own inspectors out to check on the conditions of dairies, groceries, and meat markets and proposed circulating a "whitelist" of cleaner dairies. Meanwhile, city commissioners were bombarded with demands by irate businesspeople to stop treating pure food offenders leniently. In November, 1914, the new city health officer, Walter Kleberg, "promised to revoke licenses of dairy men and dealers who sold adulterated milk," and by 1915, he had listed eight dairies as in danger of losing their licenses. None did, and while city officials dragged their heels, the WHPA took pure food offenders to court, where defense attorneys interrogated the women about the cleanliness of *their* kitchens. Strong opposition faced the women from dairymen and from a hard-to-move Board of Commissioners.[38]

Pure food advocates were pleased in February, 1915, when the commissioners accepted a proposal to hire an extra inspector at the WHPA's expense. This resulted in a curious blend of private and public policing of city entrepreneurs. Another victory came in May, when Mrs. Waters S. Davis announced that she and the WHPA president, Mrs. Jens Moller, were appointed deputy state food and drug inspectors, with "the right to go into any place in the city or county where food is produced or sold." But the power to inspect was not the power to enforce; eventually the women would have to combine public pressure with qualified voters to make city government act.[39]

The WHPA was successful in coercing the commissioners to stand firm in enforcing the city's 1907 pure food ordinance in 1916 and 1917, with the direct aid of several men's associations. The Galveston County Medical Society and the WHPA formed a joint committee headed by city pathologist and WHPA president Dr. Ethel Lyon Heard. This committee took before the city commissioners a program for the grading, inspecting, and cooling of milk. The program had the additional support of the Commercial Association, the Rotary Club, and the Labor Council. As with most unenfranchised elements of society, the women were only able to influence political change, not to control it. As long as they alone petitioned city government, little progress was made. They learned that by directing their campaign for pure milk toward voters, especially organized men's groups, they were able to accomplish collectively what they could not do alone. This was a theme that would repeat itself, even within the women's community.[40]

Pure milk was only one of many reform projects that the WHPA took on. Members were instrumental in getting city building ordinances updated, regular inspection of the city's bakeries, groceries, and restaurants, elimination of breeding grounds for flies and mosquitoes, regular medical examination of school children, public playgrounds, hot-lunch programs, and well-baby and tuberculosis clinics. The WHPA was typical of women's progressive reform organizations across the nation in that it allowed civic-minded women to act as agents of social change so that domestic politics could become public policy.[41]

While the storm of 1900 was the immediate catalyst that prompted the formation of a women's reform association, there remain questions about the origins of the reformers and the influence of the pre-1900 women's congregational societies and benevolent institutions. The critical question here is not what kinds of reforms the progressives succeeded in establishing, but rather who the women officers were who led the association. Where did they receive their "training"? What other roles, vis-à-vis suffrage, did they take on?

I have compiled and analyzed the organizational histories of sixty officers of the WHPA between 1901 and 1911. With these data, I can answer at least three questions. The majority, 55 percent, of WHPA officers belonged to a church- or synagogue-based women's society; 42 percent of the officers had belonged to Episcopalian and Presbyterian women's societies—the very societies that had first directed their ministries to the city's poor. Fifty-five percent of the WHPA officers had once served on a board of lady managers for one or more of the benevolent institutions of the 1880s and 1890s. More important, twenty-five of the twenty-eight WHPA executive officers (89 percent) had served on boards of benevolent institutions. Of the congregation-affiliated WHPA executive officers, 100 percent had served on boards of lady managers for benevolent institutions, an indication of the important link between congregation, benevolence, and civic-reform leadership. Although the officers were elected, it is clear that women who had been active in leadership positions in the 1890s, before the advent of the women's community, continued to be sought out as leaders in the city's first progressive reform association.[42]

The WHPA's activities were considerable, especially given the city's destitution in 1900, and the rewards for the members were manifold. They found that by acting collectively, they constituted a powerful lobbying force for municipal housekeeping. They brought all the organizing skills learned in their earlier institution building days to a larger forum—the city. They transferred their concern for the indigent individual to the revegetation of a denuded island. And they insisted on clean streets and alleys, pure milk, and sanitary markets, even if it meant imposing progressive standards on reluctant dairymen and grocers. They learned the arts of rhetoric, of petitioning for change, and of working around commissioners—in short, they learned practical politics. But without direct access to political power, they found their organizing talents limited to mere influence. Moreover, despite the democratic structure, their attempts to create a more pluralistic leadership were not successful. WHPA officers remained solidly upper and upper-middle class.

Unlike the WHPA, whose goals included restructuring the city, suffragists had plans for restructuring the electorate. This monothematic campaign absorbed the energies of seventy-four active and seven associate (male) members of the Galveston Equal Suffrage Association (ESA) when first organized in 1912 at the insistence of Anna Maxwell Jones and Etta Jones.[43] The association quickly gained favor, and three hundred members were on the rolls by 1915. The ESA offered opportunities for civic leadership to newcomers: women medical students, doctors, teachers, real estate agents, and semiprofessional suffrage organizers brought to the ESA backgrounds that differed significantly from those of local women. Still, many of the city elites were present. The roll of officers for the ESA in its first year contains the names of women who were known in the community for the prominence of their families and for their involvement in other areas of municipal housekeeping. Five of the seventeen officers of the ESA in 1912 had held executive positions in the WHPA, and seven of the seventeen belonged to commercially wealthy families that practiced civic philanthropy (five male members of these families became charter members of the ESA, as did Rabbi Henry Cohen). Of those ESA officers with identifiable congregational affiliation between 1912 and 1920, 55 percent were Episcopalian and 48 percent had had leadership training on the boards of lady managers of the benevolent institutions or as officers of the WHPA. With the exception of Bettie Ballinger, a Baptist who held active positions in more women's organizations than any other woman on the island, the ESA leadership did not include large numbers of women from the evangelical denominations.[44]

Suffragists supported the ideals of equal voting rights intermingled with the notion that women were the natural "housekeepers" of the community. Sally Trueheart Williams, corresponding secretary of the ESA, said publicly, "Women's place is the home. Her task is homemaking, but home

is not contained in the four walls of an individual home. Home is the community. . . . Housekeeping has ceased to be a simple matter . . . and in
asking for the right to vote, [women] are following their housekeeping to
the . . . polls."[45]

Suffragists alluded to the WHPA campaigns in Galveston for pure milk
and the need for women who knew "the relation between disease and bad
milk" to struggle for the vote in order to see that health regulations were
enforced. Despite these appeals to mothers and homemakers of every station, working-class women did not join in great numbers or become part
of the association's leadership. Perhaps they continued to see the vote as
an abstraction divorced from the realities of their lives. Purely feminist
goals were ideals that could bring few tangible and immediate rewards to
alleviate low wages or inadequate housing. While the ESA opened its leadership to professional women who had not previously been active in a reform
movement, and while it focused on the need for white women to gain access to the political process, it failed in its efforts to attract immigrant and
working-class mothers and daughters. The progressive women's community
was growing with the advent of the Galveston Equal Suffrage Association,
but evangelical and working-class women had not yet found a place among
the leadership.[46]

The need for an organization that would incorporate middle-class evangelical and working-class women alongside the traditional elite leaders of
the women's community was partially filled by the appearance in 1914 of
the Young Women's Christian Association. In Galveston as in other
southern cities, the YWCA served as an advocacy agency for working
women and was a much more conservative version of New York's Wom-
en's Trade Union League, or Chicago's Consumers' League, associations
founded by women of means to advance the economic status of working
girls through legislation and consumer education. Southern cities, slower
to experience industrialization, lagged behind their northern counterparts
in establishing women's associations that aided factory workers, clerks,
and shopgirls.[47] And Galveston dallied longer than most cities. The YWCA
had already been established in all of the nation's port cities and in most
of the larger southern cities. Galveston was the last Texas city of its size
to initiate a YWCA, but once the membership drive began, it proved to
be the most successful campaign in the city's history. On November 30,
1914, 170 women divided the city into districts (a technique that reached
back to 1875, when Trinity Guild tried to distribute aid to storm victims)
and canvassed every door for membership in the YWCA. On the first day
of the drive, seventeen teams of women signed up some 440 members.
The newspaper kept up the momentum as each daily issue detailed the
planning, the enthusiasm, and the gains made. By the third day, the women
had secured 675 members; and by the end of the week, 1,908 women had
paid at least one dollar to belong to the city's most promising women's

organization, an organization whose national membership totaled 324,000 and that had branches in fourteen countries. The YWCA continued to maintain its popularity; in 1920, it remained stable at 2,000 members.[48] A democratization process that had begun with the WHPA reached full flower with the YWCA, enlarging and expanding the boundaries of the progressive women's community.

In terms of numbers, the YWCA was the most pluralistic of the city's progressive women's associations. The WHPA never exceeded six hundred members, and the ESA attracted only half that number. Moreover, the YWCA's Board of Directors, elected by the members, comprised more women belonging to evangelical denominations than did the others. Of those board members whose religious affiliations I could identify, 37.5 percent were Episcopalian, 25 percent Presbyterian, 15.6 percent Baptist, 15.6 percent Methodist, and 6 percent belonged to the Central Christian Church. Episcopal and Presbyterian women still predominated, as they had done in the other reform associations, but evangelical women whose names had not appeared as leaders in the other reform associations were found on the list of the YWCA's elected Board of Directors. This may be explained both by the broader constituency that elected them and by the fact that the YWCA was a Christian association whose purpose was to "extend the kingdom of God." Women whose sole outlet had been churchwomen's societies no doubt felt a natural affinity toward the YWCA with its religious committee, prayer meetings, Sunday vespers, and its women missionaries in foreign lands. Of the fifty-four board members found in the records between 1914 and 1920, at least twenty-one (39 percent) had been actively engaged in women's church societies.[49]

Religious affiliation was not the only link to the broader community of women. Among the YWCA directors, fifteen (28 percent) had served on a board of female managers for a benevolent institution, twenty (37 percent) were members of the WHPA, sixteen (30 percent) were suffragists, but only three (5 percent) were members of the WCTU. Five WHPA officers were also executive officers of the YWCA, indicating that women whose talents had been proven assets in the past were elected for their experience and for their ability to propose for themselves and for the women of the city improvements not unlike those they had championed for Galveston.[50]

What did the YWCA offer women in 1915? First, it brought them protection, especially single working women. Mabel Stafford, executive director of the YWCA's southwest region, put it in the context of the times: the YWCA was like the Monroe Doctrine, which protected America from the war in Europe; it was "a stone wall protecting unattached girls from the perils of industrial life in which so many are now engaged." Galveston was never what one would call an industrial city. It sported a few manufactories but was primarily a city whose economy was based on servicing the flow of goods in and out of the port. Its principal economic base was commerce, not industry. Still, the YWCA officers estimated in 1914 that the city had fifteen hundred self-supporting women; a 1916 study raised the figure to seventeen hundred.[51]

Steps were immediately taken both to protect and to aid working women. Rented headquarters at the corner of Twenty-third and Mechanic streets offered office space for the salaried administrators and a gymnasium for "physical culture classes." A traveler's aid agent was hired to meet every incoming train and to advise women who sought lodging or employment, or who were lost or in distress. At first, a list of boardinghouses was given to new arrivals seeking work and a place to live. In 1915, the YWCA expanded its quarters to house boarders, and girls found temporary or permanent shelter in the YWCA for $3.50 a week. A cafeteria selling complete meals for about $.30 and serving six thousand people a month became the association's most popular asset. An employment bureau secured jobs for women; classes for immigrants in English, typing, stenography, salesmanship, first aid, and mathematics attracted young women determined to improve their skills in order to earn better wages.[52]

The YWCA offered a variety of social outlets in which young women participated: clubs, parties, athletic teams, picnics, entertainments, a one hundred–member glee club, and an orchestra. For young women, particularly working girls, to practice and to internalize organizational techniques, only self-governing clubs were encouraged. The officers of the Girls' Athletic Club, organized for boating, basketball, swimming, and tennis, included two bookkeepers, one insurance clerk, a stenographer, a hat trimmer, and the co-owner of an art supply store. Training the daughters of craftspeople and small businesspeople in the art of self-government was one way that civic leaders imparted middle-class values to working girls and hence potentially broadened the women's community.[53]

While social events attracted women of all ages and classes to the YWCA, the Board of Directors promoted progressive causes. Child Labor Sunday was observed annually, lecturers who spoke on the benefits of women's suffrage were frequently invited to the YWCA parlors, a women's exchange was opened for the marketing of wares made by the city's seamstresses, and teams of officers visited the factories, laundries, shops, and markets that employed women to entertain at the workers' break and encourage them to join. The YWCA's finest hour came through its association with the Red Cross during World War I. Several hundred women made hospital supplies, served in canteens, and worked in the United War Fund Drive.[54]

There are, of course, limits to the claims that may be made for the YWCA. It did not include blacks. Jewish and Catholic members were not eligible for election to the Board of Directors, which may explain the larger presence of evangelical women in executive positions. Lutheran women also were not adequately represented among its officers. It did not represent trade unions, did not espouse radical designs for intensifying the class conflict to obtain social justice, did not argue for redistributing the wealth, did not challenge the business community often enough or loudly enough to give equal pay for equal work, and did not advocate racial equality. Yet no other organization offered comparable opportunities for white women's independence in education, housing, social, and civic concerns. The YWCA stood at the heart of Galveston's progressive women's community by challenging women to reach beyond the strictures of their class. Working women of marginal means were subsidized through cheap room and board and were invited to improve themselves physically, intellectually, and spiritually. Women civic leaders were called on to socialize, teach, and volunteer their administrative skills to an organization devoted to the material advancement of women.

How much mixing between the classes occurred is difficult to reconstruct, but the opportunity for social interaction between the daughters of shopkeepers and department store owners was there. A great breakthrough was made by women of evangelical denominations into the leadership ranks of the women's community through YWCA officeholding. And, finally, it is important to remember that the opening of the YWCA doors was accomplished by the concerted efforts of the women of the women's progressive community; it was they who offered the YWCA's services to all white women, focusing on them and their needs in a practical, tangible way as no other association had done.

The origins of the women's reform movement in Galveston do not follow the model devised for the South as a whole; that is, reform was not engendered through evangelical home and mission societies or through the WCTU. Galveston was a port city with a sizable immigrant population and with relatively weak evangelical congregations. Because saloons were tolerated, its citizens showed little interest in Prohibition or other moral reform measures. Instead of concentrating on winning converts, Galveston's Episcopal and Presbyterian women in the 1880s practiced the kind of Christian charity that looked to the needs of the city's truly disadvantaged. Thus they extended women's domestic and moral authority beyond the doors of their homes and church parlors and established a precedence for community relief of the poor that led to civic benevolence. By founding community benevolent institutions whose female managers were drawn from the Protestant and Jewish congregations, an elite class of women leaders was created that pushed domestic values farther into public life in an attempt not simply to reform the moral values of individuals who were poor, but to ameliorate through practical means the social conditions that produced and adversely affected the poor. Leaders from the benevolent institutions who received pre-1900 "training" were prime candidates for leadership in the poststorm urban reform organizations and in the progressive women's community.

Addressing the urgent needs of the city for burial, revegetation, sanitation, and child welfare programs, former benevolent women leaders were able to transfer their Judeo-Christian values to the wider community through the activities of the Women's Health Protective Association. As the initial progressive women's association, the WHPA became a channel for the interests of women who wanted to create a more beautiful and a safer environment for their children. They wanted to see child mortality decline through the intervention of an *enforced* pure milk law. They wanted clean markets and bakeries even if it meant imposing their middle-class progressive standards on small shopowners and dairymen. They worked for clean alleys, shaded boulevards, school cafeterias, public parks, and health clinics. These were primarily the concerns of women with families and perhaps explains why their goals were limited to "domestic politics."

Suffragists sought to make permanent the gains made by the women progressives. Moving away from community projects to woman-centered goals, they represented the ideal of political equality. Yet their promotional language still rang with phrases from the woman's sphere. Abstractions could not compete with practicalities, however, hence the YWCA outdistanced the other Progressive era reform associations in total membership. Finally, in 1914, Galveston women created an organization that materially benefited other women, particularly those who were self-supporting. Thus the three associations complemented one another, each serving different and overlapping segments of a world of women who were divided by class, ethnicity, and religious affiliation.

Women reformers in Progressive era Galveston enjoyed the support of the elite of the community largely because their efforts improved commercial life and because they were also of that class. But the motivation for reform on the part of women cannot be attributed to class alone. Women reformers had long held a tradition to civic benevolence, stemming from an era when the women's church societies served as proto-welfare agencies. Thus the origins and advance of the women's reform movement should be viewed as a continuum of female social activism — from the care of individuals to the care and restoration of the city and finally to the enhancement of the community of women — in ever-widening circles of domestic concern.

Narrower than the separate sphere but broader than the city's individual clubs, a progressive women's community evolved out of the urban environment. It was an informal alliance comprising women who were active in the Women's Health Protective Association, the Galveston Equal Suffrage Association, and the Young Women's Christian Association. With the founding of each association, the women's community became progressively more democratic. The older, elite WHPA was followed by the ESA, which advanced newcomers to positions of leadership. With the emergence of the more pluralistic YWCA, a far broader coalition of women —

professional women, upper and middle-class matrons, as well as working girls — was harnessed for progressive work, and it was this broader community of politically and socially active women that began to create what may be described as a "movement culture" of women: women within the women's community of Galveston exhibited a solidarity that empowered them to do that which they would have been unable to do singly or in small, exclusive, or sectarian groups. This "movement culture" was manifested not in a single political party, but in several Progressive era nationally affiliated associations that were open to all white women and whose officers were elected by the members.[55] By aggregating resources, talents, and civic ambitions, a progressive women's community was made possible in Galveston and the result was a "women's movement" working for a healthier, safer urban environment with a focus on greater political and economic benefits for women.

5. The Emergence of a Black Neighborhood: Houston's Fourth Ward, 1865–1915

Cary D. Wintz

Recent scholarship on the history of racial and ethnic minorities in American cities has increased our understanding of urban America by focusing on the development of ethnic and minority neighborhoods and the experiences of the residents of these neighborhoods. Works such as John Bodnar's *The Transplanted* and Roger Lane's *Roots of Violence in Black Philadelphia, 1860–1900* have challenged our conceptions of minority life in American cities and forced us to reexamine this aspect of urban history.[1] Both of these studies examine the ethnic experience in terms of the ability of minority groups to adapt to the changing economic and social realities that they faced when they confronted an evolving capitalism in nineteenth-century urban America. For immigrant groups, this process of adaptation was largely successful; they organized themselves into effective ethnic communities that assisted their adjustment to American life. For the blacks in nineteenth-century Philadelphia, however, economic and political discrimination prevented their assimilation into the economic mainstream, undermined the viability of their institutions and neighborhoods, and resulted in the emergence of a black community characterized by the twin social pathologies of crime and violence.

Very little research has been done to determine the degree to which minorities were able to establish viable communities in nineteenth-century Texas cities. This study will address this issue by focusing on the emergence and early history of one of Houston's principal black communities, the Fourth Ward. I shall seek to clarify the misconceptions and myths that surround much of nineteenth-century black history in Houston, to provide a better understanding of the experiences of blacks in late nineteenth-century urban Texas, and to describe the institutions and people that made the Fourth Ward Houston's premier black community during the half century following emancipation. Although the Fourth Ward would not maintain its dominant position in black Houston after the 1920s, and although discrimination and prejudice limited the ability of its residents to enter the economic mainstream, this community did enjoy a significant degree of success within the limits that defined the black experience in the late nineteenth century. It achieved this principally by providing its residents and other black Houstonians with the institutions around which they would organize their lives, and through which they would confront the economic and social realities of Houston.

While most Houstonians have heard of their city's Fourth Ward and would identify it as a black community, misconceptions dominate their image of the area. Even knowledgeable Houstonians would probably describe the Fourth Ward, originally called Freedmantown, as the city's first black community. They might continue by noting that the Fourth Ward has always been the center of black Houston and that it is the "mother ward."

Doubtless, most Houston blacks have some awareness of the central role that the Fourth Ward has played in the history of their community; countless longtime black Houstonians trace their roots to its streets and shotgun houses, to its churches and its schools. Unfortunately, however, much of the history of the Fourth Ward has been shrouded in myth and legend. Even today, the emotionalism associated with defending the integrity of the "mother ward" from the developers who would transform this valuable inner city real estate into high rises and townhouses makes it difficult to uncover the real story of the emergence of one of Houston's oldest and most important black communities.

The Fourth Ward was created three years after the founding of Houston. The city charter of 1839 organized the city into four wards (a fifth and sixth ward were later added as the city grew), with the fourth extending south of Congress Avenue and west of Main Street to the city limits.[2] The primary purpose of the wards was political. Until 1905, when the city adopted a commission system of government with councilmen elected at-large, the wards were the city's council districts; each ward elected two aldermen. The Fourth Ward included not only the neighborhoods along San Felipe Street (West Dallas) that are today associated with the ward, but it extended into the heart of the city and encompassed much of today's downtown business district (although in the nineteenth century most of this area was still residential).

Blacks have lived in Houston from the city's earliest days. Many of the city's first settlers brought slaves with them, and early accounts mention that blacks, along with Mexican prisoners of war, cleared the land for the original townsite in the summer of 1836.[3]

Slaves made up a significant portion of the city's antebellum population. The censuses of 1850 and 1860 show that slaves made up 22 percent of Houston's population; in the latter years, 1,077 slaves lived in the city. Slavery was even more prevalent in the agricultural areas of Harris County (where slaves made up 49 percent of the population in 1860) and in the plantation country along the Brazos River, west and southwest of the city. Free blacks were rare in Houston before the Civil War. State and city law made it difficult for them to remain in Texas. In 1836, there were approximately 20 free blacks in Houston; in 1860 the census counted only 8.[4]

It is during the antebellum period that we find the earliest traces of the black community in the Fourth Ward. Some popular myths contend that free blacks and slaves who resided away from their masters' homes congregated in congested housing in the Fourth Ward; others report blacks living in Vinegar Hill, a community of shanties north of the bayou in what later became the Sixth Ward, or in Frosttown, northeast of the city in the Second or Fifth wards.[5] In truth, neither slaves nor free blacks were particularly concentrated in any one of the city's wards.

Despite the uncertainty about the location of the largest concentration of black residences prior to the war (if indeed there was only one concentration), we can identify the origins of the first black religious and educational institutions in the Fourth Ward. There, in 1841, Houston Methodists organized a church, located above a store on Capital Avenue between Milam and Louisiana. The sixty-eight members included thirty-two blacks. In 1843, the congregation, still including black members, built its own brick building at the same site. Eight years later, black members of the congregation began worshiping in a separate building (with a white pastor) on the Milam side of the property. In 1867, the white members of the congregation gave the blacks title to their building, which they moved to a lot they purchased at the corner of Travis and Bell, farther south in the ward. Several years later, blacks erected a new building on that property for their congregation, then known as Trinity Methodist Episcopal Church.[6]

The first evidence of black education also appeared in the Fourth Ward prior to the Civil War. Although it was never against the law to educate slaves in antebellum Texas, neither whites nor blacks made any real effort to establish a public school system for blacks before emancipation; indeed, there was not even a public school system for whites until after the Civil War.[7] Nevertheless, there is evidence that a private school for blacks operated, at least for a time, in the black Methodist church in the Fourth Ward during the late 1850s. In November, 1858, the *Tri-Weekly Telegraph* noted that "Mrs. M. L. Capshaw will resume her school in the African Methodist Episcopal Church on Monday the 22."[8] Since the 1860 census counted only eight free blacks in the city, and only one of those was of school age, we must assume that slave children and also perhaps adults made up the student body of this early black school.

The end of the Civil War brought dramatic changes to Houston's black community. Not only did over a thousand black Houstonians gain their freedom, but the city's black population surged as several thousand former plantation slaves thronged into the city during the months following emancipation.[9] Black population soared from 1,077 in 1860 to 3,691 in 1870. As table 5.1 indicates, this population was fairly evenly distributed throughout the city, although the largest number settled in the Fourth Ward (which also had the second-highest percentage of blacks in the population). These census data also underscore another major fact about the

Table 5.1
Black Population by Ward, Houston, 1870–1910

	1	*2*	*3*	*4*	*5*	*6*
			Ward			
Total population						
1870 census	738	1,638	2,812	3,055	1,139	
1890 census	1,980	3,341	7,366	8,761	6,109	
1910 census	6,954	7,572	24,705	16,772	16,584	5,943
Black population						
1870 census	250	474	1,075	1,314	578	
1890 census	777	1,262	2,661	3,682	1,997	
1910 census	1,390	2,335	7,662	6,366	4,967	1,209
Percentage black						
1870 census	33.9	28.9	38.2	43.0	50.7	
1890 census	39.2	37.8	36.1	42.0	32.7	
1910 census	20.0	30.8	31.0	38.0	30.0	20.3
Percentage of total black population						
1870 census	6.8	12.8	29.1	35.6	15.7	
1890 census	7.5	12.2	25.6	35.5	19.2	
1910 census	5.8	9.8	32.0	26.6	20.8	5.1

SOURCES: U.S. Department of the Interior, Bureau of the Census, *Ninth Census of the United States: 1870* (Washington, D.C.: Government Printing Office, 1872), p. 272; and idem, *Eleventh Census of the United States: 1890* (Washington, D.C.: Government Printing Office, 1897), p. 555; U.S. Department of Commerce and Labor, Bureau of the Census, *Thirteenth Census of the United States: 1910* (Washington, D.C.: Government Printing Office, 1913), p. 859.

NOTE: The Sixth Ward was not created until after the 1890 census.

Fourth Ward—it was never a totally black community; indeed, it never had a black majority prior to 1915.

Although the source of the black population that moved into the Fourth Ward after the Civil War is not well documented, it is not difficult to imagine where most came from. Some blacks, both slave and free, lived in the ward prior to emancipation. They and their institutions provided the roots for the black community that developed there. These newly emancipated slaves needed inexpensive housing. This was provided on the fringes of the city, often by white landowners who subdivided land for sale or built rental housing for blacks. They took advantage of profits to be made and reacted rationally to the economic problems that accompanied the disintegration of the Confederacy—the collapse of the economy and the loss of the agricultural labor supply. Birds-eye maps of Houston in the early 1870s indicate that the most accessible empty land lay southwest and southeast of the city, in the Fourth and Third wards.[10]

Blacks who had lived in the city prior to emancipation were joined by several thousand newcomers who flocked into the city from nearby and distant plantations. These freed slaves also generally found their housing on the fringes of Houston. A large number arrived from plantations along the Brazos River, entering the city by way of the old San Felipe Road, and settled in the first part of the town that they encountered.[11] The Freedmantown area of the Fourth Ward, actually platted as the Hardcastle Addition, abutted on San Felipe.

Anecdotal accounts add to this picture and provide evidence of how individual blacks established themselves in the ward. For example, Charles S. Longcope, who owned a large home in the city's Second Ward, was reported to have called his slaves to him in June, 1865, and, as he stood in his front door, read to them the proclamation that gave them their freedom. He then offered each of his former slaves a building lot in the Fourth Ward.[12]

The best evidence documenting the physical development of the Fourth Ward in the decades following emancipation is found in city maps. According to the city map of 1866, streets and building lots had been laid out along San Felipe to the city cemetery, and north of San Felipe (east of Freedmantown) to the bayou.[13] However, the platting north of San Felipe does not correspond to later street alignment, and probably never was completed. More detailed information can be obtained from the 1873 bird's-eye map of the city. This map indicates that most Fourth Ward residences were concentrated on the west side of what is now downtown Houston, while the area along San Felipe contained only a few scattered houses and remained semirural in nature.

By the end of the century, the Fourth Ward was much more fully developed. By 1890, the black population of the ward had grown to 3,682; twenty years later it had reached 6,366. The community also expanded physically. According to the 1890 city map, settlement stretched west along San Felipe several blocks past the city cemetery, north to the bayou, and eight to ten blocks south of San Felipe.[14] The 1891 bird's-eye map confirms the spread of residences west along San Felipe, but indicates that much of the area south of that street was still sparsely settled with scattered residences and remained semirural in character.[15] The area on the west side of downtown, along Milam, Louisiana, and Smith, contained the most concentrated number of residences. This layout was not, of course, solely due to an rapid increase in population: by 1890 the Fourth Ward was served by street cars, whose lines followed San Felipe, Robin, and Andrews west to the city limits, drawing with them a portion of the urban populace.[16]

By 1907 (the first year that Sanborn Fire Insurance Maps were made for the area of the Fourth Ward extending west along San Felipe), the ward had assumed much of its present character. In the area along San Felipe, several churches and schools had appeared, and many blocks had commercial buildings — cafes, groceries, bars — on the corners. The majority of the homes were one-story frame residences, although several larger, two-story homes existed on the eastern (downtown) side of the community. There were also a number of rows of cheap shotgun houses, along with simple rectangular and L-shaped houses, and several two-story tenements. The southwestern fringes of the community remained undeveloped.[17]

Maps provide a picture of the physical development of the Fourth Ward, but reveal little about the people who lived there. The census of 1870 furnishes us with a fairly good description of the black population that settled in the ward during the five years following emancipation. The value of census data is limited, however, by the thoroughness of the census questionnaires — and in 1870 they were not very thorough.[18] The description of blacks in Houston's Fourth Ward that follows is based on samples taken from the 1870 and 1900 enumerators' handwritten census lists.[19]

As table 5.2 indicates, the overwhelming majority (86.5 percent) of the blacks living in the Fourth Ward in 1870 were not born in the state (a similar percentage of white Texans were also born out of state). Black females outnumbered black males in the ward, 53 percent to 47 percent, and 57.2 percent of blacks over age fifteen were married. Only 27 percent lived in single-family households, while 46 percent shared their households with relatives or other adults. Of this latter group, about 22 percent had relatives in their household, while 78 percent housed nonrelatives, generally boarders. Nine percent of the blacks in the Fourth Ward resided as live-in domestic servants, usually in a white household, while the rest lived in apartments or boarding-houses. Finally, in 1870 — only five years after the end of slavery — 4.2 percent of the black residents of the Fourth Ward already owned their own homes.

The picture of black life in 1870 that emerges is of crowded households — only about one in four had one family per household and the average black household had 5.07 persons present.[20] This clearly reflected the rapid influx of blacks into Houston and the Fourth Ward in 1870 and the corresponding difficulty in acquiring housing. It also reflects the living conditions experienced by most other ethnic groups shortly after their arrival in America. Taking in boarders and sharing housing were common strategies used to contend with both housing shortages and high costs.

In the Fourth Ward, at least, the black family seems to have survived the period of slavery fairly well. In 1870, 57.2 percent of the population over the age of fifteen were married (as well as can be determined from inexact census records), 33.5 percent were single, and 9.3 percent were widowed, separated, or divorced. More significantly, 77.3 percent of Fourth Ward black households were headed by males, and 73.3 percent had both husband and wife present. The black family, it seems, was intact.

By 1900 significant changes had taken place in the demographics of the black population of the Fourth Ward. The majority of blacks residing in the ward in that year were born in the state (63.2 percent); females still outnumbered males (51.7 percent to 48.3 percent), but the ratio was more even than it had been thirty years earlier. In 1900, fewer blacks over age fifteen were married (only 44.8 percent) and more were widowed or divorced

Table 5.2
Black Population in Houston's Fourth Ward

| Descriptor | Percentage of Ward Population | |
	1870	1900
Sex		
Male	47.0	48.3
Female	53.0	51.7
Place of birth		
Texas	13.5	63.2
Other southern states	67.0	29.9
Marital status		
Married	57.2	44.8
Single	33.5	36.8
Widowed, separated, or divorced	9.3	16.7
Home ownership		
Owner-occupied home	4.2	12.1
Living arrangement		
Single-family house	27.0	21.3
Relative or boarders present	46.0	56.9
Live-in servant	9.3	9.2
Number of persons per household	5.1	4.8
Structure of household		
Head of household is male	77.3	67.2
Spouse of head is present	73.3	60.7
No adult relatives in household	80.0	62.3
No children in household	42.7	50.8
Whites live in household	5.3	6.6

SOURCES: National Archives Microfilm Publications, *Population Schedules of the Ninth Census of the United States: 1870, Texas,* Vol. 9, *Guadalupe, Hamilton, Hardin, and Harris Counties* (Washington, D.C.: National Archives, 1965); Bureau of the Census Microfilm Laboratory, *Twelfth Census of the Population: 1900, Texas,* Vol. 53, *Harris County.*

(16.7 percent). Somewhat surprisingly, housing had become even more crowded than it had been in 1870, perhaps reflecting the long agricultural depression in Texas and the South in the late 1880s and early 1890s and the continuing influx of blacks into the city; on the other hand, these figures may only reflect the greater number of boardinghouses that had appeared in the east and northeast sections of the ward. For whatever reason, in 1900, only 21.3 percent of Fourth Ward blacks lived in single-family households, while 56.9 percent shared their homes with relatives (now 34.5 percent) or other adults. Nine percent still resided in other households as live-in domestic servants. In thirty years, the percentage that owned their own homes had almost tripled, rising to 12.1 percent. Housing in the Fourth Ward remained crowded in 1900. In that year only one household in five contained just one family; however, the average number of persons per black household had dropped to 4.82.[21]

The most disturbing change that occurred in the demographics of the Fourth Ward during the last quarter of the nineteenth century was a measurable deterioration in the black family. Census data from 1900 reveal that only 44.8 percent of the black population over the age of fifteen were married, while the percent widowed, separated, or divorced had nearly doubled. More significantly, the number of households that were headed by males had declined to 67.2 percent, and the number of households with both spouses present had dropped to 60.7 percent. Again, it is not clear whether the deterioration of the black family was a real phenomenon caused, perhaps, by the pressures of city life or by the difficult economic times in the mid-1890s, whether it was a statistical aberration caused by the growing number of boarding-houses that attracted a transient population, or whether it merely reflected more accurate census data than were collected in 1870.[22]

If the vitality of the black family suffered during the first three decades after slavery ended, the occupational status of blacks improved slightly. In 1870, 73.5 percent of all blacks over the age of fifteen in the sample surveyed worked as unskilled, service, or domestic workers. That same year, 10.7 percent were skilled labor, while only 1.4 percent were professionals or shopkeepers. Furthermore, in 1870, 78.1 percent of black women in the Fourth Ward worked; most (67.5 percent) were domestics. By 1900, the number of unskilled, service workers, and domestics had declined to 63.8 percent, while the number of professionals and shopkeepers had risen to 9.2 percent. However, the number of skilled laborers had dropped to 5.7 percent, perhaps because the Fifth Ward now provided convenient housing for blacks who worked as skilled labor for the railroads, or perhaps because of the hostility of white-dominated labor organizations to the employment of blacks as skilled labor.[23] The number of black women who worked outside the home declined to 66.3 percent and the number employed as domestics dropped to 43.4 percent.[24]

Of particular interest in the development of the Fourth Ward is the emergence of residential segregation. Most students of Houston's history have assumed that segregation developed very quickly in black neighborhoods after the Civil War.[25] Published census data do not confirm this, however. As table 5.1 indicates, blacks were distributed fairly evenly throughout the city's wards in the late nineteenth century, no ward had a majority black population, and, indeed, the percentage of blacks in the population declined in every ward except the Second between 1870 and 1910.

Most historians, however, have dismissed published census data as being too general to depict residential segregation.[26] The smallest unit for which the U.S. Census reported data in nineteenth-century Houston was the ward; the wards, however, were too large geographically to measure neighborhood segregation adequately. Consequently, most historians have assumed that Houston reflected the residential patterns of other late-nineteenth-century southern cities that John Kellogg documented in his study of the emergence of black residential clusters on the outskirts of Lexington, Atlanta, Richmond, and Durham.[27] The consensus of those who have examined Houston's history has been that "Houston blacks characteristically clustered along a few blocks or sections of each ward creating small segregated enclaves. Seldom did black and white families occupy dwelling units on the same block."[28]

An analysis of handwritten census lists does not support this conclusion. A sample of households in the 1870 census indicates that 53.7 percent of black families in the Fourth Ward lived next door to whites. Frequently, for several blocks black and white households were completely intermixed; then there were areas where five or ten black households were grouped together, followed by several white homes. The white families that lived in the areas with the most concentrated black population were often, but not always, German or English immigrants.[29] In 1900, segregation was more widespread, and census data were more exact. In the "downtown" area of the ward, among the bars and brothels of Prairie Street and the boardinghouses of McKinney, Bagby, Milam, Travis, Clay, and Pease, blacks and whites still lived side by side — 47.8 percent of black families lived next door to whites. In the heart of the Fourth Ward, along San Felipe and adjacent streets, segregation was beginning to take hold and clusters of black homes were more common, but 24.7 percent of the black families continued to live next door to whites.[30]

Even more surprisingly, the census data indicate that in 1870, 5.3 percent of the black households had whites living in them, usually as boarders; in 1900, the number had risen to 6.6 percent. A detailed analysis of the handwritten enumerators' lists provides more details about these integrated households. In one 1870 household, for example, a thirty-five-year-old black woman who had four children and worked as a domestic rented a room in the home she owned to a sixty-year-old white carpenter from Ohio. There were other cases in which blacks resided in white households. In 1870, for example, one household headed by a sixty-six-year-old white grocer from New Hampshire contained, in addition to his wife, adult children, and grandchildren, four adult blacks (one married couple and a single man and single woman). In another case, the head of the household was a twenty-four-year-old white Texas-born clerk; included in the residence, along with his wife and infant child, were a married black couple and a young black woman. Living arrangements such as these were even more common in 1900 than in 1870.[31]

The data from the handwritten census lists that document the slow development of residential segregation in the Fourth Ward substantiate information gathered in oral history interviews in a project conducted for the Houston Center for the Humanities. Several elderly blacks interviewed in the early 1980s recalled that one or two white families (mostly foreign) lived on their block while they were growing up in the Fourth Ward in the 1920s and 1930s.[32]

In terms of its physical growth and, most likely, its residential patterns, the Fourth Ward did not differ significantly from the Third and Fifth wards in the late nineteenth and early twentieth centuries. However, during this period the Fourth Ward was distinguished from other black communities in Houston by the number of important black institutions that it housed. It was the location of most of the city's early black religious and educational institutions and many of its black businesses and professions were centered there. The first black church in Houston, Trinity Methodist Episcopal, which began in the antebellum period, was located at Travis and Bell (in what is now downtown Houston).[33] The most prominent early black church, Antioch Baptist, was also a Fourth Ward institution. Antioch was established by white missionary William C. Crane in 1866. Initially, the church held services at the First Baptist Church, then at the German Baptist Church. In the summer of 1866, a black minister, I. S. Campbell, took charge of the church and, after first holding services in a "brush arbor" erected on the banks of Buffalo Bayou, built a frame structure in 1868 at Rusk and Bagby in the Fourth Ward. Jack Yates became pastor of Antioch in late 1868 (or early 1869); in 1879, he moved the church to its present site, a brick structure on Robin Street.[34]

The influence of these early black churches on the community extended far beyond religious matters. In 1869, for example, black churches were involved in the organization of the Harris County Republican Club. This was one of the few truly integrated organizations at this time; blacks served as secretary and vice-president and held two of the five seats on the executive committee. The club held most of its meetings in Antioch Baptist Church.[35]

Black churches were also at the forefront of other civic matters. In 1872, Antioch and Trinity Methodist worked together to raise money and purchase a park for blacks in Houston. Both churches sponsored picnics and Emancipation Day celebrations on wooded land north of San Felipe in the Fourth Ward. In 1872, they acquired a permanent park site, Emancipation Park (in the Third Ward).[36]

Antioch also helped promote black education. Yates, after failing in his efforts to locate Bishop College in Houston, worked with white missionaries to establish Houston College (also known as Houston Baptist Academy) in rented facilities in the Third Ward in 1885. In 1894, the school moved to its own three-acre site west of the city limits on San Felipe.[37] The college's mission was to train black youth for the ministry as well as to provide general education. It was a college in name only, however. Virtually all of its students were enrolled in its primary, secondary, and industrial training programs.[38]

With the location of Houston College on its western edge, the Fourth Ward consolidated its position as the center of black education in Houston in the late nineteenth century. It had taken the lead in educational endeavors shortly after emancipation when the Freedmen's Bureau located two of the three schools it established in black churches in the Fourth Ward.[39] In 1870, the state legislature established the first public school for blacks in the city, Gregory Institute, located initially at Jefferson and Louisiana, also in the Fourth Ward. Eventually, the city established elementary schools for blacks in each of the wards, but until the mid-1920s, the only high school for blacks was located on San Felipe in the heart of the Fourth Ward.

The Fourth Ward tightened its hold on the educational and intellectual life of black Houston in the early twentieth century when the Carnegie Library for blacks opened its doors on San Felipe, across the street from Colored High School (and not far from Houston Negro College). The library grew out of efforts of the Library Association, which E. O. Smith organized in 1907. Initially, the library was housed in a room of the high school, but after a successful fund-raising drive (which raised money to purchase a building lot), Andrew Carnegie donated funds to erect a library building in 1910. The library opened in its new quarters three years later.[40]

The first medical facilities for blacks in Houston were also organized in the Fourth Ward. In 1910, a group of black physicians, unable to practice in Houston's white hospitals, organized the Union Hospital, located on Andrews Street near San Felipe.[41] This unit served as the city's only black hospital until Houston Negro Hospital opened in the Third Ward in 1923. Furthermore, all but one of the black doctors and dentists (and 75 percent of the black attorneys) identified by the *Red Book* in 1915 clustered their offices in the 400 block of Milam and Travis in the downtown Houston area of the Fourth Ward.[42]

In addition to housing the offices of the black population's doctors and lawyers, the Fourth Ward was also the location for a disproportionate share of black businesses in the early twentieth century. Of the 415 black-owned businesses identified in the *Red Book,* 32.8 percent were located in the Fourth Ward (which held 26.6 percent of the city's black population in 1910). More significantly, 80 percent of black professional establishments were located in the ward and 28.3 percent of its skilled or service establishments such as restaurants, grocery stores, and jewelry stores. In addition, 31 percent of the black schoolteachers lived in the ward, although only three of the city's thirteen black schools were located there. On the other hand, only 23 percent of the black churches were located in the Fourth Ward, although it was home to Antioch and Trinity—the two oldest and most prestigious.[43]

The Fourth Ward's dominant position in the early history of black Houston was determined not by the numbers who lived there (it never was home to much more than a third of the black population) but was based on the fact that until the 1920s it was the location of the most significant black institutions and housed many of black Houston's businesses and most of its professionals. The Fourth Ward dominated the city during the years that saw the exhilaration of emancipation fade before the realities of segregation and discrimination. Many of the black institutions that emerged in the late nineteenth century, including the schools and hospital and even some of the businesses, owed their existence to segregation. This, however, does not detract from the fact that blacks, like other racial and ethnic minorities, did not succumb to these prejudices, but succeeded in creating the community institutions that assisted their adjustment to the economic and social realities of American life. In Houston the Fourth Ward, while not the only black community, was the center of the most successful black efforts during the fifty years following the end of slavery. The history of these efforts and the history of this community are an essential chapter in the history of the city of Houston and of its black population.

The Fourth Ward lost its preeminence in the 1920s. The Third Ward, which surpassed the Fourth Ward in black population in 1910, began to attract more black institutions in the 1920s and 1930s. Houston Negro Hospital located there in 1923, and in the late 1920s, the second black high school opened there, as did Houston Negro Junior College, the black branch of the Houston Independent School District's first experiment with higher education and the precursor of Texas Southern University.

Meanwhile, the potential for physical growth in the Fourth Ward was severely limited. Some blacks contend that growth in the Fourth Ward came to a halt because whites refused to sell property adjacent to the ward to blacks.[44] The reality is in fact a good deal more complicated. The availability of land is a crucial issue. As the City Planning Commission observed in the late 1920s, unlike the Fifth and Third wards, which had available sufficient adjacent land for expansion, the Fourth Ward was already hemmed in by development on the south and west. These pressures increased, as evidenced by the institutional (and white) encroachment on the Fourth Ward in the 1930s. Of particular note were the clearing of land north of San Felipe for a white housing project and the southwestward spread of downtown office buildings in the second half of the century. Both of these developments accelerated the decline of the Fourth Ward and caused a large number of its residents to relocate, either to the Third or the Fifth wards, or to the new black communities that developed as the city spread. These new housing tracts are important in another respect. White builders in Houston willingly constructed new housing for blacks, usually on the fringes of the city, a lure that opened the way for additional encroachments on the former black ward. If this was not actually a malevolent attack on black Houston, it certainly reflected disregard for the interests of the people of the ward, an attitude characteristic of urban development in twentieth-century Texas cities.[45]

Indeed, the decline of the Fourth Ward reflects the changing reality of Houston politics, which Harold Platt has explored in some detail. A series of "progressive" civic reforms in early twentieth-century Houston resulted in the replacement of the ward-based system of city aldermen with a government based on a strong mayor and city commissioners elected at large. As Platt notes, this new structure diminished ward politics, diluted minority and neighborhood influence in city government, and can be viewed as a component of the movement to exclude blacks from political activity in Houston. Blacks, in short, were disenfranchised at the same time that they were dislodged.[46]

One question this study raises is, To what degree did the situation that blacks faced in Houston's Fourth Ward typify the conditions faced by blacks in other American cities? In some respects, conditions in the Fourth Ward were fairly characteristic. The structure of black households and black families in late-nineteenth-century Houston was very similar to that which Herbert Gutman found in his examination of black families in Beaufort, South Carolina, Natchez, Mississippi, Mobile, Alabama, and Richmond, Virginia.[47] On the other hand, no other study of southern cities has documented the type of racial integration that persisted in Houston's Fourth Ward into the early twentieth century. Kellogg's analysis of housing patterns, like most other studies, does not examine geographical units that were small enough to indicate accurately the degree of housing segregation. Joe William Trotter does question the degree of segregation in early-twentieth-century black Milwaukee, but does not provide sufficient data to substantiate his observation that a traditional black ghetto had not emerged by 1915.[48]

Black Houston and its Fourth Ward did differ rather significantly from other black communities in terms of both its rapid growth and its relative prosperity. The black population in Houston increased by over 1000 percent between 1870 and 1920—a growth rate much greater than that experienced by other southern cities. The Census Bureau's study of blacks published in 1932 indicates that black-owned businesses in early-twentieth-century Houston enjoyed total sales and average sales per store far in excess of those experienced by black-owned businesses in Atlanta and New Orleans (both of which had substantially larger black populations than Houston at that time). In addition, black businesses in Houston were somewhat more diversified than those in other cities—in Houston only about 61 percent of black-owned businesses were in the food or restaurant industry, while in both Atlanta and New Orleans more than 75 percent were so concentrated.[49] A rapidly growing, relatively prosperous black community may account for the continuing high incidence of integrated residential patterns in Houston's Fourth Ward. In other ways, especially in terms of family and household structure, the Fourth Ward does not appear to have been unique.

Although this examination of the rise and fall of one of Houston's oldest black communities raises almost as many questions as it answers, it nonetheless puts to rest some old myths. The Fourth Ward was neither the first nor the largest black community in Houston. A majority of Houston's black population always resided in the other wards during the late nineteenth and early twentieth centuries. Nor was the Fourth Ward the monolithic community that most believe it was. At the turn of the century, the majority of the ward's population was white, and residential segregation had not yet taken firm hold. Nor was the Freedmantown (or San Felipe) area the heart and birthplace of the ward — many of its residents and many of its institutions were located in the section of the ward that is now the heart of downtown Houston. Nevertheless, the myths of the ward's primacy in the history of black Houston are rooted in reality. For the fifty years following emancipation, it was the center of much black activity and culture, serving as the location of the first black schools, the first black churches, and many of the first black businesses. It is in this more restricted (but important) sense that the Fourth became the "mother ward" of black Houston, a role it no longer plays.

Part IV.

Suburban Idylls

6. Olmos Park and the Creation of a Suburban Bastion, 1927–39

Char Miller and Heywood T. Sanders

Suburbs offended Gus B. Mauerman. As mayor of San Antonio during the mid-1940s, he frequently vented his anger over the existence of a series of small incorporated "satellite cities" — Alamo Heights, Olmos Park, and Terrell Hills — that lay on the northern edge of the city's legal limits. Hoping to pull them closer into the orbit of San Antonio, the City Council used its powers of annexation in August, 1944, to incorporate several thousand acres of property and streets surrounding the suburbs; they became like so many Vaticans within Rome.[1]

Mauerman did not treat them with great reverence, however. He immediately proposed creating a city dump on newly acquired land between two of the suburbs, its noxious odors to be a sign of his disrespect. His next maneuver really left the communities fuming. In 1945, he brought suit against Olmos Park and Terrell Hills to force their annexation. The suit was filed when it became known that the two towns had no mechanism by which to levy taxes to support a new city and county hospital. Charging that neither community had a "real city government," that both were only inefficient "volunteer associations," Mauerman argued that the suit would finally "breach their legal defenses" and bring these "two lucrative sources of taxes" into San Antonio.[2]

Mauerman's aggressive tactics and expansionist tendencies were foiled in this case: the city ultimately dropped its suit in the face of stiff opposition. But the mayor's actions, his supporters declared, were not solely motivated by a desire to replenish city coffers. After all, the *San Antonio Express* editorialized, he was battling for a greater good: as a part of "economic San Antonio," the "suburban residents can only prosper as the community grows and prospers," a mutually beneficial state that could be realized through a "unified municipal program." The continued existence of insular suburbs retarded metropolitan progress.[3]

The very idea of bedroom communities was also an affront to a booster's vision of the character of urban society and a responsible citizenry. A town could not be a town, Mauerman and the *San Antonio Express* agreed, if it had "no parks, no libraries, no health department, no fire department, nor anything else." Since the citizens of Olmos Park and Terrell Hills enjoyed none of these privileges or protections, their political status was only partial and their communities "dormant." Only annexation could rectify this unfortunate situation; only then would the "full benefits of citizenship" accrue.[4]

But were these communities as poorly conceived and as inefficiently organized as Mauerman's antipathy would suggest? Their dormancy may have clashed with his political principles and urban boosterism, but his perspective is a poor vantage point from which to explain the context in which these suburbs were created and sustained. As an extended analysis of the history of Olmos Park reveals, there was a certain logic to being an "inactive" suburb. A town could be not a town.

An examination of this small Texas community will also cast light on the larger world of which it was a part. The development of Olmos Park, then, was inextricably bound up with and reflective of the political machinations and social problems that dominated San Antonio in the first decades of this century. As Mauerman understood, the suburb *was* a fragment of the urban whole, an observation that needs to be pushed one step farther. The forces that shaped Olmos Park and determined its relations with San Antonio were also part of a national pattern, of tensions generated by the explosive urban and suburban growth in early-twentieth-century America.[5]

The legendary aura that surrounds the site on which Olmos Park would rise, and the background of H. C. Thorman, the man responsible for its development, are an improbable combination of faded Old World elegance and brash New World ambition, a combination that, no doubt, had a certain appeal for the community's early residents.

The sixteen hundred–acre tract of land, which in the 1920s would become a posh suburb, was, in the late nineteenth century, owned by Ladislaus Uhjazzi, an Austrian count. Uhjazzi built an elaborate mansion surrounded by gracefully landscaped grounds, and his estate — legend has it — was the scene of countless soirees and cotillions. The funds that sustained the count's magnanimity, however, were derived from rental income from family lands in Austria, funds that dried up when the Austrian government prohibited profiteering by absentee landlords. This prohibition forced Uhjazzi to return to his homeland. Not long after his departure, fire consumed his sumptuous home. When H. C. Thorman purchased the land in the mid-1920s, it had for some time been known simply as Uhjazzi, a small reminder of European grace in South Texas.[6]

The life of Herman Charles Thorman, on the other hand, is the stuff of an American legend, of the rise from rags to riches. Although details of his early life are sketchy, Thorman apparently grew up on a small farm in northwestern Ohio, arriving in San Antonio in 1909 with little capital. Apparently, too, he sank what money he had in an oil exploration venture in Luling, Texas, that paid off handsomely, the proceeds providing him with the funds he needed to speculate in San Antonio real estate. By the middle 1920s, he had made his mark on the city, having developed middle-class neighborhoods in the Highlands and Fredericksburg Road areas, southeast and northwest of the city, developing, too, the Country Club Estates, middle-class housing that bordered on the San Antonio Country Club to the northeast of the city's central core. In 1925, after fewer than ten years in the business, Thorman claimed to have constructed more than twelve hundred homes, a substantial number at a time when most suburban development in the United States was on a smaller scale. Further evidence of Thorman's successful rise was the home he constructed for his family on part of Uhjazzi's former estate. Indeed, it rivaled the count's edifice. Set amid a vast grove of oak trees, complete with a two-and-a-half story glass dome foyer, the colonial mansion alone cost in excess of fifty thousand dollars. Clearly, the farm boy had made it big in the city.[7]

H. C. Thorman's success was due in part to individual initiative, but he did not operate in a historical vacuum. He was able to capitalize on the city's pattern of suburban growth, a radial pattern that the streetcars and railroads established in the late nineteenth and early twentieth centuries, one that the automobile quickly extended and began to fill in laterally during the second decade of the century. Thorman's developments to the west on Fredericksburg Road and in the Highlands district are prime examples of the new kind of suburb that the automobile made possible. Olmos Park was no exception to this trend, as both the community's physical location and spatial design illustrate.

The former Uhjazzi estate, for example, was set on the northern edge of the city limits, a location that would enable Thorman to exploit one of the most significant public works projects in San Antonio history—the Olmos Dam. At first blush, the dam would seem to have little to do with the development of a suburb, for its fundamental purpose was to establish for the first time a reliable means of flood control. Throughout its history, San Antonio had been devastated by rising waters in the San Antonio River, especially in its chief tributary, Olmos Creek. On the evening of September 9, 1921, the level of damage finally reached unacceptable proportions. After a sudden and violent storm, floodwaters rolled down the creek, rapidly spilled over the riverbanks, and inundated residential and commercial areas of the city, killing sixteen people and causing millions of dollars of damage. In the storm's aftermath, the city decided it must begin to control the San Antonio River's watershed and, in 1925, began construction of a 1,941-foot dam that spanned Olmos Creek. Its completion in late 1926 marked an important advance in public safety.[8]

The dam's completion had far-reaching economic consequences as well. As the *San Antonio Express* noted, Olmos Dam quickly "stabilized property values throughout the city, and has given San Antonio a new standing among large investors of capital," investors whose funds began to reshape the downtown business district even before the dam was finished. Indeed,

the newspaper predicted that the dam would in the end pay "greater dividends than any other expenditure which has ever been made by the city,"
a point with which H. C. Thorman fully agreed, but for somewhat different reasons. His interest in the dam lay not with its economic impact on
downtown real estate but with the role it would play in the development
of the large piece of property he had purchased just west of the dam, land
he bought as soon as he learned that the dam would be erected. For him,
the dam served as a vital bridge, for atop it ran a road that provided "a
new crosstown thoroughfare linking Alamo Heights on the east with Laurel
Heights on the west." Thorman's land was situated between these two
developments. He suspected that the new road would reorient traffic patterns along the city's north side and, in so doing, make accessible (and
profitable) land that had been previously undeveloped.[9]

Prior to the dam's construction, Thorman declared in an interview that
"no facilities existed for some considerable distance for crossing between
the east and west divisions on the north of greater San Antonio." This
meant that residential development in metropolitan San Antonio had to
"spread out to the north from downtown something after the manner of
a fan." The dam changed that outward radial thrust, Thorman concluded,
by "encouraging the filling in with residential development of some considerable proportion of the underdeveloped territory within the fan." That
the Olmos Dam and the automobile were integral to the creation of Olmos
Park is made clear in one of Thorman's advertisements for his new development. The advertisement did not focus on the Olmos Dam's flood
control potential, but rather on its use as a highway: a cavalcade of cars
is seen rushing west across the dam from Alamo Heights and toward a
banner emblazoned with the words "Park Hills Estates," one of the names
given his subdivision. Thorman stands under the banner, waving the cars
on, presumably ready to make a deal.[10]

The automobile did more than simply transport potential buyers to
Olmos Park; it also helped determine the community's spatial design. The
automobile was indispensable to the community's life, for Olmos Park was
served neither by streetcars nor by anything so pedestrian as a sidewalk.
That dependence could have led Thorman to replicate the gridiron pattern
that characterized most of San Antonio's streets, a pattern that would have
obscured the natural contours of the land for the sake of convenience and
efficiency. Instead, he designed Olmos Park to rein in the automobile, to
provide a sharp break — visual and physical — from the relentless gridiron.
After having given "careful thought to the planning of these Estates [such]
that the great natural beauty and splendid position of this property would
be enhanced," he embraced what he called the "parkway system of development." This system, which no doubt drew on the landscape theories
and practices of Frederick Law Olmsted and J. C. Nichols, laid down broad
avenues and drives that wound among the native oak trees and rolled

gently over the hills. This restful environment would be a natural tonic for the harried urban dweller.[11]

The community was further protected from the surrounding city by natural and artificial barriers. To the east and north of Olmos Park lay the Olmos Creek floodplain, land forever uninhabitable now that the dam had been built; in the future, the floodplain would be used for a city park. To the south lay additional parkland and a quarry, and portions of the western section bordered on the Missouri Pacific rail lines. Each of these helped prevent and encroachment of undesirable development and, when combined with the centripetal force that the "parkway system" exerted on movement in the community's interior, set Olmos Park apart from its environs. Physical harmony and physical exclusivity went hand in hand.[12]

Social exclusivity was also an intrinsic part of the new development and deeply imbued the legal codes governing the lives and affairs of those who moved to Olmos Park. As with other upper-class suburbs developed in the early twentieth century—such as Roland Park in Baltimore, Houston's River Oaks, and the Country Club District of Kansas City—Olmos Park adopted a rigorous and restrictive covenant to ensure racial segregation, the maintenance of high property values, and the perpetuation of these well into the future. Thorman and other developers across the nation had turned to restrictive covenants when, in 1917, the U.S. Supreme Court had declared segregation by zoning illegal. Nine years later the high court effectively sanctioned restrictive covenants when it refused to hear *Corrigan v. Buckley;* consequently, the popularity of these covenants soared. The Olmos Park covenant was thus part of a national trend and a close examination of it will suggest the complex role such documents could play in the creation of suburban bastions.[13]

In the early twentieth century, elites throughout the United States began to abandon the inner city suburbs that had arisen in the nineteenth century, seeking refuge from the steady advance of the city and its presumed social and racial ills in more distant communities. Those in San Antonio were no different, and H. C. Thorman addressed their concerns in the restrictive covenant he put into effect in Olmos Park in January, 1927. This covenant not only shaped the community's racial character, but it determined land use patterns and the kind of housing possible. These racial and economic sanctions in turn played an important role in the selling of Olmos Park, for they were prominently displayed in newspaper advertisements designed to lure those who valued such restrictions and the exclusivity they provided. In this, they were no doubt successful, for land sales in Olmos Park were brisk from the outset, and purchasers were invariably members of powerful San Antonio families.

The covenant made it clear that Olmos Park was for whites only, for no portion of the property could be "sold, conveyed or leased to any person who is not of the caucasian race." Any violation of this stipulation was punishable by law, indeed, would "work as a forfeiture of the title to the particular subdivision of property," a clear indication that the community's right to racial segregation superseded the rights of the individual property owner. This power transcended time as well: the covenant did not apply just to the original owner but was made "running with the land," and therefore applied to and was bound upon "the grantee, his heirs, devisees, executors, administrators, successors or assigns." As Thorman declared, the restrictions would "forever stand good." This covenant, as with others created around the nation, acted as a "social compact" that, in Thomas Philpott's words, "symbolized and guaranteed community solidarity," a solidarity that erected and enforced racial boundaries.[14]

Racial segregation was only one element in the Olmos Park covenant, however. It also stipulated that the new community could only be residential in nature. As the warranty deed for Olmos Park Estates puts it, "Neither the [original land] grantee nor any subsequent owner or occupant of said property shall use the same for other than residence purposes." Beneath this innocuous statement lay a host of concerns about what kind of community this would and would not be, a point addressed by the first advertisements for Park Hills Estates in late 1926: "The property has been blanketed with restrictions in order to assure development of the character which this reality warrants. It has been restricted against apartments, hotels, and business of any character." Another advertisement put it more bluntly: the restrictions were "sensibly designed to protect your home and every home from the encroachments of inferiority."[15]

This quest to produce a noncommercial haven consisting exclusively of "truly fine homes" extended even to the kinds of building materials that could be employed in construction. No residence on Stanford Drive in Olmos Park Estates, for example, could be "erected . . . except of brick, brick veneer, rock stucco or hollow tile construction," materials that characterized domestic architecture on the vast majority of the community's streets. Architectural uniformity was especially pronounced in Park Hill Estates due to the large number of homes designed by Bartlett Cocke, chief architect for H. C. Thorman's development company. But whether or not Cocke was the architect of record, each residence in Olmos Park had to comply with a series of more minor restrictions that determined, among other things, the placement and construction material of outbuildings and fences. The latter especially underscores Thorman's desire to create a physically harmonious environment: "No fence or wall other than an ornamental iron fence," the warranty deed stipulated, "shall be erected on said premises higher than three feet above the natural ground level." This stipulation suggests that the developer not only desired clean sight lines and no clutter, but something more: the community's wealth was to be framed, not obscured.

The restrictive covenant of Olmos Park was not simply concerned with the area's physical appearance or ethnic makeup, of course. Economic restrictions reinforced those that helped determine the community's residential character, all the while distinguishing Olmos Park from other suburban development in San Antonio in the 1920s.

Olmos Park's primacy in this regard was tied to three interrelated restrictions, those concerned with the size of building lots, prices per front foot, and the minimum cost established for buildings erected on the property itself. From the first, it was clear that the developer of Olmos Park wanted interested buyers to understand how different this suburb would be from other contemporary developments. Not for Olmos Park the relatively small plots of land that characterized most middle-class or upper-middle-class suburbs in San Antonio: "Sites in Park Hills Estates are much larger than those offered in other sections of the city. They are not parceled out in 50-foot units, but carry a minimum footage of 75 feet." Most lots, in fact, extended 100 feet or more, and could be as deep as 300 feet, providing the kind of expansive "grounds that are demanded by those families who build fine homes."

That such grounds were valued in their own right is clear, but there was an additional ramification — only a very few citizens of San Antonio could afford to purchase such sizable lots. The minimum price per front foot in Olmos Park, for example, was $30 and extended upward to $80, resulting in base prices for land ranging from $2,250 for a 75-foot lot to $6000 for one of 250 feet; these figures could soar to more than $20,000, depending on the lot size and location. The expansive grounds of Olmos Park, in short, can tell us much about the economic standing of those who chose to live in the community.[16]

Impressive as these figures are alone, they take on greater significance when set against the context of San Antonio real estate in the mid-1920s. A comparison of average lot sizes reveals that H. C. Thorman could indeed boast that with few exceptions his property sites were the largest of the contemporary developments. Furthermore, the cost of the land was strikingly higher — Olmos Park's minimum cost of thirty dollars per front foot was the ceiling for the vast majority of other developments advertised in the San Antonio newspapers, and none came within forty dollars of the maximum that Thorman set for his land.[17]

There was one final cost involved that further distinguished Olmos Park from its contemporary suburbs in San Antonio and, more generally, in Texas — the minimum expenditure allowed for housing construction. "Neither the grantee or subsequent owner or occupant shall erect any residence of any kind on said property at a cost less than $7,500.00," the warranty deed states, a figure that Thorman repeatedly emphasized in newspaper advertisements. That figure is remarkable on a number of levels. First, no other contemporaneous development publicly proclaimed any minimum figure, let alone one of such magnitude; that Thorman saw this as a means by which to generate sales illuminates another dimension of the exclusivity of Olmos Park. Moreover, by way of comparison, this figure more than doubled the deed restriction governing the construction of housing in Alamo Heights, an exclusive suburb to the east of Olmos Park that was initially developed before World War I. Finally, it was $500 higher than even the restriction imposed on housing in that most exclusive Houston suburb, River Oaks, which the Hogg brothers developed in the mid-1920s. Olmos Park, then, could be ranked as one of the most restrictive (and restricted) suburbs in the state and, by extension, in the nation, a status that is nothing short of extraordinary when one takes into account the general poverty of San Antonio. The elites were taking no chances.[18]

Who moved into the community that H. C. Thorman considered his "masterpiece"? Green Peyton, a novelist and journalist, offered his impressions of Olmos Park and its citizens in his *San Antonio: City in the Sun* (1946). "The expensive, independent community [lies] just outside the city limits on a hill north of San Antonio," Peyton wrote, a topographical elevation that reflected the community's social hauteur. It was in Olmos Park that the "rich oilmen and cattle ranchers live," Peyton noted, remarking as well that one would not therefore "find many sheep and goat men living in fine Olmos Park mansions. They do not have the social pretensions of the old cattle families," preferring instead to "congregate in the garish lobby of the Gunter Hotel, in shirtsleeves, still wearing their ranch hats and boots." Clearly, some people's money was more refined than others.[19] It was that sense of refinement that Thorman sought to project when he initially developed the community in the 1920s, a sense that is strikingly revealed in a comparison of the image of the ideal buyer in Olmos Park and in Spanish Acres, a contemporary development to the west.

Spanish Acres lay within what its developer considered "the Arc of Opportunity," a band of land that radiated westward along Fredericksburg Road in what is known as the Woodlawn District. Potential buyers were bombarded with appeals to the booster spirit: "Mr. and Mrs. Woodlawn District are Progressive Folks," one advertisement trumpeted, "the kind you like to have for neighbors — citizens who gladly shoulder their personal and community responsibilities." And they were youthful shoulders that bore those responsibilities in Spanish Acres. In one 1927 advertisement, a young childless couple, dressed in flapper regalia, is portrayed gazing longingly upon a row of modest homes built closely together. The message is clear: Spanish Acres and other Woodlawn developments were for those of youthful and rising expectations; it was for those whose future seemed bright but not assured. Spanish Acres was, after all, within an "Arc of Opportunity"; it was an area and a people on the move.[20]

The contrast between the image of Spanish Acres and that of Olmos Park is vividly captured in one of Thorman's first advertisements. In the foreground is gathered a conservatively dressed, mature audience; one man wears a monocle, most are in evening dress or business suits, and the women are as fashionably attired as the men. In the background, facing the audience, is H. C. Thorman in an evening jacket with satin lapels. He is gesturing toward a map of Olmos Park that is encased in a solid, enscrolled frame that is in turn set within heavy velvet drapes. The vista that unfolds on the map echoes the richness of the setting: amid rolling hills, substantial homes unobtrusively line the community's winding drives. There is, in short, nothing modest about the entire ensemble. Only people of substance would purchase property in this community, the advertisement suggests, and the magnificence of their homes would reflect their status, a status that had little to do with the expectations of youth. Rather, a home in Olmos Park signaled, as it had for H. C. Thorman, that the owners had already made it, that they had already arrived.[21]

This impressionistic evidence of the social standing and economic status of those who moved to Olmos Park is sustained by analysis of the San Antonio City Directory. Olmos Park, it seems, appealed to a growing group of San Antonio's wealthy commercial and business elite, who lived in areas either without such effective protections or that were threatened by the enlargement of the downtown business and commercial sector. Indeed, the appeal of Olmos Park signified the coming of age of the automobile and the incipient decline of the older streetcar-based subdivisions. Among Olmos Park's earliest residents, for instance, was Britain R. Webb, who moved to the suburban community from the earlier exclusive block of West French Place, which had sheltered a number of leading citizens in the early 1900s. Webb neatly symbolized both San Antonio's economic growth and the rise of the auto; he was a vice-president of the City Central Bank and Trust and regional manager for the Buick Motor Company. He was joined by such residents as Raymond Woodward, owner of Morgan-Woodward, a local Ford dealer; Joseph Edwards, an auditor for the city's Packard distributor; Clarence Gardner, treasurer of the Mountjoy Parts Company, which specialized in automobile engines; and J. Benjamin Robertson of the Luthy Battery Equipment Company. On many levels, Olmos Park was an automobile suburb.[22]

The coming of the automobile to South Texas had created a new group of commercial entrepreneurs quite distinct from the city's traditional economic elite. These new auto men were joined in Olmos Park by a new commercial elite created by the city's growth and expansion. Carl D. Newton combined a role in the City Central Bank and Trust Company with ownership of the community's Kodak outlet, Fox Photo. George Piper was a manager at the downtown Stowers Furniture Company, while both Morris Richbook and Charles Eidelberg operated Richbook's Department Store, and Alfred Beyer owned a local appliance company and later a downtown Mexican restaurant and a string of parking lots.

One final group attracted to Olmos Park closely resembled H. C. Thorman himself in terms of economic success and business interests. Henry Catto made his fortune in oil and later established a major insurance company; Urban Wagner headed the Kelwood Company, a local building and contracting firm, and shared an interest in urban development with R. Thomas McDermott, who headed two firms dealing in real estate and construction.

The initial appeal of Olmos Park was thus not to the city's traditional wealth. The growth of San Antonio and its development as a market center for a large South Texas hinterland had enlarged opportunities in retail trade, construction, and real estate. And this new wealth was attracted to the exclusivity of Olmos Park. The physical move to the new community rarely involved a substantial distance or dislocation. The bulk of new residents moved there from large homes in nearby Monte Vista. Indeed, the appeal of Olmos Park was probably not in the distinctiveness of its general location or its architecture; Monte Vista was a very similar area of large, albeit slightly older, homes. But by moving to Olmos Park, these individuals were to take advantage of a much higher degree of restrictiveness regarding land use and development and to escape the city. Olmos Park lay just beyond the historical city limits, and new residents thus avoided both city taxes and direct participation in San Antonio's governmental and political affairs.

The creation of Olmos Park as an exclusive and homogeneous upper-income preserve was readily accomplished through a series of private controls on property, building, and ownership. But the community existed in a larger political orbit and was far from insulated from the political forces affecting San Antonio and Bexar County.

The advance of suburban subdivision had been clearly facilitated during the 1920s by the spread of streetcar transportation and the coming of the automobile, as well as by the city of San Antonio's willingness to extend its services and efforts to areas outside its corporate bounds. The character of the larger city's politics provides a clear indication of the costs of growth and annexation. The dominant political organization or machine was able to control and bargain with a fixed and largely controllable electorate. While the votes of east side blacks and west side Hispanics often required a direct financial investment, they were a known (and purchasable) quantity. The middle-class Anglo residents of the growing suburban tracts were far less predictable and manipulable. They thus represented a threat to the existence of the "City Machine" and its supporters, rather than an opportunity for community growth and expansion. And the need to serve the outlying areas with expensive capital improvements and facilities was seen as a serious cost to and financial burden on the existing city of San Antonio. As a result, the city trod lightly on the issue of annexation and expansion in the 1920s and 1930s. The first serious efforts at corporate enlargement were not actually effected until 1940.[23]

In the absence of serious pressure from the larger central city, Olmos Park could manage comfortably simply as a subdivision with no specific public powers and no peculiar demands for public services. It was thus quite different from the other newly developing exclusive communities that took the form of independent polities. Beverly Hills, California, for example, was originally developed by the Rodeo Land and Water Company in the early years of the twentieth century. The Beverly Hills Hotel, constructed as a "draw" for the new community in 1912, served as both attraction and proof of exclusivity and wealth. The community's social standing and its position among the elite of the motion picture industry were confirmed by the purchase in 1919 of "Pickfair" by Douglas Fairbanks and Mary Pickford. Beverly Hills's exclusivity as a community was enhanced by its existence as an independent polity very early in its physical development. The city was incorporated in 1913. It also moved to secure its independence in terms of municipal services, providing its own police and fire protection and acquiring its own water in 1924.[24]

Similar efforts at social and governmental exclusivity in the Los Angeles area followed the Beverly Hills model. Palos Verdes Estate and Rolling Hills both incorporated as cities coincident with their actual physical development in the late 1930s, and even went so far as to use guarded gates to prevent access by nonresidents. The link between suburban exclusivity and independent local government was also maintained in a number of emerging Texas communities. Highland Park incorporated in 1913, securing its independence from Dallas. And Bellaire incorporated as a municipality in 1918, asserting its distinctiveness from Houston.[25]

The path leading to municipal incorporation for these exclusive subdivisions and suburban developments varied. Incorporation provided one sales tool for the promoter in assuring community distinctiveness and quality. Status as a municipality also guaranteed the advantages of local polity: some direct public control over taxes and public services. In the face of a desire by a larger central city to acquire high-value residential property, incorporation provided a bulwark against tax increases and efforts to soak the wealthy. And city status provided popular direction of and choice about basic city services.

The desire for low taxes and readily controlled public service clearly drove the incorporation of Beverly Hills and its later efforts to resist annexation by Los Angeles. Jon Teaford notes that "in Beverly Hills Douglas Fairbanks, Mary Pickford, Tom Mix, Rudolph Valentino, Harold Lloyd, Will Rogers, and Conrad Nagel all joined hands to defeat annexation, thereby guarding against Los Angeles' higher tax rates while preserving the Beverly Hills police force with its tolerant attitude toward stellar peccadillos."[26]

By no means all exclusive residential enclaves chose to incorporate and lead an independent existence within the metropolitan area, as River Oaks in Houston and Munger Place in Dallas indicate. But where suburban incorporation did come about, it was most often very early in the development of the enclave, as part of the developer's promotional strategy.

Olmos Park stands as an intriguing exception to this general pattern of exclusive suburban development. The physical community was well protected by covenants, deed restrictions, and Thorman's ability to pace its residential development. The subdivision could draw on public services for facilities such as water and police from the adjacent city of San Antonio with little difficulty. The city provided services to outlying areas free of charge, despite the obvious drain on its own revenues and tax base. The explanation for this seeming fiscal irrationality was rooted in the machine politics and petty political duchies of the larger city. Based on a generous use of city jobs for patronage purposes, city politicians appear to have been willing to provide services without the political complications potentially caused by a group of upper-income and reform-oriented voters. Outlying subdivisions could maintain the image of independence from the city while accepting its readily proffered services.[27]

The incorporation of Olmos Park was thus *not* rooted in some desire to secure immediate control over the enclave's future. Its development during the 1920s and 1930s proceeded without governmental status or special public services. Incorporation was, rather, the product of reaction and community fear and uncertainty well after it was developed, a direct response both to the national agenda that the New Deal set and to local reform politics. These forces would reshape San Antonio's political landscape, altering, as well, the status of Olmos Park.

The massive federal aid of the New Deal era had brought a great deal of civic improvement to San Antonio, including the improvement and beautification of what is now the city's River Walk, the paving and improvement of streets, and the construction of a new post office and athletic stadium. The period also saw an increase in activity by community elements favoring political reform and an end to machine rule. Indeed, the infusion of federal aid and the emergence of an active reform movement in San Antonio were intertwined; the former served as patronage to bolster the political standing of the latter. The reformers were given a sharp boost when Mayor C. K. Quin was the focus of a series of revelations about and indictments after the temporary hiring of city workers coinciding with the date of the Democratic primary election. The defeated incumbent Democratic congressman, Maury Maverick, led an effort to oust Quin and his commission supporters at the next city election in the spring of 1939. In a race crowded with four tickets and competition for the claim of "most good government–oriented," Maverick ran for mayor with his "Fusion Ticket."[28]

The platform of the Fusion group called for elimination of the Quin machine and the eventual change to a city manager system. Maverick also called for lower taxes, reasonable hiring practices, and a more efficient delivery of city services. But his image as a New Dealer and charges of communism were rarely out of the newspapers. His promise to construct a number of expensive physical improvement projects, such as parks, on the "colored" east side, projects funded by New Deal revenues, fueled such charges. Maverick clearly represented not simply a threat to the venerable city machine, but also to the accustomed way of doing governmental business in San Antonio.[29] In the election on May 9, 1939, Maverick and most of his Fusion Ticket beat Quin and the machine organization.

But Maverick's campaign and political triumph had a more immediate impact on the Olmos Park area. On the same day as Maverick's victory, attorney Albert Negley filed an incorporation petition for Olmos Park with the County Commissioners' Court. One local newspaper quoted Negley as arguing that "the desire of the persons living in the area to be united" was the reason for seeking municipal status. Yet the residents of Olmos Park had lived for an extended period in unincorporated limbo with no indication of a pressing desire for unification. The recollections of Olmos Park residents and the coincidence of timing suggest that the real reason for the 1939 incorporation effort lay with the threat of annexation by the city, an annexation sought by now-mayor Maverick as a means of increasing the city's wealth and tax base.[30]

The petition proved to be the opening step in a rapid incorporation effort. Olmos Park's 1,550 residents were allowed the opportunity for a vote on May 23, and they overwhelmingly supported incorporation by a vote of 237 to 6. The shift of Olmos Park from simple community to independent polity was in accord with its beginnings. The move was endorsed by its developers and early landowners, and the election was held in the rear of Thorman's office.[31]

The incorporation effort followed by about two weeks a similar successful effort in the nearby area of Terrell Hills. And it set off a spate of incorporation attempts in neighboring subdivisions on San Antonio's north side. The fear of annexation was widespread, and concern over the lax policies of city service delivery were well founded. Less than two months after the election, members of the Fusion Ticket were pressing for a radical change in the provision of fire and police services. Fire and police commissioner Louis Lipscomb threatened to end service to the incorporated suburbs unless they made some arrangements to cover the costs of service. Mayor Maverick declared that "the city of San Antonio would no longer carry the burdens for these areas beyond the city limit."

Maverick's efforts proved less than totally successful. While he headed off other attempted incorporations, Olmos Park remained outside the city and managed to secure fire protection through a contractual arrangement with the city. Indeed, Olmos Park's incorporation demonstrated substantial variance from the model of the suburban polity as provider of special or unique public services. Its elected officers served without salary, and the city itself did not impose a tax or directly raise revenue. The costs of the incorporation effort and the May election had to be borne by donations, as the city had no means of apportioning or imposing a tax.[32]

The government of Olmos Park remained a shell, with no responsibilities for providing public facilities or functions. It did so because its residents sought only to escape the taxes imposed on San Antonians and were not obliged to tax themselves to maintain the benefits or exclusivity of the community. Indeed, it was this very lack of governmental activity that would encourage another reform mayor, Gus Mauerman, to seek to annex these suburbs in 1944.[33]

Olmos Park reflects and refracts the American suburban experience. Its formation, for instance, depended on many of the same forces that had begun to reorder the economic and social structure of American cities since early in the nineteenth century. With the emergence of the streetcar and other forms of mass transit — which did not arrive in San Antonio until late in that century — cities expanded physically, following the rail lines, which encouraged the growth of streetcar suburbs. These early suburbs not only were separated geographically from the central core, they were also segregated, a segregation that was at once racial, ethnic, and economic. The tightly clustered, heterogeneous walking city was no more.[34]

But the streetcar suburbs were not all that segregated; fixed rail transit made it difficult to create and maintain large-scale exclusive suburban communities. Such could not emerge without a more exclusive form of transportation, the private automobile. The automobile, of course, extended the convenient distance between the fringe suburbs and the central core. But more than that, the car encouraged lateral mobility, which enabled well-heeled residents to avoid both the congested central city and its less desirable citizens. By 1970, this pattern of widespread, highly differentiated communities had become the norm: the United States was a suburban nation.[35]

Texas cities (and their suburbs) were also powerfully affected by the advent of the automobile. Highland Park in Dallas, Houston's River Oaks, and Olmos Park in San Antonio came to depend on the automobile, just as they came to represent a form of exclusivity, restriction, and economic segregation that catered to a new affluent urban elite. As one long-time resident of Olmos Park remembered, Olmos Park "was really a little town on the edge of a big town and was situated where it was 'out of the way' — and because of the street layout, nobody went thru' it or even came into it except us." This memory of separateness could have been voiced by those who moved to any number of elite enclaves constructed in the 1920.[36]

But within this general framework, Olmos Park offers some unique insights. It was created and came to life as an exclusive development within

Texas' poorest major city, thereby enabling the metropolitan area's business and civic elite to remain aloof from its political and social battles. This detachment was profitable, of course: they benefited from access to an urban economy and exploited that advantage, never having to pay taxes to support the larger community of which they were a part.

There are two ironies in this disengagement. The first is that it was fully supported (indeed encouraged) by San Antonio's political machine, which was only too happy to supply free urban services such as water and fire protection so as not to be troubled by Olmos Park's affluent and politically powerful inhabitants. The other irony involves the governance of Olmos Park itself. Its early residents not only wanted to be disconnected from the surrounding metropolitan community, but they pushed that tendency to the extreme when they created their own town in 1927. By not incorporating for twelve years, the residents were able to pare the town's functions to the absolute minimum. It took the threat of annexation in the late thirties and the forties to force those who lived in Olmos Park to begin to create a polity, to act like citizens.[37]

7. Protecting Community and Property Values: Civic Clubs in Houston, 1909–70

Robert Fisher

In his seminal work *The Private City,* Sam Bass Warner, Jr., identifies the tradition of "privatism" as a primary factor in the "failure of urban America to create a humane environment" for all its citizens. "Under the American tradition," Warner writes, "the first purpose of the citizen is the private search for wealth." His analysis of urban development continues: "The goal of a city is to be a community of private money makers. Once the scope of many city dwellers' search for wealth exceeded the bounds of their municipality, the American city ceased to be an effective community. Ever afterwards it lacked the desire, the power, the wealth, and the talent necessary to create a humane environment for all its citizens." Dating from the mid-nineteenth century onward, Warner observes, "the successes and failures of American cities have depended upon the unplanned outcomes of the private market. The private market's demand for workers, its capacities for dividing land, building houses, stores and factories, and its needs for public services have determined the shape and quality of America's big cities." And that dependency has come at a cost: "What the private market could do well American cities have done well; what the private market did badly, or neglected, our cities have been unable to overcome."[1]

In a later, equally important, work, *The Urban Wilderness,* Warner expands this thesis to include the entire urban experience in the United States. In case studies of the development of New York, Chicago, and Los Angeles, in essays on the history of urban planning, housing, and health care in the United States, Warner reiterates his theme. Under the ideology and practice of capitalism (no longer referred to by Warner as "privatism"), cities were fundamentally an agglomeration of businesses; they were private affairs oriented to maximizing profits and protecting property. Creating community and a humane environment, sharing resources, caring for and meeting the basic needs of all people was a by-product at best. The result was an urban history filled with conflict and control: conflict over the need for a more humane place to live, control mechanisms implemented to halt challenges to the primacy of private wealth as the determinant of what the city should be like.[2]

Warner is right when he speculates in *The Private City* that "Philadelphia's history has been repeated, with minor variations, again and again across the nation, in Cincinnati, in St. Louis, in Chicago, in Detroit, in Los Angeles, and in Houston." In Houston, however, capitalism is as much a credo as an oft-expressed conviction of the sanctity of private property rights. It functions as a flexible, simplistic guide to group action and personal achievement. Houston's boosters, for example, herald its unbridled probusiness atmosphere, "right to work" laws, low taxes, low wages, and marginal role for the public sector. It is the only major city in the nation, for example, without a zoning ordinance. Since the early twentieth century, the majority of Houstonians have seen zoning as government interference and nascent socialism. Proposals and referenda for zoning were defeated in 1929, 1948, and 1962. Instead, Houston controls land use through private means. A brief look at this aspect of the city's history illuminates the importance and limits of the credo of private enterprise in Houston and throughout Texas and the nation.[3]

Neighborhood civic clubs—numbering more than six hundred in 1980 —abound in Houston. Such widespread neighborhood organizing comes as a surprise to most. Houston seems to be little more than a massive urban sprawl, connected by freeways and a boom town atmosphere. Moreover, it has a well-deserved reputation as a highly conservative city, not the sort where one expects cooperative efforts like neighborhood organizing to abound. In 1947, for example, John Gunther in *Inside America* said that, "with the possible exception of Tulsa, Oklahoma," Houston was "the most reactionary community in the United States." Curiously, while no single image suffices for the Bayou City, extraordinary growth since the early 1940s and a laissez-faire political environment have combined to forge a mass of conservative neighborhood associations throughout the city that perform, almost as private neighborhood governments, a number of critical functions expected more of the public sector.[4]

In residential neighborhoods, once the land is developed, land use is determined, rather explicitly, by deed restrictions. Drawn up initially by the developer, such deeds include land-use controls, architectural restrictions, and, until recently, racial covenants. Under this type of land-use management, individual homeowners are ultimately responsible for enforcing restrictions. They are the ones who have to "be on the lookout." They are the ones who have to take a "violator" to court to prevent a chicken farm or a fast-food restaurant from moving in next door.[5]

Deed restrictions came into use in Houston in the 1890s with the development of residential subdivisions. Prior to the first subdivisions in Houston, as well as elsewhere, land was purchased in small parcels, usually by individual homeowners. The six inner-city wards in Houston were settled in this manner without deed restrictions. After 1890, large parcels of land were developed on Houston's periphery and these subdivisions were regulated by deed restrictions. In 1909, a brochure for Woodland Heights advertised its deed restrictions as one of the virtues of purchasing land there: "In order to keep Woodland Heights the strictly high grade residence section it is, and to guard against all undesirable features, we have placed certain restrictions on this property as to the character of the improvements and the nature of the use which are embodied in all our deeds, and are binding not only upon the purchasers, but upon their heirs and assigns."[6]

Civic clubs were quickly organized in the "streetcar suburbs" like Woodland Heights. Their raison d'être was restriction enforcement, but they also functioned as traditional neighborhood improvement associations, supplying necessary services and lobbying City Hall for street repairs, park development, and schools, just like associations in the North. As development boomed on Houston's periphery, some three miles from downtown in the 1920s, so did neighborhood civic clubs, as each new subdivision came complete with a set of enforceable deed restrictions. But Houston civic clubs in the 1920s did not pursue restrictions with the reactionary zeal of their outer-city counterparts in northern cities like Chicago or Saint Louis. Deed restrictions were seen primarily as a means of protecting property values and preserving neighborhood homogeneity, not as a method primarily intended or needed to exclude blacks.

In the North in the generation after 1880, neighborhood improvement associations, especially those in more affluent communities, whether in Baltimore, Chicago, Cincinnati, or Columbus, focused primarily on lobbying city officials for basic urban services. The excellent work of Thomas Philpott and others demonstrates, however, that many of these same associations turned their emphasis from neighborhood enhancement to protection against lower-class and black immigration. They were no longer genteel associations of the upper class lobbying City Hall for improved services; they were militant efforts by the frightened ethnic middle class to protect property values in a time when the housing market was tight and the black population was growing rapidly. From 1917 to 1921, fifty-eight homes recently purchased by black families in formerly all-white neighborhoods in Chicago were bombed. In the spring of 1919, two bombs went off each month in that city. Protectionist efforts like these also led to race riots in 1919 in Saint Louis and New York. And these were only the most dramatic reflections of such tensions in northern cities.[7]

In Houston the initial concern of the first improvement associations was also community enhancement, but here protective practices went hand in hand with enhancement from the outset. The deed in one of Houston's first "streetcar suburbs," for example, as early as 1909 included restrictions that preserved "the original beauty of the property," banned commercial development, forbade the sale of liquor in the subdivision, detailed architectural restrictions for new homes and home improvements, and "protected from colored neighbors."

By the 1920s, deed restrictions in Houston included racial clauses limiting ownership and tenancy to "Caucasians and whites only." But competition for housing between blacks and whites was slight and well controlled. The city was still relatively small in population, some 138,000 people. The number of blacks in the city was sizable, around 34,000, but the percentage of blacks, 24, was not expanding. Most important, this was the South before the Civil Rights movement of the 1960s. Segregation was the law of the land. The entire system—institutions, power brokers, police, and day-to-day relationships—enforced Jim Crow. Two clearly separate societies existed, one black, the other white. Blacks were concentrated in three older areas of the city and moving into a white area was suicidal, if not impossible. People "knew their place." Before 1948, residential racial transformation was not a "problem" for Houston's neighborhood civic clubs.

Civic clubs in Houston achieved their heyday in the decades after World War II. So did the city. From 1940 to 1960, Houston's population increased from about four hundred thousand to nearly one million. In 1948, annexations doubled the area of the city; eight years later the city doubled its geographic size again. Suburban construction boomed as well. Federal highway development made the outlying areas more accessible, and federal housing loans put the purchase of a single-family home within the reach of the middle class. Developers rushed to meet the demand.

The Braeswood area, located in the southwest sector of the city, was one of the more popular new subdivisions for upper-middle-class whites. Less expensive middle-class housing could be found in other parts of town, but the Braeswood area offered ranch homes with central air conditioning and central heat, three bedrooms, modern kitchen, and two bathrooms for around twenty thousand dollars. In many ways, the subdivision was undistinguished: small plots of land, gridiron street pattern, few trees, only a few models from which to choose. But it was pleasant enough, accessible to downtown, and on the "right" side—the west side—of the city. The Braeswood development opened in 1951, and by the end of the year there were six thousand people living there.[8]

The Southwest Civic Club (SWCC) was organized in the Braeswood area on February 13, 1951, and held its first meeting one month later. Eighty-eight residents attended. The goals of the organization were clear: enhance and protect the neighborhood and enforce deed restrictions. Like earlier neighborhood improvement associations, initial activity focused on securing physical necessities. Houston prided itself on limiting the role of government in the affairs of "private" citizens. This meant that taxes were low and public services were few. Neighborhood residents were expected to furnish their own needs. Accordingly, civic clubs coordinated neighborhood support and financing for services the city would not supply, like mosquito fogging and street lighting.

But the SWCC did lobby City Hall most effectively for improved services. Residents paid sizable property taxes compared to those in other neighborhoods and they expected something in return. A meeting on flood control in November, 1951, brought out some two hundred neighborhood residents. They resolved not to support county officials who were seeking two new tax measures unless promised road and ditch repairs were completed. The county government responded slowly, but eventually met the neighborhood's demands. Over the next few years, the SWCC effectively lobbied for traffic signs and lights, improved water pressure, road paving and repairs, a new library, park, and elementary school, and fire station. It used its political influence to relieve blocked sewers and to stop development of a sewage plant. To accomplish its objectives, the club might hold mass meetings or sponsor letter writing campaigns to pressure City Hall and county officers. But most often, club successes resulted from personal contacts between club leaders and public officials and prominent businesspeople. SWCC leaders over the years included men who were state representatives, realtors, lawyers, and urban planners, each with some contacts and varying degrees of influence in the city and county. In neighborhoods like Braeswood, the prestige and contacts of individual members, enhanced by the backing of the civic association, enabled the organization to be heard and win services.

In addition to its service acquisition and neighborhood enhancement functions, a central activity of the SWCC, as in all civic clubs in Houston, was deed restriction enforcement. The process of private deed enforcement maintained neighborhood homogeneity effectively, but not without serious drawbacks. The first steps in restriction enforcement were informal: a resident would complain to the civic club, the club president would write a letter or pay an informal visit to the "violator." Most often, people were simply unaware that they had broken the deed. In one case, a young boy was raising two lambs in his backyard for a Future Farmers of America project. The deed prohibited the keeping of livestock in the neighborhood. The resident complied, reluctantly.

Sometimes more formal action, like the threat of a civil lawsuit, was required, and it was here that a fundamental problem faced neighborhood civic clubs. Court cases were few and far between, because defendants realized the potential expense and the court's support of deed restriction enforcement. On one occasion the SWCC secured a permanent injunction against a chiropractor who was practicing in his home. On another, it took a motel operator to court, forcing his business out of the area.

But court expenses were high for the club as well as for the defendant. Over the years, the SWCC built a sizable restriction fund from membership dues. By October, 1960, it had over ten thousand dollars; the annual expense for legal fees averaged only five hundred dollars. This annual amount covered small cases in which a letter from the club's law firm was usually sufficient. One violation pursued all the way through the courts, however, could wipe out the entire restriction fund and more. Only the wealthiest civic clubs, like the River Oaks Property Owners Association, could finance frequent court battles. Deed restriction enforcement was potentially an expensive means of protecting property values.

It was also divisive. Neighbors had to keep watch over, oppose, and threaten each other with law suits. It was easy to oppose a filling station trying to move in the neighborhood. More difficult was informing neighbors that they could not extend their carport to the lot line or convert their garage into an apartment for the family of their son or daughter. Given the problems of constant enforcement, potential expense, and intra-neighborhood tension, neighborhoods with active civic clubs, not surprisingly, also ardently supported zoning proposals in 1948 and 1962. Civic clubs preferred to make enforcement of deed restrictions a public rather than a private function, one supported by tax monies and administered by local officials. But when the zoning proposals failed, the civic clubs of Houston were forced to continue to play their especially important role in neighborhood cohesion and development.

While the SWCC, like all civic clubs in Houston, established a democratic structure for resident participation, the affairs of the club were handled by a half dozen men, usually businessmen or professionals. Membership was not opened to women until 1956, and then only to women who were "resident owners of real property." The club had four elected administrative officers, ten "area directors," and "block captains." Meetings were run democratically, in that all members could vote, but, in general, resident participation and interest were slight.

The early years of the SWCC were the peak time of resident activism. The neighborhood was young, people were just getting to know each other, and basic amenities still needed to be secured. The residents wanted a community organization. In 1955, 85 percent of the residents paid $6.75 per year to join the club: $1 for membership, $1.25 for the restriction enforcement fund, and $4.50 for mosquito fogging. Meetings that addressed an "emergency issue," like flood control, could bring out two hundred residents, but even in the association's heyday most monthly meetings were poorly attended. "Everybody is willing to do everything they were asked to do, but [they] don't attend the meeting," lamented an officer in 1955. Often no more than ten or twenty people came. Block captains and a regular newsletter kept neighbors informed of club activities and this sufficed for most. Elections for club officers were rarely contested. Residents willingly accepted the suggestions of the ad hoc Nominating Committee, which was appointed by the Board of Directors. Members were grateful that someone with leadership skills and, quite often, political or business influence, was willing to assume the burden.

Over the years, the organization became even less participatory and less democratic. In 1956, the number of annual general meetings was reduced from twelve to five. The Board of Directors continued to meet monthly, however, and to direct the affairs of the club. In 1958, membership hit a low point of only 43.5 percent of neighborhood residents. The reasons were obvious. The Braeswood area was becoming more stable and most initial services and amenities had been provided. Many people, moreover, were not pleased with the club's mosquito spraying service and chose to do without the fogging. Perhaps most important, neighbors did not feel threatened. The Board of Directors proclaimed the need to "Sell the Civic Club" in the neighborhood, but to little avail. In 1963, membership was up slightly, to 48 percent, but remained much lower than in the initial years. This pattern of elite leadership and declining resident interest seems nearly universal in Houston civic clubs. The SWCC, like other neighborhood civic clubs, was, after all, fundamentally a neighborhood-based interest group, and interest groups, especially those in affluent communities like Braeswood, do not require democratic or active participation.

Despite their overt political function as neighborhood interest groups — as coordinators and lobbyists for neighborhood services and protectors of property values — civic clubs have always pictured themselves as nonpolitical. While they do not directly support candidates for public office, the most effective civic clubs, like the Southwest Civic Club, serve a parapolitical function, influencing local officials and power brokers on behalf of the neighborhood and serving as informal conduits of information about the needs of and developments in the community. The SWCC never shied away from addressing political issues. Over the years, it invited speakers and sponsored programs that reflected the conservative politics of club leaders. In the 1950s, speakers warned club members of the hazards of federal deficit spending and taxing powers. The club coordinated civil defense programs at the neighborhood level. It showed films like *The Land of the Free* and *Communism on the Map,* the latter advertised in press releases throughout the city as "a fully documented film on how the communists are spreading their doctrine throughout the world." These activities were not seen as political because residents supported them. Issues that might cause dissent within the civic club, like partisan politics, were off limits. But political activity was acceptable when it preserved, or at least did not disrupt, neighborhood homogeneity.[9]

The quest for homogeneity sparked the fundamental issue facing most outer-city neighborhood improvement associations in the 1950s — racial integration. In response to black activism and the pressures of the Cold War, segregationists organized in the North and South in both neighborhood-based and broader organizations like the Citizen Councils to resist residential and school integration. In Houston, civic clubs located in neighborhoods contiguous to the black ghettos on the east side of town actively resisted integration. For example, Riverside, east of Braeswood along Braes Bayou, was a select white neighborhood in the 1940s, "the Jewish River Oaks," some called it. With the "Shelley decision" in 1948, which declared racial covenants unenforceable, white residents in Riverside grew alarmed about the expanding black ghetto to their north.[10] In 1952, they formed the Greater Riverside Property Owners Association (GRPOA) to prevent integration. They urged white residents to sit tight, not to sell in a panic, to remain in the neighborhood, and then tried to raise money to buy property for sale and "buy out" blacks who had already moved into Riverside. These tactics, of course, had been employed thirty years earlier in Chicago and other northern cities. Signs declaring "This House is Not for Sale" were frequently seen posted on porches. Bombs exploded at the house of the first black family in Riverside in 1953.

Neither the violence nor cautionary appeals were very effective, however. Once the pattern of residential change was apparent, white homeowners sold quickly, even at lower prices, and realtors were most eager to help them do so. As a result, the white residents of Riverside moved into newly developed subdivisions in the southwest part of the city, like Braeswood, which provided good housing and appreciable distance from the black ghetto.[11]

Because Houston was expanding at a breakneck pace after World War II, competition for living space was minimal, limited only to those areas, like Riverside, that bordered the black ghettos of the city. Residents in neighborhoods like Braeswood often shared segregationist sentiments with their white counterparts in Riverside. As late as 1970, only 13 of Braeswood's 8,654 residents were black. But residents in Braeswood, like most suburban residents in the 1950s living five to ten miles from the central city and the black ghetto, were not as threatened or affected by integration pressures as residents of neighborhoods that bordered the black ghetto in both southern and northern cities. Nevertheless, organizations formed even in Southwest Houston to address this issue and to "protect property values."

In the 1950s, an umbrella organization of local civic clubs in Southwest Houston, the Allied Civic Club (ACC), was formed to deal with district-wide issues that went beyond subdivision boundaries. Among other activities, the ACC organized workshops on community leadership training and restriction violations, supported a drive toward district representation on the City Council, and became a strong advocate of zoning. The ACC also helped coordinate opposition to residential desegregation in Southwest Houston. ACC leaders recognized that, with the Shelley decision, stopping a black family from moving into a neighborhood was no longer easily accomplished. Indeed, "there is no reason now to believe that this is possible," they lamented. But the ACC could stop wholesale neighborhood transformation and panic selling; ACC leaders called this objective "neighborhood stabilization."

Where integration threatened to destabilize a neighborhood, the ACC advised its members to remain calm. "Emotional panic of white neighbors solves nothing and is, indeed, self-defeating. The way of neighborhood stabilization is much better." The ACC further advised residents to be alert to potential problem houses, such as a G.I.-financed home that did not sell quickly. If a black moved into the neighborhood, they were to call a meeting quickly with residents of the immediate area. "Urge them to sit tight," the ACC advocated. Beware of "unethical" realtors who "stir up race prejudices." If "wildcat realtors" are put out of business, then "every all-white area in Houston that wishes to remain all-white will have a much better chance." The ACC further requested that residents report wildcatters to the Houston Board of Realtors, the Better Business Bureau, and the ACC, so that such realtors could be singled out and ostracized. The advice was clear: "neighborhood stabilization" was the best way to protect property values. [12]

The SWCC, a member organization in the ACC, followed the recommendations. As late as 1970, when a black family moved into the neighborhood, the civic club president quickly wrote a letter to residents in the immediate area, advising them that "a frantic rush to get out will devalue our properties and deteriorate our neighborhood." The letter specified the realtor who sold the property and went on to praise the quality of the two black families who currently resided in the community: one a doctor, the other, an attorney, both "educated and cultured." "Sit tight and face this situation with realism, courage, and goodwill. . . . The value of your property and the future of your neighborhood depend entirely on what you people do." [13]

The strategy of neighborhood stabilization sufficed to "protect" Houston's more affluent white neighborhoods. Most blacks could not afford to move there, and for those who could, a few other areas of the city were opening that were equally attractive and more hospitable to middle-income black families. Neighborhood improvement associations in the North before and after World War II tried the "sit-tight, do not panic" strategy, but with little success in white communities contiguous to the expanding black ghetto. In Houston where white neighborhoods bordered the black ghettos, as in the Riverside area, neighborhood stabilization was equally ineffective. Throughout the nation where pressures by blacks for more and better housing were great, violent conflict ensued, bombs exploded, whites resisted militantly and then, ultimately, moved out.

This was not the case in the Braeswood area, nor in other affluent suburban neighborhoods, North and South, which were more removed from lower-class and minority inner-city areas by distance and class. In Houston, the largest concentration of blacks remained on the east side of town, away from suburbs in the west like Braeswood. Protecting the neighborhood from racial change was less important to the SWCC than were the routine tasks of service acquisition and maintenance. Throughout its history, the SWCC concerned itself with enforcing deed restrictions, keeping out commercial development, and with mosquito fogging. The extraordinary distances separating races and classes in the new multinucleic cities in the South and the metropolitan areas in the North clearly enabled affluent residents to segregate themselves more successfully and easily than before. Prior to the 1950s, such separation had been a "luxury" shared only by residents in the most affluent suburbs. But with the federal government subsidizing, through highway and housing programs, the development of low density multinucleic metropolitan centers, even moderately affluent suburban developments like Braeswood, whether within or outside the city limits, were removed and isolated from the central city as never before. In turn, improvement associations in these neighborhoods took on the responsibility of maintenance and service lobbying efforts, rather than the combative and defensive style of associations in white neighborhoods that bordered the black ghetto.

The history of the Southwest Civic Club is not unique. Rather, it is typical of the concerns and approaches of most neighborhood civic clubs in the city. While many civic club members prefer zoning because it is a publicly financed alternative to the private enforcement and watchdog functions of current civic clubs, there is little chance such a measure will be enacted in Houston in the near future. The current strength of the credo of capitalism makes it impossible. Most people in Houston, for reasons too complex to address here, and despite the obvious recent decline of quality of life in the city, are willing to allow the profit-oriented plans of private developers to determine land use and they are willing to assume the private, individual means of enforcement to regulate residential land use.

Zoning, of course, is not the answer. If the history of zoning nationwide is a good indicator, the elite who control private development decisions in Houston would strongly influence zoning decisions, although they would do so less easily and with more potential conflict than is the case now. But to continue to leave neighborhood issues — from minor concerns like streetlights and mosquito fogging to larger ones of racism, environmental quality, and transportation — to the whims of the marketplace means that solutions will continue to be determined, as has been the case historically, by those with wealth and property who will suit their needs and interests. After all, the marketplace will not help re-create a sense of community in the city; it will not promote the sharing of resources; and it will not serve the needs of all the city's citizens. If they remain, the ideology and practice of privatism will continue to perpetuate a vision of the city as an agglomeration of competing self-interests rather than, as Warner suggests, "a public environment of a democratic society."[14]

Part V.

World War II and Sunbelt Cities

8. Dallas in the 1940s: The Challenges and Opportunities of Defense Mobilization

Robert B. Fairbanks

World War II proved a watershed in Dallas history for several reasons. The wartime economy of airplane plants, ordnance factories, and military bases not only brought rapid population growth and expanded the boundaries of the metropolis, it also established the basis for a more industrialized and diversified postwar economy. Furthermore, the war accelerated social tensions and within a crisis atmosphere publicized housing problems that had thwarted Dallas blacks for years. Responses to these developments in the 1940s profoundly affected the nature of Dallas in the following decades.

The city emerged as an important southern metropolis before America's entry into World War II. Its regional dominance in wholesaling, retailing, banking, and insurance helped give Dallas the third-highest average per capita income in the nation for 1940. And the discovery of oil in East Texas, along with the state's decision to locate its Centennial Exposition in Dallas, contributed to the city's relative prosperity during the Depression years.

Much of Dallas's good fortune seemed linked to energetic leadership closely resembling the patterns of southern urban leadership historian Blaine Brownell found in his study of the urban South's commercial-civic elite. Dallas business and financial leaders, who dominated both public and private power in the first half of the twentieth century, viewed the good city as one based on stability and order, as well as on growth and prosperity.[1] For instance, Dallas boosters invested more than five hundred thousand dollars in a growth campaign during the 1920s, and then initiated a movement to change the very structure of urban government so it could respond better to the challenges brought on by urban growth.[2]

Since 1907, Dallas had prospered under a commission form of government. However, the instability of leadership during these years, as well as the lack of professionalism and fragmented authority made government by commissioners seem inappropriate in the 1920s. In an era that viewed the city as an interdependent organic whole and that stressed comprehensive, coordinated, and central administrative rule, commission government came up short. According to Harold Stone, who reviewed the old government in a 1937 study, "The Commissioners' major political trouble was not spectacular graft or patronage but the disintegration produced by the private political administrative heads, who, after being independently elected, managed their departments separately rather than collectively."[3]

Efforts to restructure Dallas's government were made in 1927, when certain business leaders, along with the *Dallas Morning News,* started advocating the city manager–council form of government. Their efforts succeeded in 1930, when local voters overwhelmingly approved a series of charter amendments reshaping local government. The Citizens Charter Association, a prime mover for the city manager–council form of government, successfully fielded a slate of nine businessman candidates for council in the first election. Shortly thereafter, all nine took their seats on the council and hired John N. Edy, former city manager of Berkeley, California, and Flint, Michigan, to lead the city.

The Charter Association's landslide and the selection of Edy did not immediately bring harmony and continuity to Dallas's politics, as former officeholders and disgruntled localists fielded successful slates in 1935 and 1937. Not until 1939 would the Citizens Charter Association begin its virtual dominance over local government.[4]

Although personnel changed during the 1930s, content and emphasis in local government remained fairly consistent. Not only did the manager-council government practice better economics and efficiency, but it readily tapped federal funds for relief and civic improvement. Local officials utilized federal monies for the fifteen million–dollar improvement of the fairgrounds, which would host the 1936 Texas Centennial Exposition. Federal funds also provided key improvements in infrastructure through providing sewers, roads, parks, and schools to a city desperately in need of them. In addition, Dallas participated in New Deal social programs. The city not only received more than four million dollars from the Federal Emergency Relief Administration for its unemployed, but it secured the only Public Works Administration public housing project in Texas, built on vacant land north of the central business district and for whites only. Later, the council created the Dallas Housing Authority (DHA), which developed a six million dollar public housing program shortly after Congress passed the Housing Act of 1937.[5]

The willingness of Dallas's leaders to participate in New Deal programs suggests that they recognized that Dallas was part of a national system of cities affected by forces beyond local control that could be addressed only with federal help. And their concern with Dallas's social needs implies a clear recognition of the interdependence of the whole metropolis; that is, poorly fed and housed blacks posed a threat to the order and stability of the entire metropolis. Bad living conditions encouraged bad citizenship, something Dallas could do without. As a result, the DHA provided more than basic shelter, since it wanted to make better citizens and not just protect the poor from the elements. Early Dallas public housing, then, attempted to provide a complete neighborhood setting, which the agency thought would promote civic consciousness and upward mobility.[6]

The city's business and financial leadership also underwent certain organizational changes in the 1930s to deal better with perceived metropolitan needs. Although the business community had dominated Dallas since its founding, civic leadership was often fragmented and unresponsive to local needs. That changed, however, after 1936, with the formation of the Dallas Citizens Council. This leading civic organization originated from Dallas's effort to secure the State Centennial Exposition. Chartered in 1937 "to study, confer, and act to help Dallas," the one hundred–man committee included only the city's leading businessmen, either company presidents or board chairmen. The council's long list of accomplishments was clearly related to the nature of its membership and its nearly unlimited financial resources. In addition to its "nonpartisan" civic leadership, the Dallas Citizens Council revitalized the Citizens Charter Association in 1939 and helped that organization dominate local government for the next three decades.[7]

Although the Dallas Citizens Council worked behind the scenes with little publicity, the Dallas Chamber of Commerce, made up of many of the same personnel, emerged as the most publicized business organization. Primarily a booster organization, it clearly articulated the dual and sometimes conflicting goals of growth and order. To ensure the latter, the chamber made numerous commitments to civic betterment and participated in many campaigns for social improvement.

Taken as a whole, the actions of the manager-council government mirrored the goals of civic growth and order articulated by business groups such as the Dallas Citizens Council and the Chamber of Commerce. The rapid growth and transformation that took place in Dallas during the 1940s provide an interesting setting in which to explore the successes and failures of commercial-civic leadership and to better understand how its actions mirrored certain assumptions about the nature of the metropolitan community in the 1940s.[8]

An *Atlantic Monthly* article in October, 1940, captured the energy of Dallas and labeled the growing metropolis "a phenomenal city." It complimented the city's economic and cultural development and concluded that Dallas was "thoroughly cosmopolitan." Despite such plaudits, local leaders feared that insufficient industrial development would prevent the city from reaching its potential as a great American metropolis. Although this absence of industry characterized all southern cities, Dallas boosters refused to accept such a condition and set out to change it.[9]

Dallas suffered other shortcomings besides inadequate industrialization. The same *Atlantic* article that praised the city's large, spreading Victorian houses and its lavish homes along Turtle Creek also portrayed another Dallas—one of dilapidated shacks housing the city's blacks and Mexican Americans. Census data confirmed the horrible housing in which many of the city's fifty thousand blacks and eleven thousand Mexican Americans lived. It showed that over seven thousand dwellings needed major repair and more than thirty-two thousand dwellings contained no private bath or toilet. Another study found that in some black slum areas, 86 percent of the dwellings failed to meet minimum standards for habitation, while 93 percent of the dwellings in Mexican American slums were unfit to live in. Disease and poverty characterized these neighborhood settings.[10]

Racial tension complicated the local housing problem for nonwhites. Although Dallas blacks lived in several distinct neighborhoods rather than one large ghetto, white racism still limited their mobility. As the city's black population increased, corresponding black neighborhoods did not appear, resulting in overcrowding and neighborhood decline. In response to these conditions, civic leaders embraced slum clearance and public housing. Fearing that limited housing opportunities in black sectors might push frustrated blacks into white areas, they attempted to improve established black neighborhoods. For instance, in 1938, the DHA scheduled its first slum clearance–public housing project in the Hall-Thomas area on the near north side, "because this has definitely been established as a negro area and it is the desire and intention of the city that it remain one."[11]

Delayed two years because of court battles, work on the project did not commence until 1940, when contractors destroyed 266 structures, displacing four hundred families. Because Dallas offered so few housing opportunities to its blacks, the slum clearance encouraged the very thing Dallas officials wished to avoid, black expansion into white neighborhoods. When displaced families started moving into formerly white property near a black enclave in South Dallas, local white homeowners responded with violence. Between September 3, 1940, and May 22, 1941, the American Civil Liberties Union counted nineteen acts of violence against black property, including thirteen bombings.

The City Council responded by trying to buy out the newly moved blacks. In addition, it established an "interracial committee" formed entirely of whites. Investigation of the situation led that committee to recommend an ordinance compelling blacks to live in segregated residential areas. The council passed such a resolution but rescinded it after a court challenge.[12]

The 1940 housing crisis had several significant consequences. First, it reaffirmed that severe shortage in black housing and underscored the impediments to the development of better housing opportunities for blacks. Second, it demonstrated how angered whites would react when impatient blacks took matters into their own hands and sought out other neighborhoods. Fear of racial conflict and of the disordered nature of Dallas slums helped keep the black housing problem in the forefront of public awareness during much of the 1940s.

During this time of racial strife, Dallas started to experience the positive impact of wartime mobilization. Between January, 1940, and February, 1941, Washington awarded more than ninety-one million dollars in defense contracts for the city. Construction firms, clothing manufacturers, and food processors received some of the first contracts.[13] About the same time, the military began expanding its presence in the area. In August, 1940, the navy selected Dallas as a site for a Reserve Aviation Squadron Base. The one million dollar base was in part acquired by the hard work of the Dallas Chamber of Commerce with the cooperation of the Dallas City Council. The latter deeded approximately thirty acres of its municipally owned Hensley Field to the navy and extended the airport's runways.[14]

Several years later, the U.S. Eighth Service Command moved from San Antonio to Dallas. The command, which provided services for the other branches of the army in a five-state area, brought a monthly payroll of more than $250,000 to Dallas. Even before that move, defense activity had so affected the city that local Chamber of Commerce officials concluded that Dallas was "the War Capital of the Southwest."[15]

New industrial developments rather than military establishments brought the most immediate prosperity to the city. By September, 1943, the federal government had spent approximately $115 million on building defense industry in Dallas. No single business activity more profoundly affected the city than aircraft manufacturing. Lockheed's Aircraft Modifier Plant at Love Field and the Southern Aircraft Company in Garland were two such plants.[16] But none had a greater impact on Dallas than the gigantic North American Aviation complex located just west of the city.

Several factors help explain why North American Aviation selected Dallas for a factory site. Chamber of Commerce officials had seriously courted the airplane manufacturer since March of 1940, emphasizing the city's good weather, open shop tradition, and the willingness of local officials to cooperate fully with the company's needs. Only after Pres. Franklin D. Roosevelt committed the federal government to expanding the aircraft industry did the Dallas leaders achieve success, however. In May of 1940, the president asked for the production of fifty thousand planes yearly and mandated government assistance to promote that goal. Roosevelt authorized large financial outlays to the newly created Defense Plant Corporation to build plants for aircraft manufacturers. Defense concerns dictated that the aircraft industry decentralize from the coasts and locate new plants inland between the Allegheny and the Rocky mountains. Except for this restriction, the aircraft companies had quite a wide range of choice in determining the final site for their new factories.

Dallas civic leaders, long interested in attracting the aircraft industry to Dallas, jumped at the new opportunities offered by wartime mobilization and strenuously lobbied for a large aircraft factory. Robert L. Thornton and Ben Critz, members of the Chamber of Commerce, visited both the North American Aviation and the Consolidated Aircraft companies in their attempt to lure them to Dallas.[17]

Their efforts proved successful. On July 5, 1940, the *Dallas Morning News* reported that Hall Aluminum Aircraft Corporation, which was shortly to merge with Consolidated, would build an airplane factory just west of Dallas near the municipally owned Hensley Field. However, that plan was aborted after merger problems between Hall and Consolidated. Because North American could immediately establish operations in Dallas, the Defense Corporation built a new war-related industrial development near Hensley Field just west of the city. Consolidated would eventually come to North Texas, but to nearby Fort Worth.[18]

Not only had the Chamber of Commerce played an important role in securing the North American plant, by selling the area and finding a 140-acre site, but local governmental bodies fully cooperated in the industrial venture. The City Council spent twenty-five thousand dollars to add a 104-acre tract to Hensley Field and the Dallas County Commissioners' Court promised to build the necessary roads to accommodate traffic. Officials in nearby Grand Prairie helped supply water and established a public housing authority to deal with anticipated housing demand. All these groups clearly understood the economic value that such a plant would bring to "Greater Dallas."[19]

Groundbreaking for the plant took place on September 28, 1940. Plant A, which produced AT Trainer Planes, opened April 7, 1941. By the end of the year, North American employed more than seven thousand workers, a figure that would increase to forty-three thousand by 1943 with the addition of Plant B. The thirty-five-million-dollar undertaking not only boosted the economy, but provided unprecedented job opportunities for women and blacks. By 1944, more than thirteen thousand women and more than twenty-four hundred blacks worked at the airplane factory.[20]

Facilitating the mammoth labor requirements was an equally impressive vocational program. It, too, resulted from the cooperation between North American Aviation and local and federal officials. Federal officials provided $125,000 worth of equipment for a training school located at Fair Park. The Dallas Technical High School, a North American Aviation defense training school, and a local vocational school for blacks supplemented the Fair Park undertaking. The federally funded schools added immeasurably to the city's economic base by training thousands as skilled industrial workers.[21]

The North American Aviation plant brought problems as well as opportunity to the Dallas area. Local residents proved insufficient to meet all the plant's labor needs, so the War Manpower Commission encouraged large-scale migration. As a result, more than twenty-five thousand families moved to Dallas between January, 1940, and September, 1943. Nearby suburbs such as Grand Prairie grew more than tenfold during that period.[22]

The rapid growth pushed the city's physical plant to the point of collapse. By 1943, Baylor and St. Paul hospitals were so overcrowded that they turned away forty patients a day. The rapid settlement of Southwest Dallas placed severe strains on the city's water system, and the local police seemed unable to control the rapid rise in juvenile delinquency. Dallas's transportation facilities, according to one federal report, were "close to the breaking point." Few buses or streetcars had been added to the transportation system, despite a ridership increase of over 30 percent; as a result, overcrowded buses and streetcars frequently broke down, causing long delays and ever-worsening riding conditions. After reviewing local conditions in 1943, one federal official concluded that "Dallas has all the earmarks of a boomtown war center."[23]

Nothing better exemplified this than the city's housing congestion. Despite the erection of the three-hundred-unit Avion Village by the Federal Works Agency in 1941, and the completion of five public housing projects by the Dallas Housing Authority in 1942, Dallas suffered a severe housing shortage in 1943.[24] Family dwellings simply were not available, a circumstance that discouraged many from coming to the city. Those who did left their families behind and found boarding in single rooms let by families with children in the service.[25]

Despite the general turmoil brought on by this rapid growth, local leaders strongly protested when the War Manpower Commission classified Dallas in 1943 as a critical labor shortage (Group 1) area. By doing this shortly after North American Aviation opened a second plant to build B24 bombers, federal officials thwarted local efforts to gain more wartime industry, for the Group 1 ranking prohibited new industry from locating in Dallas and did not permit established industries to take on new business. Chamber of Commerce officials immediately appealed the city's reclassification when it prevented Dallas from obtaining an aluminum extraction mill, something deemed necessary for the city's postwar industrial development. Dallas won its appeal, but continued to experience labor shortages and an overtaxed physical plant.[26]

During this time of both opportunity and chaos, Dallas entered into a number of cooperative ventures with the federal government. Federal funds not only built the defense plants and trained the workers, but helped provide housing and public services for Dallas residents. By 1944, federal money provided for more than seventy-three hundred units of emergency housing, including twenty-seven hundred cheaply constructed temporary units on the city's west side.[27]

Defense mobilization gave new impetus to the industrial movement in Dallas and underlined the relationship between the city's physical deficiencies and its social problems. As a result, problems incurred by mobilization helped spur the city's planning movement and culminated in the Master Plan of 1945.

Planning was nothing new to the North Texas city. When in 1943 the City Council engaged Harland Bartholomew and Associates, one of the nation's best-known planning firms, to develop a master plan, it continued a tradition that had started in 1910. In that year nationally respected planner George Kessler had produced a city plan for Dallas. And in 1927, well-known zoning expert Robert Whitten helped write the city's first comprehensive zoning ordinance.[28]

The new planning movement, which stemmed in large part from the activities of the Dallas Citizens Council, reflected popular notions about the nature of urban growth and development. Claiming that earlier planning efforts simply had not been comprehensive enough, the new plan treated Dallas as if all of its parts were so interconnected that modifications needed to affect the whole rather than some single component. As a result, the plan emphasized the interrelationships between street systems, transit facilities, parks, public buildings, city appearance, and housing. Proponents of planning also argued that much public and private building would take place immediately after the war and thought that planning assured a more orderly approach to this task. According to its advocates, planning would make Dallas more livable and attractive to newcomers. Planned physical development of the metropolis seemed particularly important to the city's economic and social good health, critical if the city were to compete successfully for industry and business after the war.[29]

Several features characterized the plan. First, the document treated Greater Dallas as if it were a discrete social-cultural system and not merely a setting in which individuals could pursue their own needs and desires. Chapter 1 traced the history of the city as a way of understanding its essential character. Only then, according to Bartholomew, could an appropriate plan be made. The plan also emphasized planning for all of Dallas and its regions, and not just developments benefiting the central business district (CBD).[30] Indeed, the plan was closely tied to an aggressive annexation movement, which more than doubled the physical size of the city during the 1940s.[31] Finally, the plan discussed at length the city's need for better housing and better neighborhoods. As a result, Report 10 of the plan focused exclusively on these issues. It particularly criticized the city's housing stock for nonwhites. For instance, it observed how black residential neighborhoods in Dallas were limited to areas of old homes, unsanitary conditions, and generally inadequate facilities. After reciting those horrible conditions, the plan concluded that "the condition of negro housing [in Dallas] is one of the most serious problems confronting the community."[32]

The housing report also observed that Dallas blacks suffered not only from inadequate dwellings, but also from a lack of proper neighborhood. Furthermore, the whole pattern of Dallas land use, with the city's generally haphazard and heterogeneous development, created neighborhood problems throughout the city. According to the plan, "No conscious direction has ever been given . . . toward meeting the needs of different ethnic and income groups, or toward controlling the physical design and location of this growth. Consequently present housing is a patchwork of individual projects, bearing little relation to cohesive, unified and homogeneous neighborhoods, or to a logical community pattern."

The lack of homogeneous neighborhoods, along with a relatively low percentage of home ownership and high residential mobility, helped explain the city's lack of neighborhood improvement activities and citizens' seeming neglect of civic affairs. Only when the city had an adequate supply of houses meeting minimum standards, adequate play space, and a setting where citizens of similar backgrounds could meet and talk would Dallas neighborhoods provide the type of experiences that would build "better citizens."[33] This emphasis on neighborhood community as a citizenship builder characterized the 1940s, and influenced the actions of professional planners and housing officials as well as the commercial-civic leadership.

The plan outlined a housing program for the entire urban area, since the housing problem went "beyond the corporate limits of Dallas." According to the plan's authors, "there is little question but that, today, more slum areas are being created on the outskirts of Dallas through substandard subdivision development than are being created in the central areas of the city through obsolescence and abandonment."[34]

Adequate subdivision control was not enough, however. Good neighborhoods, according to accepted knowledge in the 1940s, resulted from settings that encouraged interaction and local identity. Toward this end, Bartholomew's plans borrowed heavily from planner Clarence Perry's self-contained neighborhood idea. This called for clearly defined neighborhood boundaries and the establishment of schools, shopping centers, and recreation space within each neighborhood so children and adults could meet and play. Future housing should be developed on this basis, according to the plan. And older neighborhoods would be transformed into better residential communities through the use of neighborhood and improvement associations. To help with neighborhood organization, the plan established the physical boundaries of the Dallas neighborhoods.[35]

The Master Plan, then, dealt with more than merely the placement of highways and sewer lines. It tackled some of the city's toughest social issues and carefully analyzed the problems and made suggestions for improvement. However, unlike the campaign for industrialization, which ignored the conventional knowledge that southern cities were meant to be commercial rather than industrial centers, the Master Plan's housing proposals reflected the conventional knowledge about housing reform, which emphasized the importance of the homogeneous neighborhood approach to better housing.[36] This reinforced rather than challenged the city's highly segregated residential patterns, the root cause of the black housing problem.

When the war ended, North American Aviation immediately closed its doors, laying off more than seventeen thousand workers. The closing of that plant and the reconversion of other plants in the area to peacetime activity did not mark the end of either large-scale aircraft production or of other industrial activity in the city, for Dallas had gained much from the aggressive actions of its business leaders. The North American experience had left the city with a large, skilled industrial work force, which had accumulated a strong wartime performance record. In addition, a thirteen-building, 125-acre industrial complex remained even after North American Aviation abandoned the city. Dallas boosters saw this facility as a potential ally in attracting new industry into the area and in providing better facilities for local establishments wishing to expand. Indeed, that happened in 1947, when the Texas Engineering and Manufacturing Company of Dallas (TEMCO) moved into Plant A.[37]

It was not TEMCO, however, but the Chance Vought Aircraft Company that most benefited from the vacated facility. Following an impressive publicity campaign by the Dallas Chamber of Commerce and City Council's agreement to a last-minute request to expand the runway at nearby Hensley Field,[38] Chance Vought of Stratford, Connecticut, decided to relocate to Dallas. The move would transfer a major aircraft manufacturing concern to the city and provide more than forty-five hundred jobs, a number unprecedented in peacetime. The company would also transfer fifteen hundred well-paid supervisory personnel to the area. Dallas was well on its way to the industrial development for which its leaders had been pressing. Vought, as well as the entire wartime experience, was closely tied to the innovative and aggressive leadership of the city's established business elite. Civic-commercial leadership had achieved impressive results, transforming the commercial and financial center into an important southwestern industrial metropolis. The war had provided the opportunity and local leadership had taken full advantage of it.[39]

The legacy of the city's commercial-civic leadership was not so impressive, however, when it came to social problems — in particular, low-cost housing for blacks. During and after the war, housing conditions worsened for Dallas blacks. Despite a rapid increase in the black population during the war, little new housing opened up for blacks. Although the federal government built 2,681 temporary housing units at this time, they were for whites only. And after the war, facing an unprecedented housing shortage, blacks received only 176 units of the 5,325 temporary dwellings available for returning veterans.[40] Privately built permanent housing for blacks after the war proved virtually nonexistent. Despite a record-setting construction pace by Dallas builders between 1945 and 1949, few of the 30,000 houses built during this time were for blacks.[41]

Instead of gaining new neighborhoods, blacks saw old ones destroyed by public improvements such as the construction of Central Expressway

and the expansion of runways at Love Field. When a congressional committee visited the city in 1947, it heard that the twenty-six thousand black
households in the city had about 10,500 units in which to live.[42] Moreover,
a Dallas housing market review revealed that 64.7 percent of those dwellings were substandard.[43] As a result, the proportion of black families living in substandard housing was nearly three times as high as white families living in the same. The combination of virtually no new housing, de-
teriorating old housing, and the barriers imposed by white racism led
Marceo Smith, FHA racial relations adviser, to observe that "it is harder
to find homes for Negroes in Dallas than in any other city in the South."[44]
Since the city's nine black sections were already crowded and surrounded
by hostile white neighborhoods, Smith proposed that all new black neighborhoods be developed on the city's outskirts. Despite the FHA's new willingness to help private developers build housing for blacks and the proposal of at least six housing developments for blacks during the 1940s,
the private sector did virtually nothing to alleviate the shortage in the war
decade.[45]

Because of the private sector's failure to provide adequate housing for
blacks, and because insufficient housing posed a threat to the public order,
Dallas leaders turned to public housing and strongly supported it, despite
a growing resistance to it throughout much of the nation. Not only did
the business-dominated City Council agree to support and aid the development of new public housing in 1949, but the Dallas Chamber of Commerce and the Dallas home builders association endorsed public housing
for local blacks, despite strong opposition to public housing on the part
of their national affiliates. Indeed, the National Association of Home
Builders felt compelled to censor the Dallas home builders for their qualified support of the 1949 Housing Act.[46] And the Dallas Chamber of Commerce cosponsored a Negro Housing Survey with the Dallas Citizens Council in 1950, which asked that DHA construct fifteen hundred units of public
housing for blacks in the next eighteen months.[47]

The strong support for public housing for blacks no doubt was influenced by another flare-up of racial violence as blacks attempted to expand
a black neighborhood in South Dallas. Nearby whites responded by bomb-
ing eleven black homes in the disputed two-square-mile area between
February, 1950, and July, 1951.[48]

In the midst of this conflict, the DHA initiated its most ambitious
public housing program ever. Between 1950 and 1954, it built six projects
and nearly four thousand housing units for nonwhites and an additional
fifteen hundred–unit project for whites. Although the DHA located some
of its projects in blighted black neighborhoods in South Dallas, it under-
took its largest public housing project in a periphery slum area situated
in West Dallas. Located outside the city limits, the area attracted many
poor blacks and Mexican Americans after the Trinity River levees, com-

pleted in the 1930s, salvaged the bottoms from floods. A jumbled mix of shacks, abandoned gravel pits, garbage dumps, open toilets, and shallow wells dotted the landscape and made it the area's most notorious slum. The DHA's thirty-two million dollar program razed over eight hundred buildings within a 513-acre area and replaced them with thirty-five hundred public housing units, divided into three separate but contiguous projects. The Edgar Ward Place Project, the first project undertaken, provided fifteen hundred units for black families, the George Loving Place Project housed fifteen hundred white households, and the Elmer Scott Place furnished five hundred units for Mexican Americans.[49]

The DHA liked the West Dallas setting for several reasons. First, the public housing site seemed unfit for private development and could only be improved by large-scale investment. Second, it already housed blacks and provided room for further expansion. Third, public transportation made it accessible to downtown and to points of black employment, but it remained fairly isolated from established white neighborhoods. Furthermore, the self-contained public housing projects were seen as a stimulus to revitalizing all of West Dallas, a metropolitan strategy called for in the plan of 1945. Along with the public housing, the council would annex the area and provide sewers, streets, sidewalks, and fill in the gravel pits and inadequate cesspools. The addition of schools, churches, stores, and other service facilities would improve the area and make it a contributing part of the metropolis.[50]

With the completion of the West Dallas undertaking in April of 1954, the DHA ceased building public housing until the 1970s. Indeed, a public referendum thwarted additional public housing in 1962, despite the wishes of the mayor and the support of the Dallas Citizens Council. Even before that defeat, the city and its leadership had grown more conservative and seemed less willing to see Dallas as a part of the national system of cities.[51] Growing unhappiness with increasing taxes and federal "meddling" in local affairs dominated the Dallas discourse after 1955. The Texas metropolis had weathered its crisis and now set out to expand its central business district without the help of federal urban renewal monies.

On the local level, the mid-1950s marked a turning point in urban focus, too. The annexation and development of West Dallas had clearly been consistent with the metropolitan orientation found in Bartholomew's 1945 plan. After 1957, however, it appears that attention shifted from the metropolitan whole to the city's core. According to one West Dallasite, his community had become "a neglected step child," seeing little of the promised public improvement or services. Instead, local attention focused on rehabilitating areas close to the downtown area, as part of the larger program encouraging development in and around the central business district.[52]

Dallas in the 1950s, then, offered both the strengths and the weaknesses of commercial civic leadership. From an economic standpoint, the city prospered and gained true national urban prominence. But political, economic, and social barriers restricted the development of citizenship-building neighborhood community for blacks. Unwilling to overcome those obstacles, the business leadership turned its attention to something more manageable — the physical needs of the central business district. Indeed, by the 1960s, that leadership emphasized the vitality of the CBD, rather than the state of neighborhood life, as an index of the city's health and prosperity. Moreover, the entire emphasis on cooperative metropolitanism wavered in the 1960s, as did the belief in neighborhood community as a behavior-shaping force. Problems of race and housing, unfortunately, continue to haunt Dallas in the 1980s.[53]

The history of Dallas's commercial-civic leadership suggests not only the limitations of business leadership but also certain limits imposed by the metropolitan community mode of thought characteristic of Dallas in the 1940s. On one level, the vision of the metropolis as a complex and discrete social-cultural system promoted strong, decisive action by informed, central leadership. And since that leadership also subscribed to the interdependence of the whole metropolitan region, it felt compelled to improve areas and conditions that might otherwise have been ignored.

One aspect of the metropolitan community mode of thought encouraged developing local community through homogeneous (i.e., segregated) neighborhood development but limited the very possibility of responses by the commercial-civic elite. At a time when Dallas had strong and aggressive leadership willing to upset the status quo for the good of the whole, notions about city and community reinforced segregation, the root cause of Dallas's housing problems. As a result, leaders were able temporarily to relieve the immediate problem but unable to alleviate the basic causes underlying the city's housing difficulties. And these failures made it easier for Dallas's leaders to accept the inevitability of slums and to focus their attention elsewhere in the 1960s.

9. Building a New Urban Infrastructure: The Creation of Postwar San Antonio

Heywood T. Sanders

The period since the end of the Second World War has seen an explosion of urban growth in Texas and the Sunbelt. Spurred by the investment in new plants and the military during the war, by technological advances, and by broader economic change since the war, the cities of the Sunbelt have been transformed in physical and economic terms. For all of these communities, the process of urban development and outward expansion has been critically dependent on the fiscal resources and involvement of the public sector. Public capital investment for roads and expressways, bridges and overpasses, drainage and sanitary sewers has been a vital and necessary part of the business of city building. Yet cities in the Sunbelt have been long noted for their largely *private* civic ethos, for a resistance to a substantial and sustained public role. Houston's postwar boom was marked by only the most modest attempts at public sector planning and design and by the particular distinction of its consistent opposition to zoning and land-use control. And in Dallas, one recent commentary notes, "planning has traditionally been as popular . . . as no trespassing signs on the frontier."[1]

The vision of urban growth and development as a largely private matter has historically been reinforced by constraints, often self-imposed, on the ability of cities to generate and spend money. Just as the absence of a state income tax has become a political icon for Texans, so city leaders have sought to keep taxes low and public services modest. Kenneth Gray's 1960 report on politics in Houston notes that "the general citizenry of Houston is no less vigorous than businessmen and big property owners in resisting taxes."[2]

The image of the limited public fisc was further reinforced by an apparent distaste for federal grant assistance throughout the 1950s and 1960s. San Antonio was the lone participant in the federal urban renewal program among the state's largest cities. Houston and Dallas long disdained everything from social service programs to school lunch aid. As Susan Mac-Manus has noted, "Houston politicians boasted that their city's growing economy allowed it to refuse federal aid while other cities pleaded for more and more help."[3]

But the business of urban growth depends on enough public involvement and spending to pay for the maze of infrastructure and development assistance necessary to support outward growth. In Texas cities, that implied increasing local debt and selling the long-term bonds that could pay for large-scale public works and be repaid over time. Bond issues, in turn, required the approval of the local electorate, in the form of a majority vote acquiescing in greater city debt and increased taxes. The requirement of voter approval imposed a dual set of political constraints on local officials. They were obliged to craft bond proposals so as to generate majority voter support for growth-related projects while keeping the threat of higher taxes as modest as possible. Broad public support for spending plans thus had to be engineered or manipulated on a regular basis, with the generation of some sort of civic consensus on what was needed and what was affordable.

A consensus for growth and growth-related public investment has not always been easy to achieve. Despite the increasing number of academic discussions of the efficacy of urban "growth machines," the combination of support from political leadership, business and economic elites, and the voting public has not occurred without difficulty or accommodation. The rhetoric of urban growth and expansion has regularly promised a set of benefits, from the creation of new jobs and increased incomes, to the enlargement of the local tax base and a higher level of public services. But the reality of local development is often a clear division between those who stand to gain from growth and those with something to lose, and a split between voters oriented to large investments for community betterment and those who fear the cost. The city of San Antonio offers a case study in the evolution of municipal capital investment and the politics of local growth. Its history of both political conflict and shifting political control parallels broad trends among Sunbelt cities, but with a set of outcomes that render it even today quite distinct from Dallas or Houston.

San Antonio in 1930 was a city characterized by both rapid growth and sharp divisions in its population and politics. The city had enjoyed a substantial spurt of economic activity and growth in the 1920s fueled by oil discoveries in South Texas, the boom in real estate in the Rio Grande Valley, and the rapid local development of military aviation. The city's population grew from 96,600 in 1910 to more than 231,000 in 1930, placing it just slightly below Houston and Dallas. The increase in size and economic activity was mirrored in new construction and development. San Antonio added more than fourteen thousand new dwellings from 1922 to 1930 and some one thousand new commercial structures.

Population growth and private building in the city were supported by large-scale public investment in facilities and infrastructure. Major bond issues in 1924, 1925, 1926, 1927, and 1928 added $13.7 million to the city's debt and provided for the construction of parks, libraries, fire stations, and a municipal auditorium as well as new streets, bridges, sewers, drainage, and flood protection. The processes of public and private development thus proceeded apace, with new infrastructure opening up outlying land to subdivision and development.

Yet despite the impression of civic progress and enlargement, San Antonio was notable for some obvious distinctions among its neighborhoods and people. Much of the new residential development took place to the north of the downtown core, with expensive homes, large lots, and racially restrictive covenants.[4] Of the 725 miles of city streets in 1933, only 298 miles were paved. The residential areas west of the downtown housed a largely Hispanic population in some of the worst physical conditions to be found in the United States. In the words of a journalist writing in 1939,

> The Mexican slum must be seen to be appreciated. . . . The streets are not paved. Many of them are not really streets but alleys, with only a few feet of mud and stagnant water separating one long row of rickety shacks from another.
>
> Often these huts and sheds have no toilets, no running water, no drains or sewers. The walls are almost no protection against weather; wide cracks admit every winter wind.[5]

The housing conditions of the Hispanic west side were paralleled in the predominantly black east side, although (at least, by 1939) that area possessed a much higher level of infrastructure and public facilities.

The San Antonio of the 1930s thus exhibited vast disparities in wealth and neighborhood quality. It also exhibited a quite traditional form of local politics. Commentators were prone to describe the city as machine-run, dominated by a collection of small personal organizations on the east and west sides, with every month seeing "some municipal scandal to shock the innocents who still believe in the honesty of public men—if indeed, there are any innocents remaining in San Antonio."[6] The city's commission form of government was easily controlled by a succession of politicos who arranged individual support with segments of the black and Hispanic communities. For Hispanics, payment of personal poll taxes, distribution of city patronage employment, and reliance on networks of friends and relatives could be counted on for large blocs of votes. On the east side, a political organization under the control of local gambler Charles Bellinger managed deals with a succession of local officials, exchanging a few thousand votes for official ignorance of vice and a variety of more tangible neighborhood improvements.

The machines that combined to dominate San Antonio's politics notably excluded the more affluent Anglo areas to the north of the core. Much of the city's business leadership tacitly accepted the pattern of machine control, which had historically provided the public spending and improvements necessary for urban development and expansion. Capital spending projects had also aided the downtown business district, providing a new auditorium, reducing the likelihood of damaging floods, and renovating some of the city's historic buildings and tourist attractions. But a movement for elimination of machine domination and political reform appeared in 1930, and marked the full-scale emergence of a hitherto nascent split. The issue that caused the overt conflict between traditional politicians and reformers was a proposal for a bond issue, designed in part to support development in outlying areas the city was attempting to annex.

San Antonio's boundaries had been set at its incorporation as a 36-mile "box" measured from San Fernando Cathedral. Mayor C. M. Chambers proposed in August, 1929, to enlarge that area to a total of 144 square miles, adding some twenty thousand residents to the city's population and encompassing a vast area of suburbs, farms, and ranches. Contemporary accounts suggest a variety of motivations for the annexation efforts, ranging from a desire to forestall new independent suburbs to an interest in increasing tax revenues and industrial development opportunities. Division within the City Commission and the concerns of the Chamber of Commerce and suburban residents resulted in a less ambitious expansion plan that would, nonetheless, more than double the city's land area. Yet even this limited annexation effort saw a mixed public reception.

The city's attempt at annexation brought with it the wholesale opposition of a group of "suburban" residents who now faced the threat of increased taxes and little change in public services. The opposition was joined by a number of businessmen long concerned with machine politics, including Maury Maverick (later congressman and mayor), Walter W. McAllister of the San Antonio Building and Loan Association, auto dealer J. Roy Murray, and businessmen Walter Negley and Guy McFarland. The group organized as the San Antonio Citizens League, heir to a succession of reform groups over the years, and moved to oppose the annexation and the city's plans for a bond issue.

Mayor C. M. Chambers proposed a major package of bond issues in March, 1930, designed to provide improvements for newly annexed areas and to deal with a variety of long-standing public needs. Of a total of $4,975,000, street paving accounted for $1 million, river and drainage improvements made up another $1 million, and other public works for streets and sewers consumed most of the balance. One item of $700,000 was devoted to parks, although it also included a modest sum for airport improvements. The bond proposals were very much on the order of those passed in the 1920s. And the economic impact of the Depression lent a particular symbolic relevance, with the mayor promising "Bonds or Bread Lines."[7] The importance of the bonds to the city's growth and development was also forcefully argued by the city commissioners. A newspaper advertisement signed by the incumbents noted the need to serve both annexed areas and older sections and asked the city's taxpayers, "If you are in earnest about maintaining and further assuring San Antonio's progress, go to the polls and vote FOR these bonds."[8]

The city's bond plans were endorsed by a host of local individuals and organizations, including the local Building Trades Council of the AF of L, the Chamber of Commerce, and one of the city's two daily newspapers. The support thus involved most of the traditional elements of local growth machines.

The opposition to the bonds was centered in the new Citizens League and an antitax group, the Taxpayers' League. The issues they raised would not appear out of place at a "tax revolt" meeting today. Maury Maverick, for example, campaigned against improper spending, demanded an audit of the city's books, and argued that monies "had been diverted to build the library for negroes and for improvements to Woodlawn Lake park [on the west side]." Other opponents argued that the city was too far in debt and "five years ahead of its needs in building construction."[9] But at base the campaign against the bond issues was aimed at the distribution of political power within the city, most simply stated by opponent William Wurzbach in demanding that "the crooked political machine should be destroyed."[10]

As a referendum on the local machine organizations, the vote for the bonds sustained the status quo. The full set of spending proposals carried by tiny margins, the vote on the street paving bond divided 17,612 for and 17,413 against. The distribution of that vote proved a key measure of variation in local sentiment and organization. The votes for the bonds proved heaviest on the city's Hispanic west side, one precinct voting 88 percent in favor and another machine stronghold voting some seven to one for. The vote on the east side, where Charles Bellinger's organization swung the black vote, was also in favor although at a more modest margin. The "antis" appeared most concentrated on the city's north side, among middle- and upper-income voters. One typical precinct opposed the bonds by a division of 60 percent to 40 percent. And among the Anglo homeowners on the city's southeast side, in the Highland Park area, the "no" vote reached 63 percent.

The vote on the bonds demonstrated the sharp splits within the city's business elite and among its voters. A number of important businessmen stood with the machine organization despite the tales of poll tax manipulation and patronage and politics. Yet others sought to create an independent political organization and a reform slate dedicated to wiping out the purported machine control. The split among the electorate followed class and ethnic lines, with the machine's traditional support among black and Hispanic have-nots opposed by much of the city's middle- and upper-income Anglo population. Maverick's campaign rhetoric hit on the central truth of the distribution of voting power and political benefits. The machine could garner votes in minority neighborhoods and, in turn, produce "a library for negroes" and improvements for a major west side park, and it could do so with the property taxes of Maverick and his neighbors.

The ultimate outcome of the 1930 bond election became, along with the annexation plan, a judicial issue. And the Citizens League succeeded in the courts where it had failed at the polls. The city did not issue bonds in 1930, and the forces of reform succeeded in maintaining the city's boundaries and its moderate level of debt and taxation. The 1930 vote proved to be the opening shot in a continuing battle over public spending, growth, and political control. The political divisions within the city largely defined the outcomes of bond elections throughout the 1930s, and the persistent opposition of reform and antitax forces effectively constrained the city's fiscal plans.

The city's efforts at capital investment were delayed until 1934, when the national unemployment situation and the city's own capital needs combined to lower the direct cost of infrastructure improvements. The City Commission sought to match federal WPA funds with revenues from sewer service to "permit the extension of sewers to thickly populated unsewered sections of the city."[11]

The legacy of the 1930 vote was a promise to limit the issuance of bonds to $400,000 rather than the $1.4 million possible, presumably with the aim of demonstrating civic frugality. Yet even with the promise of matching federal assistance and a limited dollar amount, the 1934 sewer bond vote failed by a margin of 36 percent. The 1934 failure was followed by another in the fall of 1935. A largely private effort to spend $500,000 on civic improvements — a stadium, Alamo monument, coliseum, and museum enlargement — was designed to serve as the city's participation in the Texas Centennial activities. Despite the appeals to "patriotic and civic motives," the bonds were defeated by a margin of three to one.[12] The defeat of the Centennial bonds represented a victory for the city's machine organizations. City commissioners did not endorse the Centennial plans and did not attempt to swing organization votes for them.

City officials reversed themselves two months later with a plan for yet another bond issue. The December, 1935, package was largely devoted to basic infrastructure such as streets and sewers, intended primarily for the west and east side areas. Again, the promise of matching WPA grant funds was pressed as a rationale for the $350,000 proposal. But the political realities of improvements distributed to machine strongholds were far more persuasive reasons. In the words of the *San Antonio Express,* "Success of the bond issue, plenty of work for voters before the spring municipal election, improvements which can be 'pointed to with pride,' all these are reasons why the present city administration which preserved a detached attitude towards the recent unsuccessful bond issue for celebrating the Texas Centennial, is anything but detached towards Monday's election."[13] The addition of a strong machine effort to the voting equation and the apparent lack of strong opposition from reform forces proved sufficient to carry the bond proposals by margins of four and five to one.

The final bond proposition of the 1930s came before the voters in the fall of 1936. A scheme for $450,000 in bonds to generate some $2 million in WPA funds was proposed, dominated by a $100,000 fire station project to complement the Alamo in the downtown area. The division of sentiment on the bonds precisely mirrored that of 1930. Incumbent city officials promised a modest tax increase and thousands of new jobs and argued that the plan involved no politics. Arrayed in opposition were the Citizens League and the Taxpayers League, again opposed to an increase in city taxes, the dominance of the machine, and "the greed of the city hall for bond money."[14]

The results of the 1936 election demonstrated the problem the city faced with the split between "machine" and "reform" forces. The bulk of the bond proposals, a total of $325,000, received a majority endorsement. But the $125,000 balance for park and market house improvements was defeated. The strongholds of the city organization provided impressive margins for all issues. Four precincts on the city's Hispanic west side combined in a vote of eighty-three to one in favor. But in reform locales, particularly the north side neighborhoods of Laurel Heights and Denver Heights, the vote count stood at four or five to one against.[15]

The modest success of some of the bond issues at the polls again did not ensure public spending. Citizens League officials threatened legal action against the incumbent city officials over voting irregularities, and the bonds were not sold until the following July.

After a boom in construction and urban development during the 1920s, the city's public investment efforts all but collapsed during the 1930s. The Depression obliged any number of cities to alter their fiscal plans and caused a host of defaults on municipal bonds. Yet San Antonio's failure to meet public investment needs was rooted in political division and dissent. After millions of dollars of public spending during the previous decade, the 1930s saw only $650,000 in city bonds issued. The failure of the local electorate to endorse a succession of bond proposals reflected a political split within the city and its business community. Those opposed to "machine rule" and high taxes were successful at least in limiting the growth of debt and in altering the city's annexation policies. Yet the "machine," whatever its ability to manipulate the public fisc and the electoral machinery, regularly produced concrete and material benefits for the minority neighborhoods on the city's east and west sides.

Texas cities boomed during the Second World War, with an influx of service personnel, industry, and population. San Antonio's status as the center of army aviation was the springboard for substantial growth during the war, with the city adding thousands of new residents. Still, the deficiencies in public facilities and infrastructure that had plagued the city throughout the 1930s only increased. An assessment in 1951 as part of a

new city plan noted that a large proportion of the city's streets were unpaved or poorly paved, a "considerable area of the city [was] unserviced
by sanitary sewers," and that "little has been done in San Antonio over
the last 25 years to provide facilities for removing surface waters."[16] The
city did, however, possess substantial capacity to sell bonds and generate
debt to meet its backlog of improvement needs.

The first thrust at dealing with that backlog and the growth of the war
era came with a massive postwar improvement plan developed by the City-
County Planning Board in 1945. The planning group called for expenditures
on a new expressway system, airport expansion, fire stations, World War
II memorial, and museum and aquarium projects. But the City Commission added its own spending ideas, creating a bond package of twenty-two
projects totaling $7.26 million.

The differences between the improvement preferences of the elite-
dominated planning board and the city's elected officials involved the persistent issues of cost, impact, and location. The commission's projects included a number of parks projects distributed on the west, east, and south
sides and spending for new streets, buildings, and an incinerator. The finance committee of the planning group clearly favored a smaller total cost,
those items tied to the promise of federal grant assistance, and investments
that "favored the north side of town."[17]

The conflict over the size and purpose of the postwar bond package
came to involve a wide swath of the community. Contractor H. B. Zachry,
who chaired the planning board's finance committee, pressed for only the
smaller set of projects, with a price tag of $3.64 million. But other local
reform leaders coalesced as the Greater San Antonio Committee to back
passage of the full package. And the support of the city's elected officials
was balanced by the vocal opposition of county officials. The new decade
clearly had not altered the debate and division within the city over debt
and spending issues. It also had not changed the split within the local electorate along class and ethnic lines.

The fate of the bonds at the polls in September, 1945, was mixed. The
major propositions, those backed by Zachry and the Taxpayers Defense
League, squeaked by with bare majorities. Most of the smaller propositions failed to receive the necessary simple majority, often by just a few
hundred out of almost twelve thousand votes. Despite the city's low debt
level and modest rate of taxation, the bond election results indicated a continuation of the local political divisions and capital investment stasis of
the 1930s.

The most telling evidence for the problematic character of public spending in San Antonio came from the precinct returns. The areas annexed
to the city after 1940 provided substantial opposition to the bonds. The
antipathy remained constant on the Anglo north side, although that area
provided slightly higher margins for airport, expressway, and museum

plans. The principal support for the bonds came from the black precincts on the city's east side and from the traditional machine strongholds of the Hispanic west side. And the vocal opposition of county officials and city tax commissioner Alfred Callaghan raised questions about the possibilities for *any* future capital investment schemes.

A second major bond proposal came before the voters some eight months later, involving $4.4 million for the expansion of the city's sewer lines and treatment plant and drainage improvement. The issue was portrayed in the most dramatic terms as vital to public health and safety: "Simply, San Antonio's storm and sanitary sewer systems are inadequate and inefficient. Those systems cannot protect the city against infectious and contagious diseases that result from filth created by stagnant waters and exposed raw garbage and sewage. . . . San Antonio has far to go to bring its sewer systems abreast of its present needs, let alone provide for the city's future growth."[18] Despite the threat of dread disease, voters once again rejected bonds and once again the opposition of Callaghan and his organization played a major part.

The bonds for the sewer improvements were presented to the voters again in December, 1947. This time they were successful, endorsed by a substantial citywide majority. This campaign involved a much broader effort at securing endorsement and support than the first and, apparently, a much higher level of political activity.

That success was followed by a 1949 proposal for highway development and right-of-way acquisition to support a major local expressway program. The expressway proposal was carefully crafted to appeal to a substantial segment of the voters and property owners. The city promised that bond passage would not affect the property tax rate, due to the maturity of outstanding debt. The bonds were also linked to additional aid from the state and federal governments, which would assist in paying for expressway construction. Mayor Jack White pressed the bonds on the electorate, arguing that they were the "kind of progressive measure that will help make San Antonio the city it should be."[19]

The symbols of low-cost growth and development thus played a role in the public appeal. But perhaps more important was the relatively unified political front of its supporters. Through what must have been an impressive political bargaining exercise, the bonds garnered the endorsement of both the leaders of San Antonio's personalistic machine organizations (Sheriff Owen Kilday, Judge C. K. Quin) and its reform-oriented politicians, including former mayor and congressman Maury Maverick.

The lessons of the city's first few efforts to expand public capital investment and development in the postwar period were clear. First, given a history of low voter turnout and widespread political apathy, the outcomes of bond referenda were problematical. Second, the passage of bonds all but demanded some accommodation with the various machine organizations in the city. The opposition of one group or even a single important political official with a personal agenda could hamstring public plans and investments. Ultimately, the solution to both the bond referendum problem and the city's larger problems required an alternative form of political and electoral organization that could both reduce official conflict and deliver the votes.

The larger political environment of the city during this period was marked by a series of swings in City Commission composition and politics, as "reform" supporters contested with the personalistic machines. The city adopted the manager form of government in 1951 and voted in a reform council slate. But the council coalition soon fell apart, and in 1953, "control was taken by a council the majority of which neither understood nor cared about the meaning of good government."[20]

The seesaw battle for political control had an obvious impact on the city's ability to finance public infrastructure investment. Local voters faced four proposals that summed to a record nineteen million dollars, largely for expressways and street improvements. With an all-time high turnout, the bonds were consistently defeated, although the expressway issue came the closest to passage.

The pattern of defeat indicates yet another chapter in the continuing machine-reform split. The city's middle- and upper-income neighborhoods generally favored the plans, but some of the outer north side precincts voted against, as did the Harlandale area on the south side. Interestingly, the black east side precincts voted overwhelmingly against the bonds. A major source of opposition to the issues came from one of the city's largest property owners, businessman Morris Kallison, and from Thurman Barrett, owner of a major lumberyard and a gravel, masonry, and concrete supply firm. This division within the city's business community reflected both differences in political allegiance and a split over the tax and fiscal impact of growth policies. Kallison, the city's eighth-largest tax-payer, with property valued at close to $2.5 million in 1955, contended that "councilmen had broken promises to lower taxes and refrain from bond issues."[21]

The failure at the polls in January, 1954, certainly did not doom the expressway plans. The "deal" offered by the combination of state and federal funding was simply too good for the city to pass up, even in the face of bond opposition. The program reappeared on the ballot in July, with a sole eleven million dollar bond issue devoted to the expressway program. Newspaper coverage of the issue now greatly emphasized the availability of outside financing and the fiscal opportunity. The *San Antonio Express* editorialized that "the $11 million in city bonds will assure expenditures here of up to $44 million in federal-state highway construction funds over the next five years," and that "the state is purposely offering the city the best highway deal in Texas because it has to date lagged so far behind the other metropolitan areas in expressway development. . . . Failure to take advantage of this unprecedented civic opportunity would be unthinkable."[22] The coalition supporting the expressway proposal was enlarged from the previous vote, and an attempt was made to involve city employees as a campaign organization. The result was a substantial victory at the polls and the beginnings of a major expressway network for the city.

San Antonio's experience in the early years of the postwar period demonstrates the difficulties of garnering widespread public support for capital investment in the face of a fragmented polity with vestiges of machine organization. The public funds required for urban growth and development were by no means assured in a fractious environment, and the city's ability to compete for industry and new development was hampered. The tax rate for debt in 1955 was *half* of what it had been five years previously. The city's total net debt stood at $14.5 million in mid-1954, only slightly higher than the $10.8 million of ten years previously.

The contrast with other Texas cities was quite dramatic. San Antonio's debt per capita was the lowest among the seven largest cities in the state, at about $31 per person. Fort Worth's debt came to $98 per person, Dallas's figure was about $94 per capita, while Houston had some $144 in debt for each of its residents. San Antonio's total debt was thus about one-fifth the level of Houston's. The results of this fiscal condition could be seen in a stalled expressway program, limited street improvements and access to the central business district, and a continuing problem of inadequate water, sewer, and drainage systems in the area brought into the city during the 1940s and early 1950s. San Antonio thus faced an array of capital needs independent of its interest in supporting further growth or the support of new industry or development plans. It also lacked a political base on which to build the public support for substantial debt and capital spending. San Antonio's civic problem at the end of 1954 was a combination of political disorganization and public investment requirements.

The solution to this combination of political and fiscal necessities came in the form of a new political organization that was to reshape the city's electoral politics and its public policies. A group of reform-oriented individuals, largely drawn from the local business community, banded together in December, 1954, as the Good Government League (GGL), with a commitment to redeem the city manager plan and the promise of good government. The group developed a slate of council candidates committed to a progressive, business-oriented view of city government and management and directly contested for control of the council. The first results were quite impressive. Eight GGL candidates secured seats on the nine-member council by margins of roughly three to one. With substantial support from the Anglo middle-class precincts on San Antonio's north side, the GGL effectively forged a new electoral coalition that could dominate the personalistic machines.

The impact of the GGL's electoral muscle was immediately visible in bond elections and infrastructure politics. The new council placed a total of fifteen million dollars in bond proposals on the ballot in November, 1955, and campaigned for them as a referendum on the effort to restore "good government." Editorials promoted this theme, arguing, "After a 10-year battle, the citizens have won good government. . . . This is the golden opportunity to preserve the gains."[23] The growth-oriented GGL council also repeated the importance of bond issues to the city's economic future, contending that "industries looking for new locations certainly would not select a city with run-down streets, run-down sanitary sewers, a sewage disposal plant in need of enlargement and other deficient municipal services."[24]

But amidst all the rhetoric about community betterment, keeping the tax rate stable, and the virtues of the new good government administration, local newspaper coverage was notable in its change from earlier periods. The *Express* editorialized, "So let's name names and get down to cases," blasting Morris Kallison and bond opponents as "the diehard remnants of the disgruntled obstructionists who for 10 years have fought a losing battle against council-manager government and every related civic effort for community progress."[25] The editorial, headed "Fight the Saboteurs of City Progress!" was accompanied by a cartoon showing a smiling boy labeled "progressive city government" under the protection of a large policeman called "public opinion" and safe from the bemused countenance of another boy marked "selfish interests." The 1955 bond fight, much like the earlier GGL victory, was not handled by the local press as a news or public issue, but rather as a battle between civic virtue and the forces of evil and municipal poverty. The passage of the bulk of the bond proposals, particularly those for new infrastructure, thus marked a dominant role for the new GGL coalition and new intervention by the press in the business of financing urban growth.

The electoral success of the GGL organization and its political coalition sharply altered the landscape of local politics. The organization effectively dominated council politics until the early 1970s. Its impact on bond elections and fiscal politics are equally marked. From a time when bond proposals faced certain opposition and an uncertain electoral fate, the passage of infrastructure spending plans became a virtual certainty.

There were occasional chinks in the GGL's success, such as the defeat of a police headquarters and parks bond in late 1957. But the only serious setback came in the 1960 defeat of a nine million dollar streets and expressway proposal. That defeat was the product of what was to be one of the most divisive and long-standing conflicts in the recent history of the city—a plan (first presented in the 1945 package of bond issues) to construct the "North Expressway" between the downtown core and the northside airport. The expressway fight, involving threats to Brackenridge Park, Trinity University, the city's most exclusive "in town" suburban jurisdiction, and a historic area, came to involve a broad range of groups and individuals who were the GGL's natural allies, including the powerful San Antonio Conservation Society.

Perhaps the ultimate tribute to the power of the GGL's political organization came with the eventual outcomes. A modified expressway bond program passed overwhelmingly six months after the initial defeat, and the North Expressway, now known as U.S. 281 or the McAllister Freeway (after GGL stalwart Mayor Walter McAllister), was eventually built with state and federal funds even after federal law was changed to ban its eligibility as part of the Interstate Highway program.

The GGL's impact was not simply one of better and more effective promotion of bond proposals, or of a new style of campaign politics. The organization effectively restructured the patterns of voting on spending propositions and generated a clear shift in bond voting. The 1945 bond issues, for example, received their greatest relative support in west side precincts that included the city's lower-income Hispanic areas. Voters on the city's north side provided only lukewarm support for everything from expressways to a new aquarium.[26] The east side black precincts, which had provided the support for the organization and its proposals during the 1930s, now voted consistently against spending items. And the southern and southeastern parts of the community, which had long opposed bond plans, continued to do so. Without the consistent and substantial support of north side precincts, bond issues faced little likelihood of passage.

The general distribution of electoral sentiment persisted into the early 1950s. Thus the 1954 street bonds proposal received its greatest proportional support on the west side (simple correlation or $r = +0.34$), a slightly negative reception on the north ($r = -0.07$), and opposition on the east side ($r = -0.27$). But the passage of the expressway bonds in July, 1954, saw the beginning of a new pattern of voting that marked a divide in political preferences. For the first time, a large percentage of north side voters endorsed major capital-investment plans. The simple correlation between support for the expressway and a balance of city/north side dummy variable was $+0.41$ (n = 66). And substantial north side support then remained constant for bond issues throughout the 1950s. Thus, by 1957, there still existed a strong relationship between north side location and support for expressway spending ($r = +0.68$; n = 69).

The emergence of the GGL in late 1954 and 1955 thus brought about a quantum increase in support for bonds among the city's Anglo middle class. Whether as a result of the active involvement of the GGL's precinct volunteer organization or the perception that "politics" had now been removed from City Hall and from spending decisions, middle-class north side voters now ensured regular passage of infrastructure bonds.

At the same time, the GGL's new support did not extend to the Hispanic west side. The correlation between bond issue voting after 1955 and west side location became either zero or negative, indicating that these precincts were providing no particular support for bond plans. The political reform represented by the Good Government League did not necessarily extend to the city's poorest Hispanic residents. Bond issues that once regularly included projects for east and west side neighborhoods were increasingly devoted to the basic highway, sewer, and water infrastructure needed for growth. And the GGL, faced with opposition from or electoral indifference on the part of the city's minority residents, apparently felt little pressure to deal with the public facility deficiences of their neighborhoods. The price of controling reform was thus a selective attention to public concerns, one that sought not solely to benefit one section or another but to spur outward expansion and the presumed community benefits of "growth."

The fiscal impact of the GGL's electoral success and policy preferences was enormous. From a net debt of $14.4 million in 1954, the city's debt climbed rapidly to $37.6 million in 1959, $52.7 million in 1969, and about $120 million in 1979. By 1984, San Antonio owed more than $181 million in general obligation city debt. The new patterns of bond voting were sufficient to assure regular public endorsement of the debt needed to finance growth and development.

Yet the increase in the city's debt did not imply a profligacy of GGL-endorsed city councils or a wild spending binge. Public financing for growth was kept well within taxation limits that were acceptable to a conservative business elite, and the total size of bond issues was tailored to fit within those limits. Thus "Progress for San Antonio," the official description of the 1955 bond projects, noted that "the Committee agreed that a tax rate of $1.96 will be required to pay for current operations of the City, duly provide for preventive maintenance, and support the proposed bond issue. It was concluded that this is a sound rate."[27]

The $1.96 tax rate for $100 of assessed value had no magic import to local voters or property owners. Indeed, it represented a *decrease* from the tax rate that prevailed in 1945 and through the early 1950s. The $1.96 rate cap was breached, but only modestly, in 1968, when taxes hit $2.10. But that level dropped in the face of city-supported growth and other revenue devices. Property tax rates dropped to $1.65 per $100 in the last half of the 1970s, where it stood in the early 1980s. Thus, despite the ravages of inflation and demands of a rapidly increasing population and city area, San Antonio was able to lower the tax rate required to repay its debt and provide for basic city services.

The goal of keeping property taxes low and eventually decreasing them was managed by a "top down" capital planning process that set the total of bond issues not at what was needed, required, or publicly demanded, but at the level fixed by the tax rate. So the city's $65.5 million bond program in 1970 neatly fit within a tax rate for bond retirement actually *lower* than the rate prevailing in 1950. It mattered little that "the hard working

citizens' committee that met numerous times to pull together the bond proposals found justifiable needs amounting to some $218 million at today's
level of cost estimates."[28]

San Antonio managed to pay the public costs of growth and development despite a relatively modest tax burden by paying highly selective attention to public needs during the GGL era. The city invested in items like
highways, airports, and urban renewal, where its own spending was matched
by federal and state aid, and supported outlying development by extending water lines, sewer facilities, and storm drainage. The city's older neighborhoods were effectively ignored until the 1970s, and "frills" like parks,
libraries, and recreation facilities received only modest attention. These
items were kept in the overall bond programs as a means of securing wider
public interest and support. But they were far overshadowed in monetary
terms by spending for urban infrastructure.

The parks, libraries, and cultural facilities that constituted a major part
of bond proposals in the 1930s had all but disappeared during the GGL
period. The $15 million spending package of 1955 included only $1.6 million for parks and recreation improvements. Yet that stood as a high-water
mark in proportional terms. The major bond package in 1964 devoted
only 11 percent of its total for parks and libraries, and by the 1970 bond
program, that proportion stood at about 10 percent. San Antonio's elected
officials and business leaders restricted the city's capital investments to infrastructure. They then skewed those infrastructure investments to favor
certain parts of the city and projects with growth or economic development promise.

The 1955 bond program, which represented the ascension of the GGL
to control, was dominated by almost four million dollars for street projects, the single largest item. And those street projects were limited to "the
main arteries and most heavily traveled streets in the City."[29] Thus the bulk
of the bond program served the newly developing north side areas by widening major streets and offering easy access to the downtown business district. A small part of the street bonds was devoted to paving poor streets
in residential areas. But that program involved the city's providing but a
third of the paving cost, while property owners paid for two-thirds. The
result was that unpaved streets in poor neighborhoods where residents could
not pay remained unpaved.

The street projects in the 1964 and 1970 bond packages continued the
same sort of highly selective attention to the city's needs. Street improvements consisted largely of widening and enlarging major arterial routes,
or those specific roadways needed to serve major development projects or
large employers. Thus the phrase "serving Kelly Field," the city's major
air force installation and its largest source of jobs, is repeated again and
again in descriptions of street projects.

The 1970 bonds were particularly oriented to the improvement of the downtown core and the promotion of far north side expansion. More than $4 million was planned for the "completion of an inner loop around the downtown business district," while another $1.2 million was committed to a street widening designed to "serve residents of the fast growing northwestern section."[30]

The GGL's dominance of the city's political system meant that bond issues were crafted to serve a limited set of public purposes. Supported by a council-manager city government that promised efficient, professional city government free from "politics," the city's capital investments were devoted almost solely to outlying growth and downtown improvements. The same city that could afford an $11 million convention center in 1964 and a $5.5 million Tower of the Americas in 1966 could not afford to pave many of its streets, to solve a flooding and drainage problem that persists even today, nor to assure an adequate parks or library system. The political solution to San Antonio's ethnic and class divisions of the 1930s, 1940s, and 1950s thus brought about a new set of voting outcomes, a new style of politics and local governance, and a persistent indifference to a broader set of community needs and requirements. The vehicle for passing bond issues garnered votes at a cost in civic indifference.

The management of San Antonio's electorate and its capital finances by the GGL and its supporters provided the necessary means for meeting the public requirements for growth. Yet San Antonio's fractious politics in the 1940s and early 1950s placed it at a decided disadvantage in its self-proclaimed competition with other Texas cities and the larger Sunbelt. While San Antonio's divided electorate failed to support bond programs or forced a limit to their size, Dallas and Houston were able to progress at the business of building urban infrastructure. The passage of substantial bond programs in those cities during the period of San Antonio's stasis supported a much larger investment of state and federal funds in the critical areas of streets and highways. Thus in 1952, the Texas State Highway Department invested almost $14 million of state and federal dollars in Harris County (Houston), some $2 million in Dallas County, and only $675,000 in Bexar County (San Antonio). Although San Antonio was occasionally able to catch up to Dallas in terms of state highway investment during the 1960s, it lagged far behind Houston and its aggressive freeway-building efforts.

A major key to Houston's success was the domination of that city's business community and Chamber of Commerce in formulating, promoting, and passing a steady succession of bond programs. In 1960, when a nine million dollar street and highway bond issue failed in San Antonio, Houston was spending twenty-four million dollars for public capital improvements and preparing to use some fifty-five million dollars endorsed in a 1959 bond vote. A broad consensus in support of bond programs bul-

warked by the intimate involvement of the business community allowed
Kenneth Gray to conclude in 1960 that "voters usually approve city requests
for bond issues if business groups and the press support the proposals."[31]
But the generation of electoral support was eased by holding elections on
Saturdays, keeping overall turnout low, and utilizing the employees of ma-
jor firms and corporations as part of political organization. Just as in San
Antonio, the creation of public support for bond issues and urban devel-
opment required well-crafted appeals *and* direct political intervention.

San Antonio thus conformed to a widespread Sunbelt pattern in "managing" the local electorate. In cities like Albuquerque and San Jose, the
business of growth was simply too important to be left to the vagaries of
the popular will at the ballot box.

Albuquerque began the postwar period with a relatively modest population size, serious spending constraints under state law, and a backlog of
public works projects ranging from water line extensions to storm drainage, street paving, and downtown access. Its municipal politics had long
been dominated by Democratic mayor and governor Clyde Tingley. He
sought a limited public fisc and preferred to invest in parks and a beach
on the Rio Grande. Bond issues were modest in size, yet not regularly supported by the city's electorate. As in San Antonio, the emergence of a
middle-class political reform movement and a slate-making organization
titled the Albuquerque Citizens' Committee (ACC) provided the basis for
a shift in local political control and capital-investment policies.

The ACC set about altering Tingley's fiscal orientation and secured leg-
islative permission for new tax sources with the result that "Albuquerque,
after a number of very lean years, [had] enough income to begin catching
up on its obligations."[32] The expansion of the public sector was particularly notable in terms of bond proposals. The ACC's 1959 bond program
came to some $21 million, largely devoted to sewers for outlying areas ($6.1
million), storm drainage ($3.7 million), and street improvements ($1.25 million). In 1962, the public approved $18.5 million in bonds, and in 1966
the city's voters readily endorsed a $22 million bond package.

The boom in city capital investment, coupled with state and federal
assistance, supported a sustained upward expansion and population growth.
The "reform" of the city's politics thus did not simply mean the end of
Tingley's personal control of freedom from some "machine"; it meant a
dramatic shift in political control and policies to a system dominated by
local growth interests, often those with a pecuniary interest in capital spending and urban development. If bond issues were regularly presented to the
public as being limited to projects of broad community interest, they were
passed by a combination of middle-class acceptance and traditional campaign techniques.

Both bond elections and regular city contests involved substantial financial contributions from those with an interest in growth and city infra-

structure development. A combination of architectural and engineering firms and local contractors provided fiscal sustenance for campaigns and support for prospective officials committed to both growth and the appropriate distribution of city work. Indeed, in the face of a new scheme in the early 1960s for distributing engineering contracts, a new city political organization, the People's Committee for Better Government, was formed and assisted to victory by these local infrastructure producers. Albuquerque's ability to sustain capital improvements and weather the storm of environmental sentiment in the early 1970s was due in no small measure to the political efficacy of a small group of highly interested firms that could generate money, votes, and a consistently progrowth city policy.

The local politics of postwar growth proved strikingly similar in San Jose, California. A county seat that served as a fruit canning and agricultural processing center for the Santa Clara Valley, San Jose in 1950 had a population of about ninety-five thousand and a tiny debt of exactly $20 per capita (less than half the level of San Antonio). A personalistic political machine that dominated the city's politics during the 1930s was challenged by a reform "Progress Committee" in 1944, and the city gradually embraced a growth-oriented strategy under an activist city manager. The dominance of growth forces and the efforts of manager Anthony "Dutch" Hamann resulted in a sharp alteration of fiscal policies. A major bond issue in 1950 paid for expansion of the city's sewage treatment plant, and a 1956 bond plan supported the construction of a new city hall that lured development outside the downtown core area. But with a $22.35 million bond package in 1957, the city entered a new era of electoral politics.

The 1957 bond program established a precedent for substantial public capital investment, elaborate efforts at promotion and sales, and a commitment to funding basic infrastructure. It also saw the beginnings of a formal bond campaign organization, eventually known as the "Book of the Month Club." The "Club" has best been described by one of San Jose's former mayors: "This loose combine . . . was composed of a number of contractors, developers, businessmen with a smattering of less well-heeled public officials. Their ability to put up seed money that attracted other money to advertise gave us the push to get ahead."[33] The club included the city manager and the police chief, as well as a group of developers, bankers, and the local newspaper publisher. Eleven of its twenty-four continuing members in the 1960s were directly linked to the business of infrastructure building, including the city's largest contractor (who had received the construction contract for the new city hall), the dominant civil engineering firm, and a number of paving contractors and materials suppliers.

The organization's efforts went far beyond mere promotion and campaign contributions. It operated on a regular meeting schedule to plan the city's capital improvements, land acquisitions, and development policies and to choose candidates for city elections. It thus neatly served as planning board, financial manager, and political party in defining local growth programs and politics.

The growth engendered by the Book of the Month Club and its costs proved a central element in its downfall. Public revelations about its existence, the retirement of Hamann in 1969, and a more conflictual local politics resulted in the demise of the club and the total defeat of bond programs in 1970 and 1975.

San Antonio's postwar political history thus parallels that of many of its Sunbelt counterparts. Growth and public investment did not simply happen as a product of some economic predestination or resource endowment. They required a local public sector made active and aggressive in supporting building and development and the generation of substantial debt and obligation. That new public role, in turn, required a "reform" of local government institutions and politics. The local political organizations that had served low-income communities through jobs, favors, and public projects were effectively eliminated. In their place came a system that supposedly embraced rational decision making and professional management values and that stood above petty politics. The middle-class notion that economy and efficiency were paramount criteria of local governance held sway.

But this type of "reform" involved not a new kind of local politics so much as a change in control and beneficiaries. San Antonio's Good Government League and its counterparts in other Sunbelt cities provided a means of managing and containing the political conflicts that had historically surrounded growth and spending decisions. They preempted the symbols and rhetoric of the general public interest and communitywide improvement. And they managed local voting behavior as well, bringing a new middle- and upper-income coalition to the polls that could dominate bond issues, referenda for changes in the charter, and general city elections. Local conflict over political benefits and fiscal policies was not reduced; it was simply submerged.

The growth and development of San Antonio in the postwar era saw its population increase from 254,000 in 1940 to more than 900,000 in 1989, with an increase in land area from 36 square miles to more than 350. Its expansion was by no means an inevitable result of natural endowments, resource wealth, or locational advantage. It was, rather, the product of a set of public policies that maintained low taxes and cheap and abundant public infrastructure and kept housing prices low while serving the desires of new and expanding employers.

The quest for economic development and a bigger population, the hallmarks of a "big city," have, in turn, brought increasing traffic congestion, a boost in storm water runoff and flooding, and the continuing need for new sewers, sewage treatment plants, and water supplies. San Antonio today must not only cope with its future needs, it must also remedy a host of deficiencies in public facilities, as the public investments of the GGL era skewed public goods to only a limited segment of the city's residents. While the metropolitan area's most affluent residents have been able to escape the problems of their neighbors in independent suburbs, new, walled subdivisions, and enclaves of private investment, the broader and more pervasive legacy of inadequate public services and infrastructure will remain as much a part of San Antonio as its fabled river.

Notes

INTRODUCTION

1. William E. Claggett, "Dallas: The Dynamics of Public-Private Cooperation," in R. Scott Fosler and Renee Berger, eds., *Public-Private Partnership in American Cities* (Lexington, Mass.: Lexington Books, 1982), p. 245.

CHAPTER 1 — THE RISE OF URBAN TEXAS

1. T. R. Fehrenbach, *Lone Star* (New York: Macmillan, 1968), p. 213; Glen Lich, "The Rural Scene in Texas: Half-Created/Half-Perceived," in Glen Lich and Dona B. Reeves-Marquandt, *Texas Country: The Changing Rural Scene* (College Station: Texas A&M University Press, 1986), pp. 3–15; Larry McMurtry, *Texas Observer,* October 23, 1981; Susan P. Schoelwwien, *Alamo Images: Changing Perceptions of a Texas Experience* (Dallas: Degolyer Library and Southern Methodist University Press, 1985).

2. Fehrenbach, *Lone Star,* p. 559.

3. *Newsweek,* December 30, 1985, p. 23.

4. Dora Crouch, Daniel J. Garr, and Axel I. Mindigo, *Spanish City Planning in North America* (Cambridge, Mass.: MIT Press, 1982), pp. 23–65, describe the urban pattern of which San Antonio's layout was a part.

5. Walter Prescott Webb, *The Great Plains* (New York: Grossett and Dunlap, 1931), p. 208.

6. Wayne Gard, "Retracing the Chisholm Trail," *Southwestern Historical Quarterly,* extra number (May 1, 1956), p. 12; David Galenson, "The Profitability of the Long Drive," *Agricultural History* 51 (October, 1977): 754–58; David Galenson, "The Origins of the Long Drive," *Journal of the West* 14 (July, 1975): 3–14.

7. Howard Chudacoff, *The Evolution of American Urban Society* (Englewood Cliffs, N.J.: Prentice-Hall, 1981), provides a general survey of the process of urbanization nationwide.

8. Timothy Mahoney, "Urban History in a Regional Context: River Towns on the Upper Mississippi," *Journal of American History* 72 (September, 1985): 320.

9. David R. Goldfield, "The New Regionalism," *Journal of Urban History* 11 (February, 1984): 180.

10. Ibid., pp. 180–83.

11. Kenneth W. Wheeler, *To Wear a City's Crown: The Beginnings of Urban Growth in Texas, 1836–1865* (Cambridge, Mass.: Harvard University Press, 1968), pp. 47–48. We have not included El Paso in this study for, as Bradford Luckingham has argued, its economic connections and urban rivals lie to the west, with Albuquerque, Phoenix, and Tucson. Bradford Luckingham, "The Southwest Urban Frontier, 1880–1930," *Journal of the West* 18 (July, 1979): 40–50.

12. Andrew F. Muir, "Railroads Come to Houston, 1857–1861," *Southwestern Historical Quarterly* 64 (July, 1960): 42–63.

13. James P. Baughman, "The Evolution of Rail-Water Systems of Transportation in the Gulf Southwest, 1836–1890," *Journal of Southern History* 34 (August, 1968): 357–81; Harold L. Platt, *City Building in the New South: The Growth of Public Services in Houston, Texas, 1830–1915* (Philadelphia: Temple University Press, 1983).

14. William L. MacDonald, *Dallas Rediscovered* (Dallas: Dallas Historical Society, 1978), pp. 1–18.

15. Ibid., p. 19; Ralph W. Widener, *William Henry Gaston: A Builder of Dallas* (Dallas: Historical Publishing Company, n.d.) pp. 15–16, 20–23.

16. Wheeler, *To Wear a City's Crown.*

17. Mayor Will C. A. Thielepape to James P. Newcomb, December 13, 1868, James P. Newcomb Letters, San Antonio Public Library; Donald E. Everett, "San Antonio Welcomes the 'Sunset' — 1877," *Southwestern Historical Quarterly* (July, 1961): 47–60.

18. Wheeler, *To Wear a City's Crown,* pp. 111–12; Terry G. Jordan, *German Seed in Texas Soil: Immigrant Farmers in Nineteenth-Century Texas* (Austin: University of Texas Press, 1966), pp. 74–75, 102–103, 135–36, 142, 152, 170–73.

19. John Coatsworth, "Obstacles to Economic Growth in Nineteenth-Century Mexico," *American Historical Review* 83 (February, 1978): 80–100.

20. Ibid; Friedrich Katz, "Labor Conditions on Haciendas in Porfirian Mexico: Some Trends and Tendencies," *Hispanic American Historical Review* 54 (February, 1974): 1–47.

21. Wheeler, *To Wear a City's Crown,* pp. 111–12; Muir, "Railroads Come to Houston," p. 54.

22. The following discussion of San Antonio between the wars is drawn from David R. Johnson, "The Failed Experiment: Military Aviation and Urban Development, 1910–1940," in Roger W. Lotchin, ed., *The Martial Metropolis: U.S. Cities in War and Peace* (New York: Praeger, 1984), pp. 84–108.

23. Ibid.

24. Nowlin Randolph, *The Citizens' League Will Win Again* (Marjorie McGehee Randolph, publisher, 1973), pp. 6–8.

25. For details of the intense rivalry between Fort Worth and Dallas in the late nineteenth century, see Michael Q. Hooks, "The Struggle for Dominance: Urban Rivalry in North Texas, 1870–1910," Ph.D. diss., Texas Tech University, 1979.

26. Dallas's decennial growth rate from 1900 to 1910 equaled 116 percent; Fort Worth's was 174 percent. Calculated from U.S. Census of Population.

27. The analysis that follows is tentative; there has been no systematic study of the rivalry between Fort Worth and Dallas for the years between 1910 and 1940.

28. Frank W. Johnson, *A History of Texas and Texans* (Chicago: American Historical Society, 1914), II, 824.

29. Walter J. Humann, "Agri-Business, Manufacturing, and Other Industries," in Evelyn Oppenheimer and Bill Porterfield, eds., *The Book of Dallas* (Garden City, N.Y.: Doubleday, 1976), p. 28; *Handbook of Texas,* I, 457–58.

30. W. W. Overton, Jr., "Finance," in Oppenheimer and Porterfield, eds., *Book of Dallas,* p. 107.

31. Humann, "Agri-Business, Manufacturing, and Other Industries," pp. 32–34.

32. Overton, "Finance," p. 111.

33. Elmer H. Johnson, *The Basis of the Commercial and Industrial Develop-*

ment of Texas: A Study of the Regional Development of Texas Resources, Research Monograph no. 9, Bureau of Business Research, University of Texas Bulletin (Austin: University of Texas, 1933), pp. 78, 91, 143 (fig. 66).

34. Marilyn McAdams Sibley, *The Port of Houston: A History* (Austin: University of Texas Press, 1968), p. 112.

35. Harold L. Platt, "Houston at the Crossroads: The Emergence of the Urban Center of the Southwest," *Journal of the West* (July, 1975): 53; David G. McComb, *Galveston: A History* (Austin: University of Texas Press, 1986).

36. Platt, "Houston at the Crossroads," pp. 52–54.

37. Sibley, *Port of Houston,* pp. 121–25.

38. Ibid., pp. 134–37.

39. Ibid., p. 164.

40. Platt, "Houston at the Crossroads," p. 55.

41. Harvey Molotch, "The City as a Growth Machine: Toward a Political Economy of Place," *American Journal of Sociology* 82 (September, 1976): 309–32.

42. William D. Angel, Jr., "To Make A City: Entrepreneurship on the Sunbelt Frontier," in David C. Perry and Alfred J. Watkins, eds., *The Rise of the Sunbelt Cities* (Beverly Hills, Calif.: Sage Publications, 1977), p. 126.

43. Jesse H. Jones, *Fifty Billion Dollars: My Thirteen Years with the RFC* (New York: Macmillan, 1951), pp. 402–17; Kelly Riddell and Joe R. Feagin, "Houston and Government: The Growth of the Petrochemical Industry and the War Production Board," paper presented to the Southwest Sociological Association (March 20, 1987), places the growth of this industry in the context of sociological theory.

44. Sibley, *Port of Houston,* p. 202.

45. The traditional version of NASA's decision to locate in Houston discounts Houston's political leverage and lays the greatest weight on locational factors and cultural amenities. See Stephen B. Oates, "NASA's Manned Spacecraft Center at Houston, Texas," *Southwestern Historical Quarterly* 67 (January, 1964): 350–75; and Sibley, *Port of Houston,* p. 206.

46. Oates, "Manned Spacecraft Center," p. 355; Angel, "To Make a City," pp. 123–24, 127n.

47. Angel, "To Make a City," p. 126.

48. Ibid., p. 124; David G. McComb, *Houston: A History* (Austin: University of Texas Press, 1981), pp. 142–43.

49. Oates, "Manned Spacecraft Center," pp. 373–75 (quoted on p. 375); Marvin Hurley, *Decisive Years for Houston* (Houston: Houston Chamber of Commerce, 1966), pp. 215–16.

50. Carl C. Rister, *Oil! Titan of the Southwest* (Norman: University of Oklahoma Press, 1949), p. 311.

51. Ibid; Humann, "Agri-Business, Manufacturing, and Other Industries," p. 35.

52. Martin V. Melosi, "Dallas–Fort Worth: Marketing the Metroplex," in Richard M. Bernard and Bradley R. Rice, eds., *Sunbelt Cities: Politics and Growth since World War II* (Austin: University of Texas Press, 1983), p. 176. In contrast to Dallas's unified (and well-heeled) effort to secure the centennial, stands San Antonio's divisive (and confusing) response. Instead of tapping private sources, the city asked the public to support a five hundred thousand dollar bond, which apparently neither the public nor the city's administration itself actually supported. The voters rejected the proposal by a 3–1 margin. *San Antonio Light,* October 15, 1935.

53. Melosi, "Dallas–Fort Worth," pp. 176–77.

54. E. C. Barksdale, *The Genesis of the Aviation Industry in North Texas* (Austin: Bureau of Business Research, University of Texas, 1958), p. 2.

55. Ibid., pp. 1–5; Jones, *Fifty Billion Dollars,* chap. 22.

56. Jones, *Fifty Billion Dollars,* pp. 15–24; Tom Lee McKnight, *Manufacturing in Dallas: A Study of Effects* (Austin: Bureau of Business Research, University of Texas, 1956), p. 35.

57. Stanley A. Arbingast, *Texas Resources and Industries: Selected Maps and Distribution* (Austin: Bureau of Business Research, University of Texas, 1955).

58. David R. Johnson, John A. Booth, and Richard J. Harris, *The Politics of San Antonio: Community, Progress and Power* (Lincoln: University of Nebraska Press, 1984), chap. 1.

59. Elmer Johnson, *Commercial and Industrial Development of Texas,* argues for the primacy of the environment, of location. A rebuttal of this kind of argument can be found in Burton J. Folsom, Jr., *Urban Capitalists: Entrepreneurs and City Growth in Pennsylvania's Lackawanna and Lehigh Regions, 1800–1920* (Baltimore: Johns Hopkins University Press, 1981), and in Carl Abbott, *Boosters and Businessmen: Popular Economic Thought and Urban Growth in the Antebellum Middle West* (Westport, Conn.: Greenwood Press, 1981). One might well argue that Galveston's location was destiny—precariously situated on a sandbar, its harbor's depth at the mercy of tide (and sand), its people's lives dependent on the absence of tropical storms and hurricanes. That it proved a powerful competitor is directly related to the skill and adaptability of its citizenry; that it ultimately failed to supplant Houston was due in the end to a quirk of nature directly tied to its location.

60. See the U.S. Census population tables for the comparisons. On the intensity of the Dallas–Fort Worth rivalry, see Barksdale, *The Genesis of the Aviation Industry,* pp. 2–3, 8.

Chapter 2—Frugal and Sparing

1. Studies that examine the diverse nature of boosterism include Carl Abbott, *Boosters and Businessmen: Popular Economic Thought and Urban Growth in the Antebellum Middle West* (Westport, Conn.: Greenwood Press, 1981); Burton J. Folsom, Jr., *Urban Capitalists: Entrepreneurs and City Growth in Pennsylvania's Lackawanna and Lehigh Regions, 1800–1920* (Baltimore: Johns Hopkins University Press, 1981); J. Rogers Hollingsworth and Ellen J. Hollingsworth, *Dimensions in Urban History: Historical and Social Science Perspectives on Middle-Size American Cities* (Madison: University of Wisconsin Press, 1979); and William H. Pease and Jane H. Pease, *The Web of Progress: Private Values and Public Styles in Boston and Charleston, 1828–1843* (New York: Oxford University Press, 1985).

2. Jesús F. de la Teja, "Elite Formation in Early San Antonio: The Privileges of the Canary Islanders," manuscript, 1985, pp. 2–3; Kenneth W. Wheeler, *To Wear a City's Crown: The Beginnings of Urban Growth in Texas, 1836–1865* (Cambridge, Mass.: Harvard University Press, 1968).

3. Wheeler, *To Wear a City's Crown,* pp. 110–11; Terry G. Jordan, *German Seed in Texas Soil: Immigrant Farmers in Nineteenth-Century Texas* (Austin: University of Texas Press, 1966), pp. 118–91.

4. Wheeler, *To Wear a City's Crown,* pp. 150–60.

5. Crosby A. Houston, "San Antonio's Railroads in the Nineteenth Century," Master's thesis, Trinity University, 1963, p. 14; Thomas A. Jennings, "San Antonio in the Confederacy," Master's thesis, Trinity University, 1957; Dale A. Somers, "James P. Newcomb: Texas Unionist and Radical Republican," Master's thesis, Trinity University, 1964, pp. 97–98, 124–25, 143; S. G. Reed, *A History of the Texas Railroads and of Transportation Conditions under Spain and Mexico and the Republic and the State* (Houston: St. Clair Publishing Co., 1941), pp. 90–92; Cecilia Steinfeldt, *San Antonio Was: Seen through a Magic Lantern* (San Antonio: San Antonio Museum Association, 1978), pp. 133–40; Minutes of the City Council, Journal C, August 4, 1863, in city clerk's office, City Hall.

6. Will C. Rogers III, "A History of the Military Plaza to 1937," Master's thesis, Trinity University, 1968, pp. 18–20, 21, 23; Ann M. Watson, "San Antonio on Track: The Suburban and Street Railway Complex through 1933," research project, Trinity University, 1982, pp. 8–9, 28–31; Steinfeldt, *San Antonio Was,* p. 201.

7. Watson, "San Antonio on Track," pp. 9, 31.

8. Harold L. Platt, *City Building in the New South: The Growth of Public Services in Houston, Texas, 1830–1910* (Philadelphia: Temple University Press, 1983), pp. 27–29.

9. *San Antonio Express,* February 19, 1871; Edward Degener to James P. Newcomb, June 21, 1870, Washington, D.C. to San Antonio, in the James P. Newcomb Letters, San Antonio Public Library (hereafter Newcomb Letters); Degener to Maj. W. B. Moore, September 22, 1870, San Antonio to Austin, in Newcomb Letters; Somers, "James P. Newcomb," p. 102.

10. S. W. Pease, "They Came to San Antonio," mimeograph, Daughters of the Republic of Texas Library (n.d.), pp. 33, 91; *Biographical Encyclopedia of Texas* (New York: Southern Publishing Company, 1880), pp. 51–52; Jordan, *German Seed in Texas Soil,* pp. 108–85.

11. Mayor Will C. A. Thielepape to Newcomb, December 13, 1868, Newcomb Letters; Minutes of the City Council, Journal C: August 3, September 11, and November 16, 1868, March 29, July 13, August 2, October 20, and December 18, 1869, and January 10, 1870, city clerk's office, City Hall.

12. A. I. Lockwood to Newcomb, February 24, 1872, Newcomb Letters.

13. Thielepape to Newcomb, December 6, 1868, Newcomb Letters; "An Act to Incorporate the San Antonio City Street Railroad Company, May 19, 1871," in *Gammel's Laws of Texas,* V; 1567–71; *San Antonio Herald,* October 3, 1872.

14. Minutes of the City Council, Journal C: January 23, February 1, 4, 1869, and Journal D: April 4, December 14, 1870, March 21, 1871, December 2, 1872, city clerk's office, City Hall.

15. Ibid., Journal C: February 22, 23, March 2, 1868, and Journal D: May 22, 1871, April 27, 1875.

16. Ibid., Journal D: August 10, 1870.

17. Somers, "James P. Newcomb," pp. 97–98, 124–25, 143.

18. Letter to the editor, *San Antonio Herald,* September 20, 1870.

19. Thielepape to Newcomb, July 13, 1870, Newcomb Letters; *Gammel's Laws of Texas,* VI, 762–803.

20. Steinfeldt, *San Antonio Was,* p. 144; William W. Gamble to W. J. Locke,

September 14, 1871, Thomas M. Paschal to Newcomb, September 11, 1871, and S. G. Newton to Newcomb, January 14, 1873, Newcomb Letters.

21. Any attempt to reconstruct the history of San Antonio's religious groups for this period is complicated by the fact that a massive flood in 1921 destroyed many nineteenth-century records. In general, the records of liturgicals seem to have survived better than those of pietists, but none of the local church archives for this era are very complete. The evidence that survives indicates that the Catholics (Mexican, Irish, and German), Episcopalians, and Presbyterians were the largest religious groups in the city in the late 1860s and early 1870s. My inferences regarding their views on issues of public morality are based on the conclusions of Richard Jensen, *The Winning of the Midwest: Social and Political Conflict, 1888–1892* (Chicago: University of Chicago Press, 1979), pp. 298–356, and on a survey of church records during which I identified the religious affiliations of 43 of 115 key community influentials. Of those identified, 49 percent were German and Irish Catholic, 39 percent were Episcopalian, and 12 percent were Presbyterian.

22. *San Antonio Herald,* September 14, 1870; Malcom G. Anderson to Newcomb, September 11, 1871, Newcomb Letters.

23. *San Antonio Herald,* September 15, 16, 20, 1870.

24. Ibid., September 15, 1870.

25. Ibid., September 16, 1870.

26. Ibid., September 20, 1870.

27. The analysis of the ethnic, political, and business relationships of these individuals is based on comparisons of their activities as reported in the local press.

28. *San Antonio Herald,* September 23, 1870; Stanley Welch to Newcomb, September 21, 1870, Newcomb Letters.

29. *Gammel's Laws of Texas,* VII, 138–39.

30. Minutes of the City Council, Journal D: February 17, 1871, city clerk's office, City Hall; *San Antonio Express,* February 19, 1871; Stanley Welsh to Newcomb, May 12, 1871, Newcomb Letters.

31. Minutes of the City Council, Journal D: September 2, 4, 16, 1871, city clerk's office, City Hall; A. W. Kempton to Newcomb, September 11, 1871, Newcomb Letters.

32. August Siemering to Newcomb, September 12, 1871, Newcomb Letters.

33. John C. Hanson to Newcomb, February 25, 1872, Newcomb Letters.

34. A. I. Lockwood to Newcomb, March 4, 1872, and J. H. Kampmann to Newcomb, March 9, 1872, Newcomb Letters; Minutes of the City Council, Journal D: January 23, April 1, 8, May 6, 1872, city clerk's office, City Hall.

35. *San Antonio Herald,* August 31, September 8, 10, 1872.

36. Ibid., October 2, 10, 11, 1872.

37. Ibid., October 23, 1872.

38. Ibid., September 10, 1872; *San Antonio Express,* October 25, November 10, 1872. On Republican delusions about German voters, see James N. Fisk to Newcomb, October 27, 1871; on their wholesale desertion of the Republicans in the 1872 elections, see Godfrid Lieck to Newcomb, January 6, 1873, Newcomb Letters.

39. *San Antonio Express,* November 10, 1872.

40. *San Antonio Herald,* December 12, 1872.

41. Minutes of the City Council, Journal D: November 18, 1872, city clerk's office, City Hall; *San Antonio Herald,* November 28, 1872.

42. Ira M. Dobbin to Newcomb, April 30, 1873, Newcomb Letters.

43. *San Antonio Herald,* May 3, 1873.

44. Ibid., June 14, 1873.

45. Minutes of the City Council, Journal D: July 23, September 16, November 6, 1874, city clerk's office, City Hall.

46. Ibid., Journal C: November 25, 1867, Journal D: June 16, November 14, 1871, January 23, December 26, 1872, June 18, July 12, August 3, 1875.

47. Ibid., Journal D: November 8, December 14, 1870, February 1, August 26, October 7, 14, 28, 1872, June 24, July 22, 1873, July 25, 1874.

48. Ibid., Journal D: December 2, 1872; *San Antonio Herald,* December 7, 1872; *San Antonio Express,* December 8, 1872.

49. Lockwood to Newcomb, November 10, 1872, Newcomb Letters.

50. See Minutes of the City Council, Journal C: January 31, 1870, and Journal D: January 21, 1873, city clerk's office, City Hall.

51. Ibid., Journal D: January 21, 1873.

52. Ibid., July 12, 1873.

53. Ibid., June 24, 1873.

54. Ibid., September 23, 1873.

55. Ibid., June 2, 23, 1874.

56. This interpretation is based on an analysis of the ethnic and residential backgrounds of the Democratic slate published in the *San Antonio Herald,* January 4, 1875.

57. *San Antonio Express,* January 5, 1875.

58. Backgrounds of these candidates determined from the Population Schedules of the Ninth (1870) Census, roll 1575, Bell and Bexar Counties; for their previous political activities, see Jennings, "San Antonio in the Confederacy," pp. 56–57; "Catalog of the Officers of the City Government, 1837–1879," in *Charter and Revised Ordinances of the City of San Antonio* (San Antonio: M. M. Mooney, 1880), pp. 153–66; and various letters from Malcom Anderson (Theophilius's brother) to Newcomb, in the Newcomb Letters.

59. This interpretation is based on an analysis of the ethnic and residential backgrounds of the Independents' ticket published in the *San Antonio Herald,* January 5, 1875.

60. Minutes of the City Council, Journal D: January 15, 1875, city clerk's office, City Hall.

61. Ibid., January 20, 21, 22, 1875; *San Antonio Herald,* January 21, 22, 23, 1875.

62. *San Antonio Herald,* January 22, 1875; Minutes of the City Council, Journal D: February 3, 1875, city clerk's office, City Hall.

63. French to the Council, Minutes of the City Council, Journal D: April 6, 1875, city clerk's office, City Hall.

64. Ibid., April 20, 1875.

65. Ibid., January 20, 1875.

66. Ibid., July 20, 1875.

67. Ibid., August 17, 1875.

68. Ibid., June 1, July 6, 20, September 7, 21, November 2, 16, 24, 1875.

69. Ibid., May 10, 18, July 20, 1875, October 17, 1876, February 6, April 3, 18, 28, June 19, 1877, July 2, 1878.

70. Ibid., October 6, 1875; Bernice Strong, "Alamo Plaza, 1875–1890: Era of Change," manuscript, 1984, pp. 12–13.

71. Minutes of the City Council, Mayor's Budget Message, Journal D: March 21, 1876, city clerk's office, City Hall.

72. This analysis of the occupational backgrounds of the Independent and Democratic candidates in the 1875 election was gleaned from information reported in the 1870 manuscript census and newspaper advertisements between 1870 and 1875. Various deficiencies in these sources, such as numerous reporting errors and omissions in the census, no doubt contributed to the large number of individuals I could not identify on both tickets. However, since no city directory was published for San Antonio until 1877, no better sources exist for this type of analysis.

73. Minutes of the City Council, Journal D: January 4, 1873, city clerk's office, City Hall; *San Antonio Express,* January 29, 30, 1876; Houston, "San Antonio's Railroads," pp. 130–34, 143–44, 145, 147–48; Reed, *History of the Texas Railroads,* pp. 196–98.

74. Minutes of the City Council, Journal D: March 21, 1876, city clerk's office, City Hall.

75. Ibid., March 19, October 17, 1878.

76. *San Antonio Express,* November 27, December 3, 1878; letter to the editor from Taxpayer, in ibid., December 6, 1878.

77. Based on a survey of the residences of the men attending the organizational meeting of the Taxpayers' Association, reported in ibid., December 7, 1878.

78. Based on a comparison of those attending the association's organizational meeting with the list of 115 key community influentials compiled for the period 1870–85.

79. *San Antonio Express,* December 14, 1878.

80. Ibid. (December 14, 22, 1878).

81. Based on an analysis of the vote as reported in the Minutes of the City Council, Journal D: January 21, 1879, city clerk's office, City Hall.

82. Ibid., Journal E: February 4, 18, 1879.

83. *Charter and Revised Ordinances of the City of San Antonio,* pp. 6, 149–51.

84. Minutes of the City Council, Journal E: April 26, 1879, February 28, 1880, city clerk's office, City Hall.

85. Ibid., French to the Council, April 20, 1880.

86. Ibid., Journal E: March 21, 1882; *San Antonio Express,* February 15, March 23, 1884.

87. *San Antonio Light,* May 20, 1884; *San Antonio Express,* June 27, 1884.

88. Minutes of the City Council, French to the Council, Journal E: April 16, 1881, city clerk's office, City Hall.

89. For commentary on these points, see *San Antonio Express,* January 2, November 16, 23, 1875, May 10, 1884.

90. On the relationship between a city's economic structure and the character of its business/booster community, see David R. Goldfield, *Cotton Fields and Skyscrapers: Southern City and Region, 1607–1980* (Baton Rouge: Louisiana State University Press, 1982), esp. pp. 5–9, 98. While not a southern city, San Antonio's economic functions and relationships with the national market, when combined with the southern origins of many of its local leaders, made its development in the late nineteenth century closely resemble the model Goldfield is proposing.

CHAPTER 3 — BOSS TWEED AND V. O. KEY IN TEXAS

1. V. O. Key, Jr., *Southern Politics* (New York: Vintage, 1949).

2. An exception is Bradley R. Rice, *Progressive Cities: The Commission Government Movement in America, 1901–1920* (Austin: University of Texas Press, 1977).

3. Bradley R. Rice, "The Galveston Plan of City Government by Commission: The Birth of a Progressive Idea," *Southwestern Historical Quarterly* 78, no. 4 (April, 1975): 366–408.

4. Samuel P. Hays, "The Politics of Municipal Reform in the Progressive Era," *Pacific Northwest Quarterly* 55, no. 4 (October, 1964): 157–69; James Weinstein, *The Corporate Ideal in the Liberal State* (Boston: Beacon Press, 1968), chap. 4; and Amy Bridges, "Another Look at Plutocracy and Politics in Antebellum New York City," *Political Science Quarterly* 97, no. 1 (Spring, 1982): 57–71.

5. Edward Banfield and James Q. Wilson, *City Politics* (New York: Vintage, 1966), chap. 11, for the political culture of reform.

6. Martin Shefter, "Regional Receptivity to Reform: The Legacy of the Progressive Era," *Political Science Quarterly* 98, no. 3 (Fall, 1983): 459–83. Shefter excludes from his analysis those states which had not yet been admitted to the Union in 1896; this would exclude most of the states discussed here. His argument should apply even more strongly, however, to those states which did not participate in the 1896 election.

7. Harold Platt, "City-Building and Progressive Reform: The Modernization of an Urban Polity, Houston, 1892–1903," in Michael H. Ebner and Eugene M. Tobin, ed., *The Age of Urban Reform: New Perspectives on the Progressive Era* (Port Washington, N.Y.: Kennikat Press, 1977), pp. 28–42. The three "regional" explanations rest on quite different understandings of region. In the first, the region is defined by selected characteristics of individuals who live in it. In the second and third, the region is described by its relation, as a whole, to the larger political economy.

8. This account is based on Rice, "Galveston Plan"; the quotes are from pp. 401, 388.

9. Quoted in Michael J. Schingle, "Albuquerque Urban Politics, 1891–1955, Aldermanic vs. Commission Government," senior thesis, University of New Mexico, 1976, p. 18.

10. Harold A. Stone, Don K. Price, and Kathryn H. Stone, *City Manager Government in Nine Cities* (Chicago: Public Administration Service, 1950), p. 428.

11. Ibid., p. 179.

12. *Houston Chronicle,* July 31, August 2, 1942.

13. Rice, "Galveston Plan," pp. 396–98.

14. P. J. Trounstine and T. Christensen, *Movers and Shakers: The Study of Community Power* (New York: St. Martin's, 1982), p. 84.

15. Platt, "City-Building," p. 41.

16. William H. Riker, *Democracy in the United States* (New York: MacMillan, 1953), p. 66.

17. Trounstine and Christensen, *Movers and Shakers,* p. 83.

18. Rice, "Galveston Plan."

19. Platt, "City-Building," p. 41.

20. Minutes of the Houston Charter Commission, March 24, 1938, Houston Municipal Research Library.

21. Leonard E. Goodall, "Phoenix: Reformers at Work," in L. Goodall, ed., *Urban Politics in the Southwest* (Tempe: Arizona State University Institute of Public Administration; 1967), pp. 110–26 (quote on p. 114).

22. Stone, Price, and Stone, *City Manager Government,* p. 143.

23. Dorothy I. Cline, *Albuquerque and the City Manager Plan, 1917–1948* (Albuquerque: University of New Mexico Press, 1951), p. 12.

24. Stone, Price, and Stone, *City Manager Government,* p. 414.

25. Ibid., pp. 273–74.

26. Minutes of the Houston Charter Commission, March 3, 1938, Houston Municipal Research Library.

27. John A. Booth and David R. Johnson, "Power and Progress in San Antonio Politics, 1836–1970," in David R. Johnson et al., eds., *The Politics of San Antonio: Community, Progress and Power* (Lincoln: University of Nebraska Press, 1983), pp. 3–27.

28. Had the reformers known more history, they might have anticipated this. A similar set of charter revisions was enacted for New York City in the 1850s, and immediately led to eager machine building by each of the city's administrators. See my *A City in the Republic: Antebellum New York and the Origins of Machine Politics* (New York: Cambridge University Press, 1984), p. 136.

29. Rice, *Progressive Cities,* pp. 91–93.

30. Ibid., p. 91.

31. Thus Rice's conclusion in *Progressive Cities* is that commission government was a transitional style in the history of reform government.

32. Goodall, "Phoenix," p. 114.

33. George J. Mauer, "Oklahoma City: In Transition to Maturity and Professionalization," in Goodall, *Urban Politics,* p. 89.

34. Cline, *Albuquerque,* pp. 16–26.

35. Stone, Price, and Stone, *City Manager Government,* p. 169.

36. Speech on KTRH radio, October 18, 1946, Holcombe Papers, Box 4, Houston Municipal Research Library.

37. Speech on KTHT radio, July 21, 1947, Holcombe Papers, Box 4.

38. *La Tribuna,* November 13, 1924, Holcombe Papers, Box 1.

39. For union endorsements, see Holcombe Papers, Box 1, folders 1 and 2. Holcombe had endorsements in the early 1920s from the Culinary Workers, the United Brotherhood of Carpenters and Joiners, and various railroad workers' unions.

40. Speech, April 7, 1949, Holcombe Papers, Box 4, Folder 8, and Campaign Speech, on KTRH radio, November 1, 1946, Holcombe Papers, Box 4.

41. Testimony dated October 30, 1947, Holcombe Papers, Box 4, p. 67.

42. Campaign speech, 1924, Holcombe Papers, Box 1.

43. Political Campaign Collection, Houston Municipal Research Library, Box 1. There are pledge cards for 1926, 1946, and 1948. The letter to municipal employees, sent with pledge cards, is from 1948. See also Holcombe Papers, Box 1, for a 1924 survey of municipal employees and the report of the police superintendent on his pledge card campaign in the department.

44. Stone, Price, and Stone, *City Manager Government,* p. 428.

45. Ibid., p. 434.

46. Labor support was not without its contradictions. Labor divided in the 1931 election, with the result that in 1933 the Zilker group excluded union candidates from its ticket. Moreover, the ticket was "conspicuously supported by the head of the open-shop committee of Austin builders and real estate developers" (ibid., p. 438). If Miller and his fellows nevertheless received labor support, it is a confirmation of Key's assertion that contradictory coalitions are more easily maintained in the absence of parties.

47. Austin, an exception, had nonpartisan elections, and so a significant number of black voters.

48. Ibid., p. 437. This was in contrast to the Mexican Americans, who, a "veteran campaigner" explained, "listen, accept favors, and then vote independently" (ibid., p. 436).

49. On the mayor's official duties, see David Olson, "Austin: The Capital City," in Leonard E. Goodall, ed., *Urban Southwest;* for Miller's mayoral campaigns, see Floylee H. Hemphill, "Mayor Tom Miller and the First Year of the New Deal in Austin, Texas," Master's thesis, University of Texas, 1976.

50. Stone, Price, and Stone, *City Manager Government,* p. 431.

51. Ibid., p. 430.

52. Ibid., p. 432.

53. Key, *Southern Politics,* p. 16.

54. Ibid., p. 61.

55. John W. Pratt, "Boss Tweed's Public Welfare Program," *New York Historical Society Quarterly* 45 (1961): 396–411.

56. Minutes of the Houston Charter Commission, Box 2, June 20, 1938, Houston Municipal Research Library.

Chapter 4 — Women, Religion, and Reform

1. Mary Ritter Beard, *Woman's Work in Municipalities* (1915; reprint, New York: Arno Press, 1972), p. 318; *Galveston Tribune,* undated Special Edition that appeared either March 17 or 18, 1915 (hereafter *Galveston Tribune,* Special Edition). I wish to thank Samuel S. Hill, Kathleen C. Berkeley, Charles Reagan Wilson, John B. Boles, Harold M. Hyman, and Bradley R. Rice for their helpful comments on earlier drafts of this chapter. Funding for this project was aided by an Ottis Lock Research Grant.

2. *Galveston Tribune,* Special Edition.

3. Ibid.

4. Joseph F. Kett ("Women and the Progressive Impulse in Southern Education," in Walter J. Fraser, Jr., R. Frank Saunders, Jr., and Jon L. Wakelyn, eds., *The Web of Southern Social Relations: Women, Family, and Education* (Athens: University of Georgia Press, 1985), pp. 166–80) points out that social progressives "sought to ameliorate social conditions without fundamentally altering distribution of political and economic power among classes" (p. 166). See also Dewey W. Grantham, *Southern Progressivism: The Reconciliation of Progress and Tradition* (Knoxville: University of Tennessee Press, 1983), pp. 200–10.

5. Grantham, *Southern Progressivism,* p. 200; Anne F. Scott, "Women, Religion, and Social Change in the South, 1830–1930," in Samuel S. Hill, Jr., ed.,

Religion and the Solid South (Nashville: Abingdon Press, 1972), pp. 108, 110, 115–17; Anne F. Scott, "Historians Construct the Southern Woman," in Joanne V. Hawks and Sheila Skemp, eds., *Sex, Race, and the Role of Women in the South* (Jackson: University Press of Mississippi, 1983), p. 107; Anne F. Scott, *The Southern Lady: From Pedestal to Politics, 1830-1930* (Chicago: University of Chicago Press, 1970), pp. 144–48; Jean E. Friedman, *The Enclosed Garden: Women and Community in the Evangelical South, 1830-1900* (Chapel Hill: University of North Carolina Press, 1985), pp. 111-18. Scott emphasizes particularly the connection between Methodist home and foreign mission societies, the Women's Christian Temperance Union (WCTU), and suffrage. The WCTU did not begin to recruit southern unions until Pres. Frances Willard made a journey to the South in 1881. Thereafter, southern states enthusiastically supported the WCTU, even with its prosuffrage stance. However, Willard had enacted in 1881 a "Do-everything policy" that did not require local participation in suffrage work. Ruth Bordin, *Frances Willard: A Biography* (Chapel Hill: Univeristy of North Carolina Presss, 1986), pp. 113–15; Barbara Leslie Epstein, *The Politics of Domesticity: Women, Evangelism, and Temperance in Nineteenth-Century America* (Middletown, Conn.: Wesleyan University Press, 1981), pp. 118–21; Joseph R. Gusfield, *Symbolic Crusade: Status Politics and the American Temperance Movement* (Urbana: University of Illinois Press, 1970), p. 89; Paula Baker, "The Domestication of Politics: Women and American Political Society, 1780-1920," *American Historical Review* 89 (June, 1984): 638. See also Jacquelyn Dowd Hall, *Revolt against Chivalry: Jessie Daniel Ames and the Women's Campaign against Lynching* (New York: Columbia University Press, 1979), pp. 22, 25, 36, 66, for a discussion of the significance of the WCTU to the Texas women's suffrage movement and of Methodist mission societies to interracial cooperation.

6. Friedman, *The Enclosed Garden,* pp. 112–18; Mrs. W. M. Baines, *A Story of Texas White Ribboners (WCTU)* (N.p., [1936]), pp. 60–61; Grantham, *Southern Progressivism,* p. 202. For a definition of evangelical Protestantism, see Samuel S. Hill, ed., *Encyclopedia of Religion in the South* (Macon, Ga.: Mercer University Press, 1984), pp. 239–44. Dewey Grantham, Anne F. Scott, Jacquelyn Dowd Hall, and Jean Friedman also recognize the importance of postwar educational opportunities for women, industrialization in some areas of the New South that created a leisured middle class, the growth of the women's club movement, and greater professional opportunities for women. Because this chapter deals specifically with women's social activism stemming from the congregational (church and synagogue) societies, discussion herein is limited to that aspect of the origins of Progressive era reform.

7. See, for example, Sophonisba Preston Breckinridge, *Madeline McDowell Breckinridge: A Leader in the New South* (Chicago: University of Chicago Press, 1921); "Minnie Fisher Cunningham," in Barbara Sicherman et al., eds., *Notable American Women: The Modern Period* (Cambridge, Mass.: Belknap Press of Harvard University Press, 1980), pp. 176–77; John E. Talmadge, *Rebecca Latimer Felton: Nine Stormy Decades* (Athens: University of Georgia Press, 1960); Paul E. Fuller, *Laura Clay and the Woman's Rights Movement* (Lexington: University Press of Kentucky, 1975); Kenneth R. Johnson, "Kate Gordon and the Woman-Suffrage Movement," *Journal of Southern History* 38 (August, 1972): 365–92; Scott, *The Southern Lady,* pp. 173–76.

8. See John Patrick McDowell, *The Social Gospel in the South: The Woman's Home Mission Movement in the Methodist Episcopal Church, South, 1886–1939* (Baton Rouge: Louisiana State University Press, 1982); Noreen Dunn Tatum, *A Crown of Service: A Story of Woman's Work in the Methodist Episcopal Church, South, from 1878–1940* (Nashville: Parthenon Press, 1960); Virginia A. Shadron, "Out of Our Homes: The Woman's Rights Movement in the Methodist Episcopal Church, South, 1890–1918," (Master's thesis, Emory University, 1976; Sara Estelle Haskin, *Women and Missions in the Methodist Episcopal Church, South* (Nashville, Tenn.: Publishing House of the M. E. Church, South, 1923); Inez Boyle Hunt, *Century One, a Pilgrimage of Faith: Woman's Missionary Union of Texas, 1880–1980* (Woman's Missionary Union, 1979); Mrs. W. J. J. Smith, *A Centennial History of the Baptist Women of Texas, 1830–1930* (Dallas: Woman's Missionary Union, 1933); Katherine L. Cook, "Texas Baptist Women and Missions, 1830–1900," *Texas Baptist History* 3 (1983): 31–43; Patricia Summerline Martin, "Hidden Work: Baptist Women in Texas, 1880–1920," Ph.D. diss., Rice University, 1982; Lois A. Boyd and Douglas Brackenridge, *Presbyterian Women in America: Two Centuries of a Quest for Status* (Westport, Conn: Greenwood Press, 1983), pp. 217–24; Ernest Thrice Thompson, *Presbyterians in the South,* 3 vols. (Richmond, Va.: John Knox Press, 1973), III, 385–91; Mary S. Donovan, "Women and Mission: Towards a More Inclusive Historiography," *Historical Magazine of the Protestant Episcopal Church* 53 (December, 1984): 297–305; Catherine M. Prelinger, "Women as Episcopalians: Some Methodological Observations," *Historical Magazine of the Protestant Episcopal Church* 52 (June, 1983): 141–52.

9. Don Harrison Doyle, "Urbanization and Southern Culture: Economic Elites in Four New South Cities (Atlanta, Nashville, Charleston, Mobile), c. 1865–1910," in Orville Vernon Burton and Robert C. McMath, Jr., eds., *Toward A New South? Studies in Post-Civil War Southern Communities* (Westport, Conn.: Greenwood Press, 1982), pp. 11–36.

10. Ibid., p. 25. Historians recognize the existence of denominational subregions in the South, but patterns of denominational preferences among New South cities have yet to be explored. See "Geography of Southern Religion," in Hill, ed., *Encyclopedia of Religion,* pp. 284–88.

11. William G. McLoughlin, *Revivals, Awakenings, and Reform: An Essay on Religion and Social Change in America, 1607–1977* (Chicago: University of Chicago Press, 1978), p. 132; David Edwin Harrell, Jr., "Religious Pluralism: Catholics, Jews, and Sectarians," in Charles Reagan Wilson, ed., *Religion in the South* (Jackson: University Press of Mississippi, 1985), p. 70. C. Vann Woodward in *Origins of the New South, 1877–1913* (Baton Rouge: Louisiana State University Press, 1951), pp. 449–51, puts the percentage of Baptists and Methodists in the rural South in 1915 at 82.

12. Ira Berlin and Herbert G. Gutman, "Natives and Immigrants, Free Men and Slaves: Urban Workingmen in the Antebellum American South," *American Historical Review* 88 (December, 1983): 1175–1200; Howard Miller, "Texas," in Samuel S. Hill, ed., *Religion in the Southern States: A Historical Study* (Macon, Ga.: Mercer University Press, 1983), p. 321.

13. For a discussion of Texas reform movements, see Alwyn Barr, *Reconstruction to Reform: Texas Politics, 1876–1906* (Austin: University of Texas Press, 1971), pp. 86–87, 91–92. Barr states that Prohibition strength in the 1880s came from

Northeast and Central Texas, not from the Gulf Coast. After the defeat of Prohibition in the state assembly in 1887, the movement remained quiet until the Progressive era. The Texas Prohibition movement of the Progressive period is discussed in Lewis L. Gould, *Progressives and Prohibitionists: Texas Democrats in the
Wilson Era* (Austin: University of Texas Press, 1973), p. 51. Still the best published
account of Texas women's suffrage movement is A. Elizabeth Taylor, "The Woman
Suffrage Movement in Texas," *Journal of Southern History* 17 (May, 1951): 194–
215. See also David G. McComb, *Galveston: A History* (Austin: University of Texas
Press, 1986), p. 61; Woodward, *Origins of the New South,* p. 125; Bradley R. Rice,
*Progressive Cities: The Commission Government Movement in America, 1901–
1920* (Austin: University of Texas Press, 1977), pp. 6–7; U.S. Census Office, *Report
on the Social Statistics of Cities. Part II: The Southern and Western States* (Washington, D.C., 1887), p. 321; U.S. Bureau of the Census, *Thirteenth Census of the
United States . . . 1910.* Vol. 9: *Manufactures, 1909* (Washington, D.C., 1912), p.
1203. Galveston in 1906 had thirty-one Protestant churches with a total reported
adult membership of 5,504. Of these, Southern Baptists comprised 534 (9.7 percent, rounded to nearest tenth); Lutherans, 758 (13.8 percent); members of the
Methodist Episcopal Church, 681 (12.3 percent); members of the Methodist Episcopal Church, South, 627 (11.4 percent); members of the Presbyterian Church in
the U.S.A., 75 (1.4 percent); members of the Presbyterian Church in the U.S., 400
(7.3 percent); and Episcopalians, 1,278 (23.2 percent). Except for Episcopalians,
who included blacks in their membership, these figures exclude black churches and
miscellaneous Protestant churches. In Jewish congregations only heads of families
were counted, which provides no basis for an estimate of total membership. Galveston's synagogue membership included 220 heads of families. U.S. Bureau of
the Census, *Religious Bodies: 1906.* Pt.1: *Summary and General Tables* (Washington, D.C., 1910), pp. 24, 442. See also Miller, "Texas," pp. 313–33.

14. The Galveston churches and synagogue represented in this study are First
Baptist Church, Grace Episcopal Church, Trinity Episcopal Church, First Evangelical Lutheran Church, Zion Lutheran Church, First United Methodist Church,
First Presbyterian Church, and Congregation B'nai Israel. The four benevolent institutions are the Galveston Orphans' Home, Lasker Home for Children, Letitia
Rosenberg Home for Women, and the Johanna Runge Free Kindergarten. The four
post-1900 reform organizations are the Women's Health Protective Association,
the Women's Christian Temperance Union, the Galveston Equal Suffrage Association, and the Young Women's Christian Association. See Vernon E. Bennett, *An
Informal History of the First Baptist Church, Galveston, Texas* (Galveston: Privately printed, 1970); Minutes of the First Baptist Church of Galveston, 1866–83,
microfilm, Rosenberg Library, Galveston; "Women's Work in the First Baptist
Church, Galveston, Texas," typescript, First Baptist Church, Galveston; *Grace Epis-
copal Church: A Hundred Years of Grace* (Galveston: Privately printed, 1974); Ladies
Aid Society Minutes, Grace Episcopal Church, 1911–22, Grace Episcopal Church,
Galveston; William Manning Morgan, *Trinity Protestant Episcopal Church,
Galveston, Texas, 1841–1953* (Houston and Galveston: Anson Jones Press, 1954);
Minutes of the Vestry of Trinity Church Guild Minutes, 1902–19, Trinity Church
Guild Dues Book 1902–28, all in Trinity Episcopal Church, Galveston); S. M. Bird,
Twenty Years in Trinity Parish (Galveston: Press of J. W. Burson Co., 1891); Ben-
jamin A. Rogers, *Memorial Sermon on the Rev. Stephen Moylan Bird, D.D. . . .*

(Galveston: Privately printed, 1894); C. M. Beckwith, *A Word from the Rector of Trinity Church to His Vestry on the Occasion of Their First Meeting after the Easter Election, 1896* (Galveston: Clarke and Courts, 1896); "125th Anniversary of Trinity Episcopal Church, Galveston, Texas, February 6, 1966," pamphlet, Rosenberg Library, Galveston; *Constitution and By-Laws of the Ladies Hebrew Benevolent Society of Galveston, Texas* (Galveston: Clarke and Courts, 1903); Minutes of the Ladies Hebrew Benevolent Society, 1879–1918, Congregation B'nai Israel, Galveston; A. Stanley Dreyfus, "The Hebrew Benevolent Society: A Saga of Service," typescript, A. Stanley Dreyfus Papers, Rosenberg Library, Galveston; *A Brief Review of the Past and Survey of the Present of the First Evangelical Lutheran Church of Galveston* (Galveston: Privately printed, 1925); *One Hundredth Anniversary of the First Evangelical Lutheran Church* (Galveston, 1950); *50th Anniversary of Zion Lutheran Church* (Galveston, 1942); Mrs. J. E. Murphy, "The History of Methodism in Galveston, 1839–1942," typescript, Moody Memorial Methodist Church, Galveston; Constitution and By-Laws of the Ladies Aid Society of the First Presbyterian Church, Galveston, Texas, n.d.; Minutes of the Ladies Aid Society of the First Presbyterian Church, Galveston, 1893–1909; Treasurer's Report of the Ladies Aid Society of the First Presbyterian Church, Galveston, 1893–96, all in First Presbyterian Church Records, Rosenberg Library, Galveston; *Charter and By-Laws of the Galveston Orphans' Home* (Galveston: Clarke and Courts, 1913); Minutes of the Board of Lady Managers, 1885–1913, Galveston Orphan's Home Records, Rosenberg Library, Galveston; *Charter, Constitution, and By-Laws of the Society for the Help of Homeless Children of Galveston, Texas* (Galveston: Clarke and Courts, 1894); the Woman's Home Charter, August 10, 1893; Minutes of the Board of Lady Managers, 1894–1911, both in Letitia Rosenberg Woman's Home Records, Rosenberg Library, Galveston; Minutes of the Board of Lady Managers, 1904, Lasker Home for Children Records, Rosenberg Library, Galveston; "Mrs. Johanna Runge," typescript biography, subject files, Rosenberg Library, Galveston; Women's Health Protective Association File, 1901–16, Morgan Family Papers, Rosenberg Library, Galveston; "W.C.T.U. Here Serves Whole Community," *Galveston Daily News,* October 22, 1922; Galveston Equal Suffrage Association Records, 1912–20, and the Young Women's Christian Association Records, both in the Rosenberg Library, Galveston.

15. Recent studies of northern women's antebellum societies have found little indication that individual women progressed from church to benevolent to reform societies, yet in postbellum Galveston, there is sufficient evidence to suggest that this was the case. See Anne M. Boylan, "Women in Groups: An Analysis of Women's Benevolent Organizations in New York and Boston, 1797–1840," *Journal of American History,* 71 (December, 1984): 502, 514; Nancy A. Hewitt, *Women's Activism and Social Change: Rochester, New York, 1822–1872* (Ithaca, N.Y.: Cornell University Press, 1984), p. 22; Catholic church records in Galveston are a rich source for the study of charitable activities, but although Catholics formed an important segment of the community in this regard, there are two reasons why a more detailed study of their activities has not been presented here. First, charitable work in the fields of education, hospitals, and asylums was almost entirely in the hands of the women's religious orders; opportunities for Catholic laywomen to become involved in benevolent institution building (an important first step to civic involvement) were almost nonexistent. Second, it is clear that Protestant and Jewish women

did not encourage Catholic laywomen to join them in managing their orphanages, kindergartens, and old-age homes. Consequently, only a handful of Catholic women were found in the post-1900 secular civic leadership. It is difficult to conclude, therefore, that Catholic laywomen advanced from their church societies to the secular world, as did Protestant and Jewish women. See Elizabeth Turner, "Benevolent Ladies, Club Women, and Suffragists: Galveston's Women's Organizations, 1880–1920," Ph.D. diss., Rice University, in progress; *History of the Diocese of Galveston and St. Mary's Cathedral,* (Galveston: Knapp Bros., Printers, 1922), pp. 102, 110; Carlos E. Castañeda, *Our Catholic Heritage in Texas, 1519–1936* (Austin: Von Boeckmann-Jones, 1958), VII, 285, 361–65; Catholic Youth Organization, *Centennial: The Story of the Development of the . . . Diocese of Galveston* (Houston: Centennial Book Committee, 1947), pp. 157, 163; *Galveston Daily News,* February 26, April 2, 1922; *General Directory of the City of Galveston, 1899–1900* (Galveston: Morrison and Fourmy, 1900); *Directory of the City of Galveston, 1909–1910* (Galveston: Morrison and Fourmy, 1910); John O'Grady, *Catholic Charities in the United States: History and Problems* (Washington, D.C.: National Conference of Catholic Charities, 1930), pp. 405–406; and Jay P. Dolan, *The American Catholic Experience: A History from Colonial Times to the Present* (Garden City, N.Y.: Image Books, Doubleday, 1985), pp. 324, 328.

16. Some of the indicators for elite status are inclusion in city "blue books," representation on corporation boards of directors as found in city directories, location of residence, and inclusion in city biographies or "mug books." For a discussion of elites in a southern city, see James M. Russell, "Elites and Municipal Politics and Government in Atlanta, 1847–1890," in Burton and McMath, eds., *Toward A New South?* pp. 37–70. Using church directories, comparisons were made between members of the various churches and those persons listed in the two published blue books, *The Galveston Blue Book: A Society Directory, 1896* (Houston: J. R. Wheat, 1896), and *The International Blue Book Publications, 1912–1914: Southeast Texas* (Houston: M. J. Sullivan and Company, 1912). Also helpful was Sam B. Graham, ed., *Galveston Community Book: A Historical and Biographical Record of Galveston and Galveston County* (Galveston: Arthur H. Cawston, 1945). For an excellent overview and bibliography of the extensive writings of the social gospel, see Ronald C. White, Jr., and C. Howard Hopkins, *The Social Gospel: Religion and Reform in Changing America* (Philadelphia: Temple University Press, 1976), p. xii. Three historians of religion in the South have assumed different positions on southern churches' involvement in the social gospel movement. Samuel S. Hill, in *South and the North in American Religion* (Athens: University of Georgia Press, 1980), pp. 130–31, states that, while southern churches were aware of social problems and the need to take action, "yet by no stretch of the imagination can it be said that a strong Social Gospel tradition lived as an element in regional religious life." Kenneth Bailey, in *Southern White Protestantism in the Twentieth Century* (New York: Harper & Row, 1964), notes that, "although the social gospel movement was much weaker in the South than in the North, yet social concern was more manifest among southern religious leaders than has been generally recognized" (p. 43n). By contrast, McDowell, in *The Social Gospel in the South,* challenges these positions and sees ethically and socially responsible Methodist women advancing a "concern for social reform" through the agency of the Women's Home Mission Society (p. 2).

But does the women's home mission program in the South represent a segment of the national social gospel movement? The history of churchwomen's considerable activities is just now being brought into better focus, and their influence and role in mission outreach is surprising even to religious historians. Tagging this activity social gospel, however, may confuse and distort what seems to have been a truly female or gender-related manifestation of the churches' long-held tradition of charitable works. See Mary S. Donovan, *A Different Call: Women's Ministries in the Episcopal Church, 1850–1920* (Wilton, Conn.: Morehouse-Barlow, 1986); Bird, *Twenty Years in Trinity Parish*, pp. 22–27; and Rogers, *Memorial Sermon on the Rev. Stephen Moylan Bird*, pp. 13–15. For a discussion of elitism, piety, and charity, see Kathleen McCarthy, *Noblesse Oblige: Charity and Cultural Philanthropy in Chicago, 1849–1929* (Chicago: University of Chicago Press, 1982), pp. 3–5. Epstein, in *The Politics of Domesticity*, p. 3, shows that the middle classes, who were "neither wealthy or desperately poor," found in evangelicalism and temperance "two of the central issues around which struggles over culture and ideology were conducted." Epstein offers a positive appraisal of the work of the WCTU in the Northeast, but she notes that "the WCTU stopped short of identification with feminism" (p. 147). Greater distance between suffragists and women Prohibitionists is also found in the work of Jack S. Blocker, Jr., "Separate Paths: Suffragists and the Women's Temperance Crusade," *Signs* 10 (Spring, 1985): 460–76. For a description of men who joined the Galveston Equal Suffrage Association, see Larry J. Wygant, "'A Municipal Broom': The Woman Suffrage Campaign in Galveston, Texas," *Houston Review* 6, no. 3 (1984): 117–34; and *Galveston Tribune*, Special Edition.

17. Earl Wesley Fornell, *The Galveston Era: The Texas Crescent on the Eve of Secession* (Austin: University of Texas Press, 1961), pp. 77–88. See also Bailey, *Southern White Protestantism*, p. 2, who notes that Lutherans, Catholics, and Episcopalians were the three major denominations in the South with extraregional affiliation. In Galveston, these three denominations held the majority of congregants, which may help explain why churches within the city were not influenced by the "cultural captivity" of southern rural evangelism and therefore were more receptive to "northern" concepts of relief of the urban poor directed by churches. See John Lee Eighmy, *Churches in Cultural Captivity: A History of Social Attitudes of Southern Baptists* (Knoxville: University of Tennessee Press, 1972), and Rufus B. Spain, *At Ease in Zion: Social History of Southern Baptists, 1865–1900* (Nashville: Vanderbilt University Press, 1961), for a discussion of Southern Baptists in the post–Civil War period. For a discussion of northern churches and their response to poverty, see Nathan Irvin Huggins, *Protestants against Poverty: Boston's Charities, 1870–1900* (Westport, Conn.: Greenwood Press, 1971); Walter I. Trattner, *From Poor Law to Welfare State: A History of Social Welfare in America* (New York: Free Press, 1974).

18. Morgan, *Trinity Episcopal Church*, pp. 558, 563.

19. Constitution and By-Laws of the Ladies Aid Society of the First Presbyterian Church, First Presbyterian Church Records, Rosenberg Library, Galveston.

20. Minutes of the Ladies Aid Society of the First Presbyterian Church, October 1, 1891, First Presbyterian Church Records (hereafter, Minutes, LASFPC).

21. *Charter of the City of Galveston with the Amendments thereto and Revised Ordinances* (Galveston: Clarke and Courts, 1888), p. 209.

22. Elizabeth Wisner, *Social Welfare in the South: From Colonial Times to World War I* (Baton Rouge: Louisiana State University Press, 1970), p. 30; *Lee County v. Lackie,* 30 Arkansas, 764 (1875) (quotation). The poor farm was finally closed in 1913: *Galveston Daily News,* May 1, 1913.

23. Minutes, LASFPC, 1890–97, 1900. Few private organizations existed for the financial protection of women. Relief came primarily from families, fraternal orders, ethnic groups, labor organizations, and sometimes churches, but only for their own members. None of these groups made helping the city's disadvantaged their sole purpose. Destitute women residents of Galveston who had no affiliation of any kind were assigned to the county poor farm. Trinity Guild and the LASFPC tried to save women from this ignoble existence. Charter of the French Benevolent Society of Galveston, May 2, 1871, French Benevolent Society of Galveston Records, Rosenberg Library, Galveston. For a discussion of the function of fraternal orders in community life, see Don Harrison Doyle, *The Social Order of a Frontier Community: Jacksonville, Illinois, 1825–70* (Urbana: University of Illinois Press, 1878), p. 188; Lynn Dumenil, *Freemasonry and American Culture, 1880–1930* (Princeton: Princeton University Press, 1984); Joseph W. Hale, "Masonry in the Early Days of Texas," *Southwestern Historical Quarterly* 49 (1945–46): 374–83. Wisner, *Social Welfare in the South,* p. 30, and Helen Evans, "Provisions for Public Relief in Texas, 1846–1937," Master's thesis, Tulane University School of Social Work, 1941, offer detailed explanations of public relief systems in the South and in Texas.

24. LASFPC minutes, May 1, 1890, July 6, Aug. 3, Nov. 2, 1893; Morgan, *Trinity Episcopal Church,* pp. 563–65.

25. I compiled lists of officers from organizational records, charters, city directories, newspaper articles, and blue books; I found religious affiliations in congregational directories and women's society records.

26. The first WCTU chapter was founded in 1888 but did not survive; the second chapter was organized in 1914: *Galveston Daily News,* October 22, 1922. The Texas Equal Suffrage Association was organized in 1893, but like the WCTU died until its reemergence as the Galveston Equal Suffrage Association in 1912. Morrison and Fourmy's *General Directory of the City of Galveston* (1893); Wygant, "'A Municipal Broom,'" pp. 117–34.

27. Herbert Molloy Mason, Jr., *Death from the Sea* (New York: Dial Press, 1972), pp. 182, 198, 200, 221; John Edward Weems, *A Weekend in September* (1957; reprint College Station: Texas A&M University Press, 1980), pp. 89, 159, 169; Bradley R. Rice, *Progressive Cities: The Commission Government Movement in America, 1901–1920* (Austin: University of Texas Press, 1977), p. 3; David G. McComb, *Galveston: A History* (Austin: University of Texas Press, 1986), p. 132; *Galveston Daily News,* September 16, 1900.

28. Shirley Abbott, *Womenfolks: Growing Up Down South* (New York: Ticknor & Fields, 1983), pp. 1–3.

29. *Galveston Daily News,* March 3, 1901. The WHPA was a member of the Texas Federation of Women's Clubs from 1902 until 1908: *Galveston Daily News,* December 3, 1902, April 8, 1908.

30. *Galveston Daily News,* May 12, 1906, December 11, 1921.

31. The announcement for the first WHPA meeting read, "The time [has] now come when the Galveston women, rich and poor, club women and non-club women,

must work hand in hand and heart to heart to make Galveston a beautiful town and a law-abiding place, and the only way to do this is to have the co-operation of every woman in the city": *Galveston Daily News,* March 3, 1901.

32. Fuller accounts of the origins and continuation of the woman's sphere may be found in Barbara Berg, *The Remembered Gate: Origins of American Feminism* (New York: Oxford University Press, 1978); Nancy F. Cott, *The Bonds of Womanhood: Woman's Sphere in New England, 1780–1835* (New Haven, Conn.: Yale University Press, 1977); Barbara Welter, "The Cult of True Womanhood, 1820–1860," in Welter, *Dimity Convictions: The American Woman in the Nineteenth Century* (Athens: Ohio University Press, 1976), pp. 21–41; Carl Degler, *At Odds: Women and the Family in America from the Revolution to the Present* (New York: Oxford University Press, 1980), chap. 10; William L. O'Neill, *Everyone Was Brave: The Rise and Fall of Feminism in America* (Chicago: Quadrangle Books, 1969), chap. 5; Sheila M. Rothman, *Woman's Proper Place: A History of Changing Ideals and Practices, 1870 to the Present* (New York: Basic Books, 1978), pp. 127–32.

33. Morrison and Fourmy's *General Directory of the City of Galveston* (1899–1900).

34. *Galveston Daily News,* December 11, 1921. The WHPA operated a nursery that provided plants to citizens at cost, supporting these endeavors through horse shows, garden contests, and rose sales. By 1912 more than ten thousand trees, twenty-five hundred oleanders, and twenty thousand rose bushes had been planted throughout the city.

35. Ibid., February 22 (quotation), 23, 1913; "Report of a Sanitary Survey of the City of Galveston, Texas," pamphlet, April, 1913, WHPA File, Morgan Family Papers, Rosenberg Library, Galveston.

36. *Galveston Daily Herald,* March 5, 1913; *Galveston Daily News,* January 7, 1914.

37. *Galveston Daily News,* January 9, November 4, 1914; clipping, January, 1915, WHPA File, Morgan Family Papers, Rosenberg Library, Galveston.

38. *Galveston Tribune,* December 1, 1914, May 4, 1915.

39. *Galveston Daily News,* July 6, 1915, November 3, December 1, 7, 1916; City Commission Minutes, December 1, 21, 1916, Galveston City Hall.

40. Galveston *Daily News,* December 11, 1921. See, for example, Baker, "The Domestication of Politics," p. 640; Marlene Stein Wortman, "Domesticating the Nineteenth-Century American City," *Prospects: An Annual of American Cultural Studies* 3 (1977): 531–72; Grantham, *Southern Progressivism,* pp. 200–208.

41. Of the sixty officers, twenty-eight held executive positions (president, vice-president, secretary, treasurer, auditor, executive committee member), and thirty-two chaired committees. I could not determine the religious affiliation of fourteen, or 23 percent. The remaining forty-six officers, or 77 percent, belonged to eight religious groups: Baptist, Catholic, Episcopal, Jewish, Lutheran, Methodist, Presbyterian, and Swedenborgian. If the WHPA officers of unknown religious affiliation are removed, the number of officers who belonged to women's church and synagogue societies reaches 72 percent, 54 percent of whom were affiliated with Trinity Guild and the LASFPC.

The most striking evidence of the influence of Trinity Guild, the Ladies Aid Society of the First Presbyterian Church, and the four benevolent institutions can be seen in the histories of the first four presidents of the WHPA, Mrs. H. A. Landes,

Mrs. Joseph Clark, Mrs. Bertrand Adoue, and Mrs. George D. (Jean) Morgan. Three of the four belonged to Trinity Guild, one served as president from 1875 to 1883, another became president of the guild in 1918, and a third belonged to both Trinity and Grace Episcopal sisterhoods and served as president of Grace Episcopal's sisterhood in 1901. The fourth WHPA president had been a member of the Ladies Aid Society of the First Presbyterian Church in the 1890s. All four of the WHPA presidents had been officers on one or more of the boards of lady managers for the benevolent institutions. Only two Methodists and two Baptists held positions of leadership within the WHPA, and no officers of the local WCTU were officers of either the WHPA or the Galveston Equal Suffrage Association. For a discussion of the distance between temperance and feminism, see Blocker, "Separate Paths," pp. 460–76.

42. *Galveston Tribune,* June 14, 1913.

43. Morrison and Fourmy's *General Directory of the City of Galveston* (1916). I compiled percentages by matching the officers of the ESA listed in newspapers with their religious affiliation as found in church records and with their prior service in the WHPA. The congregational affiliations of suffragists have been more difficult to establish. Of the thirty-three ESA officers between 1912 and 1920, I identified twenty (61 percent) as members of congregations; thirteen (39 percent) remain unidentified. Of those women with congregational affiliation, eleven (55 percent) were Episcopalian; nine (27 percent) suffrage officers had served as officers of the WHPA; and seven (21 percent) had belonged to boards of lady managers. Two of the Galveston ESA officers went on to become officers in the state suffrage association; one, Minnie Fisher Cunningham, assumed the presidency of the Texas Equal Suffrage Association from 1915 to the passage of the nineteenth amendment: Wygant, "'A Municipal Broom,'" pp. 117–34; "Minnie Fisher Cunningham," in Sicherman et al., eds., *Notable American Women: The Modern Period,* pp. 176–77; Taylor, "The Woman Suffrage Movement in Texas," p. 204.

44. *Galveston Daily News,* February 16, 1912. Perle P. Penfield, a medical student at the University of Texas Medical Department in Galveston, wrote that a woman "to fulfill her duties to her own bit of the community . . . must become a party to the expression of its will, as she is a party to the conditions it imposes, and to become so she must become a voter." Perle P. Penfield, "Woman Suffrage," undated clipping in the Galveston Equal Suffrage Association Records, Rosenberg Library, Galveston.

45. I compiled these percentages from YWCA records and from WHPA and ESA lists of officers and members found in local newspapers.

46. Penfield, "Woman Suffrage"; Wygant, "A Municipal Broom.'"

47. Degler, *At Odds,* p. 322.

48. *Galveston Daily News,* November 23, 24, December 1, 3, 4, 7, 1914, and *Galveston Tribune,* December 7, 1914, all in YWCA Scrapbook, 1914–15, Galveston YWCA Records, Rosenberg Library, Galveston. See also *Directory of the City of Galveston* (1920).

49. I compiled these percentages by matching officers found in the YWCA Records with religious affiliation found in church records. See also Mary S. Sims, *The Natural History of a Social Institution—the Young Women's Christian Association* (New York: Woman's Press, 1936), p. 28.

50. *Galveston Daily News,* November 30, 1914, YWCA Scrapbook, 1914–15

(quotation); U.S. Census Office, *Census Reports,* Vol. 8: *Twelfth Census of the United States . . . 1900. Manufactures* (Washington, D.C.: 1902), p. 866. Between 1890 and 1900, Galveston's "industrial establishments" increased from 190 to 295 (a 55.3 percent increase), but the number had dropped to 64 in 1904, after the 1900 storm. By 1909 the number of manufactories had risen to 81. According to the 1910 census report, among the Texas cities that ranked fifth or lower in size, "the largest industries in 1909 were the flour mills and gristmills in Galveston": U.S. Bureau of the Census, *Thirteenth Census of the United States . . . 1910.* Vol. 9: *Manufactures, 1909* (Washington, D.C.: 1912), p. 1204; *Galveston Daily News,* December 1, 1914, May 8, 1915; clipping, February 2, 1916, YWCA Scrapbook, 1916.

51. Clipping, December 31, 1914, *Galveston Daily News,* July 9, 1915, *Galveston Tribune,* September 23, 1915, and clipping, March 1, 1916 all in YWCA scrapbooks, 1914–15, 1916.

52. Clipping, June 28, 1915, YWCA scrapbook, 1914–15; Morrison and Fourmy's *Directory of the City of Galveston* (1916).

53. Clippings, March 24, 1917, October 26, 1918, YWCA scrapbook, 1917–18.

54. For a discussion of a women's community as seen through Chicago's settlement house, see Kathryn Kish Sklar, "Hull House in the 1890s: A Community of Women Reformers," *Signs* 10, no. 4 (1985): 658–77. On the political potential of the woman's sphere, see Estelle Freedman, "Separatism as Strategy: Female Institution Building and American Feminism, 1870–1930," *Feminist Studies* 5 (Fall, 1979): 512–29.

55. I owe an intellectual debt to Lawrence Goodwyn, *The Populist Moment: A Short History of the Agrarian Revolt in America* (Oxford: Oxford University Press, 1978), for the concept of "movement culture" as it relates to the Populist Movement.

Chapter 5 — The Emergence of a Black Neighborhood

1. John Bodnar, *The Transplanted: A History of Immigrants in Urban America* (Bloomington: University of Indiana Press, 1985); Roger Lane, *Roots of Violence in Black Philadelphia, 1860–1900* (Cambridge, Mass.: Harvard University Press, 1986).

2. David G. McComb, *Houston: A History* (Austin: University of Texas Press, 1981), p. 51.

3. See Writers' Program of the Works Projects Administration (WPA), *Houston: A History and Guide* (Houston: Anson Jones Press, 1942), p. 38. The source most often quoted as the basis of this claim is a nephew of Houston's founders; See O. Fisher Allen, *The City of Houston from Wilderness to Wonder* (Temple, Tex.: privately published, 1936), pp. 1–2.

4. Only one of eight free blacks residing in Houston in 1860 lived in the Fourth Ward, a thirty-three-year-old woman named Charlotte, who lived with a seventy-year-old white woman.

5. Descriptions of antebellum black life in Houston are vague, at best. Some travelers' accounts mention black activity, and the newspapers frequently complained about unsupervised slaves. See Charles O. Green, *Fighters of Houston, 1838–1915* (Houston: Dealy-Adey Company, 1915), pp. 137–41; Jesse A. Ziegler, *Wave of the*

Gulf (San Antonio: Naylor, 1938) pp. 56–58; Orphia D. Smith, "A Trip to Texas in 1955," *Southwestern Historical Quarterly* 59 (July, 1955): 27; and *Weekly Telegraph* (Houston), September 17, 1856.

6. WPA, *Houston,* pp. 249–50.

7. James Martin SoRelle, "The Darker Side of 'Heaven': The Black Community in Houston, Texas, 1917–1945," Ph.D. diss., Kent State University, 1980, p. 20; Mary Susan Jackson, "The People of Houston in the 1850's," Ph.D. diss., Indiana University, 1974, p. 143.

8. *Tri-Weekly Telegraph,* November 17, 1858.

9. Ibid., June 30, July 7, August 15, 1865.

10. *Bird's Eye View of the City of Houston,* 1873, Metropolitan Research Center, Houston Public Library (hereafter MRC).

11. *Tri-Weekly Telegraph,* June 30, 1865.

12. WPA, *Houston,* p. 288.

13. W. E. Wood, *Map of Houston, Harris County, Texas,* January 15, 1866, MRC.

14. *Topographical Map for Commerce of Houston, Texas,* (Baltimore: Wm A. Flamm, 1890), MRC.

15. *Houston, Texas (Looking South),* 1891, MRC.

16. Ibid.; *Freedmen's Town Historic District,* National Register Department, Texas Historical Commission, Austin, 1984.

17. *Sanborn Fire Insurance Maps for the City of Houston, Texas* (Chicago: Sanborn Fire Insurance Company, 1907); *Freedmen's Town.*

18. The major problem with the 1870 handwritten census lists is that the questionnaires provide no information about the marital status of the population. Consequently, it is necessary to reconstruct family relationships based on the names, ages, and sex of family members. The 1870 lists also do not provide the addresses of those surveyed. It is necessary to assume that the enumerators went from house to house in a logical manner. It is impossible, however, to determine from the census records in which part of the ward an individual resided. National Archives Microfilm Publications, *Population Schedules of the Ninth Census of the United States: 1870, Texas,* Vol. 9, *Guadalupe, Hamilton, Hardin, and Harris Counties* (Washington, D.C.: National Archives, 1965).

19. Ibid.; Bureau of the Census Microfilm Laboratory, *Twelfth Census of the Population: 1900, Texas,* Vol. 53, *Harris County.* For the 1870 census, my sample consisted of every fourth black person over the age of fifteen and every fourth black household. For the 1900 census, my sample consisted of every eighth page of census data, every third black individual over the age of fifteen, and every third black family.

20. *Population Schedules, 1870.*

21. *Twelfth Census, 1900.*

22. As previously noted, the 1870 census questionnaires did not clearly indicate the marital status of the population; it was necessary to estimate whether individuals were married, single, widowed, or divorced.

23. See Robert E. Zeigler, "The Workingman in Houston, Texas, 1865–1914," Ph.D. diss., Texas Tech University, 1972, p. 51.

24. *Population Schedules, 1870; Twelfth Census, 1900.*

25. SoRelle, "The Darker Side," pp. 46–47; Zeigler, "The Workingman," p. 53.

26. SoRelle, "The Darker Side," p. 46.

27. John Kellogg, "Negro Urban Clusters in the Postbellum South," *Geographical Review* 67 (July, 1967): 310–21.

28. SoRelle, "The Darker Side," pp. 46–47.

29. *Population Schedules, 1870.*

30. *Twelfth Census, 1900.*

31. Ibid.; *Population Schedules, 1870.*

32. Author's taped interview with Sylvia Harrison, November 11, 1981, in author's possession.

33. WPA, *Houston,* pp. 249–50.

34. Hunter O. Brooks, *Historic Highlights of the Antioch Missionary Baptist Church of Christ, Inc. 1866–1976* (Houston: Antioch Community Trust, 1976), pp. 1, 2.

35. SoRelle, "The Darker Side," p. 40.

36. Rutherford B. H. Yates, Sr., and Paul L. Yates, *The Life and Efforts of Jack Yates* (Houston: Texas Southern University Press, 1985), pp. 31–35.

37. Ibid., pp. 44–45; Brooks, *Historic Highlights,* p. 3.

38. *Catalogue of Houston College, 1919–1920,* MRC.

39. SoRelle, "The Darker Side," p. 21.

40. WPA, *Houston,* pp. 273–74.

41. *Freedmen's Town.*

42. *The Red Book of Houston: A Compendium of Social, Professional, Religious, Educational and Industrial Interests of Houston's Colored Population* (Houston: Sotex Publishing Company, [1915]), pp. 164–71.

43. Ibid., pp. 91–93, 121–22, 164–73.

44. Yates and Yates, *Jack Yates,* p. 23.

45. *Report of the City Planning Commission, Houston, Texas,* (Houston: Forum of Civics, 1929), p. 25. This willingness on the part of Houston builders to build for a black market did not occur as readily in other Texas communities (especially San Antonio). See Jack E. Dodson, "Minority Group Housing in Two Texas Cities," in Nathan Glazer and Davis McEntire, eds., *Studies in Housing and Minority Groups* (Berkeley & Los Angeles: University of California Press, 1960), pp. 103–105.

46. Harold L. Platt, *City Building in the New South: The Growth of Public Services in Houston, Texas, 1830–1915* (Philadelphia: Temple University Press, 1983), pp. 158–59, 204–208.

47. Herbert G. Gutman, *The Black Family in Slavery and Freedom, 1750–1925* (New York: Vintage Books, 1977), pp. 484–87, 497, 498–500.

48. Kellogg, "Negro Urban Clusters"; Jow William Trotter, Jr., *Black Milwaukee: The Making of an Industrial Proletariat, 1915–1945* (Urbana: University of Illinois Press, 1985), pp. 21–24.

49. U.S. Department of Commerce, Bureau of the Census, *Negroes in the United States, 1920–1932* (Washington, D.C.: Government Printing Office, 1935), pp. 518, 520–24.

CHAPTER 6 — OLMOS PARK
AND THE CREATION OF A SUBURBAN BASTION, 1927–39

1. *San Antonio Light,* September 8, 1956, p. 13; Arnold Fleischmann, "Sunbelt Boosterism: The Politics of Postwar Growth and Annexation in San Antonio,"

in David C. Perry and Alfred J. Watkins, eds., *The Rise of the Sunbelt Cities* (Beverly Hills, Calif.: Sage Publications, 1977), pp. 154–55. "Satellite cities" was one of the more generous terms San Antonio politicians used when discussing the suburbs. In 1952, city manager C. A. Harrell called them "parasite cities"; Fleischmann, "Sunbelt Boosterism," p. 157.

2. *San Antonio Light,* August 8, 1944, p. 1, June 19, 1945, p. 1. For an extended discussion of the Texas laws regarding annexation and the use to which they were put by Texas cities, see Letitia A. Gómez, "Growth Management and Annexation: San Antonio's Struggle with Growth," Master's thesis, Trinity University, 1987. The dump that Mauerman proposed was never built.

3. *San Antonio Express,* June 20, 1945, p. 1, June 21, 1945, p. 2; Olmos Park Town Council Minutes, June 20, 1945, Olmos Park City Hall.

4. *San Antonio Express,* June 21, 1945, pp. 1, 2.

5. Kenneth T. Jackson, *The Crabgrass Frontier* (New York: Oxford University Press, 1985); Joel Schwartz, "Evolution of the Suburbs," in Alexander Callow, ed., *American Urban History* (New York: Oxford University Press, 1982), pp. 492–514.

6. *North San Antonio Times,* December 23, 1976.

7. Ibid., December 16, 1976; *San Antonio Express,* February 8, 1925, December 5, 1926, May 18, 1954.

8. *San Antonio Express,* November 14, 1926.

9. Ibid., December 5, 1926.

10. Ibid., November 28, 1926.

11. Ibid., November 14, 21, December 26, 1926.

12. Ibid., November 21, 1926.

13. Richard Kluger, *Simple Justice* (New York: Knopf, 1976), pp. 120, 246–47; Thomas Philpott, *The Slum and the Ghetto: Neighborhood Deterioration and Middle Class Reform, Chicago 1818–1930* (New York: Oxford University Press, 1978), pp. 189–96, 255–56; Jackson, *Crabgrass Frontier.*

14. Warranty Deed, "Olmos Park Estates," Bexar County Deed Records, vol. 954, p. 395; Philpott, *The Slum and the Ghetto,* p. 189; Jackson, *Crabgrass Frontier.*

15. Warranty Deed, vol. 954, p. 395; *San Antonio Express,* December 5, 26, 1926.

16. *San Antonio Express,* January 2, February 6, 1927.

17. Comparisons include developments in the Woodlawn District, ibid., January 9, 30, 1927.

18. Warranty Deed, "Olmos Park Estates," Bexar County Records, vol. 954; Debbie Allen, "Alamo Heights: From Suburb to City," Manuscript, December, 1984; Charles O. Cook and Barry J. Kaplan, "Civic Elites and Urban Planning: Houston's River Oaks," *East Texas Historical Journal* 15, no. 2 (1977): 31.

19. *San Antonio Express,* November 21, 1926; Green Peyton, *San Antonio: City in the Sun* (New York: McGraw-Hill, 1946), pp. 18, 22.

20. *San Antonio Express,* February 27, 1927, pp. A5, A2.

21. Ibid., January 2, 1927.

22. The information on which this discussion is based is drawn from the *San Antonio City Directory,* 1924–1934. Our thanks to Kay Reamey for her research assistance in this regard.

23. David R. Johnson et al., eds., *The Politics of San Antonio* (Lincoln: University of Nebraska Press, 1983), intro.

24. Reyner Banham, *Los Angeles: The Architecture of the Four Ecologies* (New York: Harper & Row, 1971); Robert A. M. Stern, *The Anglo-American Suburb* (London: Architectual Design, 1981), pp. 78–79; David Gebhard and Robert Winter, *A Guide to Architecture in Los Angeles and Southern California* (Santa Barbara, Calif.: Peregrine Smith, 1977), pp. 120–24.

25. Stern, *Anglo-American Suburb,* p. 80; William L. McDonald, *Dallas Rediscovered* (Dallas: Dallas Historical Society, 1978), p. 204.

26. Jon Teaford, *City and Suburb* (Baltimore: Johns Hopkins University Press, 1979), p. 101.

27. Johnson, et al., *Politics of San Antonio,* pp. 16–19; *San Antonio Light,* June 30, 1939.

28. Richard Henderson, *Maury Maverick: A Political Biography* (Austin: University of Texas Press, 1970), pp. 188–93.

29. *San Antonio Express,* April 14, 27, 1939.

30. Ibid., May 9, 1939; Thomas Trachta to Char Miller, March 4, 1985; interview with Mrs. Frances Conlon, March, 1985.

31. *San Antonio Express,* May 24, 1939.

32. Ibid., June 20, 30, 1939.

33. Ibid., June 21, 1945; *San Antonio Light,* June 19, 1945. Olmos Park has continued to exist as an independent polity. The city now assumes a larger responsibility for public services, providing for its own police force and selling water it buys from San Antonio. And those services, particularly the police, are carefully employed to protect both the image and the property of Olmos Park residents — maintaining a thirty-mile-per-hour speed limit in keeping with the development's quiet residential character and carefully regulating overnight parking to ensure quiet and the privacy of the citizenry.

34. Jackson, *The Crabgrass Frontier;* Schwartz, "Evolution of the Suburbs"; Carl Abbott, *The New Urban America: Growth and Politics in Sunbelt Cities* (Chapel Hill: University of North Carolina Press, 1981). Henry Binford, *The First Suburbs: Residential Communities on the Boston Periphery, 1815–1860* (Chicago: University of Chicago Press, 1985), presents an alternate vision of the ways that cities and suburbs could grow.

35. Jackson, *The Crabgrass Frontier;* Schwartz, "Evolution of the Suburbs"; Abbott, *New Urban America;* Raymond A. Mohl, *The New City: Urban America in the Industrial Age, 1869–1920* (Arlington Heights, Ill.: Harlan Davidson, 1985), pp. 31–32, 44, 199; Stern, *Anglo-American Suburb,* pp. 10–12, 75–87.

36. McDonald, *Dallas Rediscovered;* Charles Orson Cook and Barry J. Kaplan, "Civic Elites and Urban Planning: Houston's River Oaks"; Johnson et al., *The Politics of San Antonio,* intro.; Trachta to Miller, Mar. 4, 1985, letter in author's possession.

37. Some of the urban costs associated with the elite's disengagement from San Antonio's politics (and its exploitation of that disengagement) are chronicled in Ralph Maitland, "San Antonio: The Shame of Texas," *Forum* (August, 1939): 51–55; Julia Kirk Blackwelder, *Women in the Depression: Caste and Class in San Antonio* (College Station: Texas A&M University Press, 1984).

CHAPTER 7 — PROTECTING COMMUNITY AND PROPERTY VALUES

1. Sam Bass Warner, Jr., *The Private City: Philadelphia in Three Periods of Its Growth* (Philadelphia: University of Pennsylvania Press, 1968), pp. x–xi. An earlier version of this chapter, now substantially amended, appeared in my book, *Let the People Decide: Neighborhood Organizing in America* (Boston: Twayne, 1984).

2. Sam Bass Warner, Jr., *The Urban Wilderness: A History of the American City* (New York: Harper & Row, 1972), pp. 3–7.

3. Warner, *The Private City*, p. xi; Barry Kaplan, "Houston: The Golden Buckle of the Sunbelt," in Richard M. Bernard and Bradley R. Rice, *Sunbelt Cities: Politics and Growth since World War II* (Austin: University of Texas Press, 1983); Robert Fisher, *Let the People Decide: Neighborhood Organizing in America* (Boston: Twayne, 1984).

4. Gunther cited in Don Carleton, "McCarthyism in Houston: The George Ebey Affair," *Southwestern Historical Quarterly* 80 (October, 1976): 167.

5. In 1965 the city of Houston was given authorization by the state of Texas to enforce deed restrictions. The funds available to the city legal department, however, were insufficient to handle the task, thus almost all restriction enforcement remains a "private" matter.

6. Woodland Heights promotional brochure, 1909, Houston Metropolitan Research Center (MRC), Subdivision file.

7. Roderick D. McKenzie, *The Neighborhood: A Study of Local Life in Columbus, Ohio* (Chicago: University of Chicago Press, 1923); Thomas Philpott, *The Slum and the Ghetto: Neighborhood Deterioration and Middle Class Reform, Chicago 1818–1930* (New York: Oxford University Press, 1978).

8. Southwest Civic Club (SWCC) manuscript, MRC. I also used papers on the Southwest Civic Club written by Kathy Sexton, Cindy Herbert, and others in my urban history course, at the University of Houston–Downtown, spring, 1981. The information that follows about the SWCC is based on the historical records of the club, which were made available to me by John Shanahan and which are now housed at the Houston Metropolitan Research Center.

9. Robert Bailey, Jr., *Radicals in Urban Politics: The Alinsky Approach* (Chicago: University of Chicago Press, 1972), p. 30, says parapolitical "refers to the formal voluntary associations which are not mobilized primarily for political purposes but which may become political when matters of interest to them are being considered by decision-makers."

10. Clement Vose, *Caucasians Only: The Supreme Court, the NAACP, and the Restrictive Covenant Cases* (Berkeley and Los Angeles: University of California Press, 1959).

11. *Houston Chronicle*, April 18, 1971, sec. 4, p. 1; Jack E. Dodson, "Minority Group Housing in Texas," in Nathan Glazer and Davis McEntire, eds., *Studies in Housing and Minority Groups: Special Research Report to the Commission on Race and Housing* (Berkeley & Los Angeles: University of California Press, 1960), p. 106. An invaluable study of the transformation of the Riverside area is Barry J. Kaplan, "Race, Income and Ethnicity: Residential Change in a Houston Community, 1920–1970," *Houston Review* 3 (Winter, 1981): 178–203.

12. Bertram Mann, a past president of the Allied Civic Club, was kind enough to speak with me about and share some of his materials on the history of the association.

13. President, Southwest Civic Club, letter, 1970, SWCC Manuscript, MRC.

14. Philpott, *The Slum and the Ghetto;* Warner, *The Urban Wilderness,* p. 5.

CHAPTER 8 — DALLAS IN THE 1940S

1. Blaine A. Brownell, *The Urban Ethos in the South, 1920–1930* (Baton Rouge: Louisiana State University Press, 1975). A summer grant from the Graduate School of the University of Texas–Arlington allowed me to complete this essay.

2. Bureau of Business Research, *An Economic Survey of Dallas County* (Austin: College of Business Administration, University of Texas, 1949), p. 103; Louis P. Head, "Dallas Joins Ranks of Manager Cities," *National Municipal Review* 19 (December, 1930): 806–809.

3. Harold A. Stone et al., *City Manager Government in Dallas* (Chicago: Public Administrative Service, 1939), p. 13.

4. By "localist" I mean those opposed to bringing in outsiders like Edy and opposed to overdependence on federal monies. For more on Dallas's politics in the 1930s, see Carolyn Jenkins Barta, "The Dallas News and Council-Manager Government," Master's thesis, University of Texas, 1970; Roscoe C. Martin, "Dallas Makes the City Manager Plan Work," *Annals* 198 (July, 1938): 64–70; Stone, *City Manager Government in Dallas.*

5. Federal Works Agency, *Final Statistical Report of the Federal Emergency Relief Administration* (Washington, D.C.: Government Printing Office, 1942); Dallas Housing Authority, *Designed for Living: The Housing Authority of the City of Dallas, Texas, 1938–1947* (Dallas, n.d.).

6. The community emphasis comes through clearly in the DHA's early reports. See, for instance, "Annual Report of the Dallas Housing Authority, 1942," Dallas Housing Authority Office.

7. Carol Estes Thometz, *The Decision-Makers: The Power Structure of Dallas* (Dallas: Southern Methodist University Press, 1963), pp. 30–50; Warren Leslie, *Dallas: Public and Private* (New York: Grossman Publishers, 1964), pp. 60–85.

8. For more on the metropolitan community mode of thought, see Robert B. Fairbanks, "Better Housing Movements and the City: Definitions of and Responses to Cincinnati's Low Cost Housing Problem, 1910–1954," Ph.D. diss., University of Cincinnati, 1981, pp. 71–127. See also R. D. McKenzie, *The Metropolitan Community* (1933; reprint, New York: Russell & Russell, 1967).

9. David L. Cohn, "Dallas," *Atlantic Monthly,* October, 1940, pp. 453–60.

10. Ibid.; Bureau of the Census, *16th Census of the United States, 1940, Population and Housing. Dallas Texas and Adjacent Area* (Washington, D.C.: Government Printing Office, 1942), p. 32.

11. Minutes, Dallas Housing Authority (DHA), November 8, 1938, DHA Office. The strong case for improved segregated black housing had been made in a 1927 school textbook by Justin Kimball. According to Kimball, slum housing was "like a canker or eating sore" on Dallas. "The rest of our city can no more live and grow and prosper with such a condition, than our body can be well when it has an angry,

bleeding inflamed sore on some part of it. The rest of the body will be injured in health and strength; so will the rest of the city sooner or later, suffer the penalty for bad housing conditions among any large group of its population, however humble". Justin F. Kimball, *Our City: A Community Civics* (Dallas: Kessler Plan Association of Dallas, 1927), p. 199.

12. Memorandum to the American Civil Liberties Union from Thurgood Marshall, July 28, 1941, American Civil Liberties Archives, Princeton University Library; "Racial Dynamism in Dallas," *New Republic,* March 24, 1941, p. 6.

13. "Contracts Total $91,000,000," *Dallas,* March, 1941, p. 11.

14. "Dallas Gets Naval Base," *Southwest Business* 19 (October, 1940): 6.

15. "Eighth Service Command to Begin Move November 15," *Dallas,* November, 1942, p. 9; "Dallas—The War Capital of the Southwest," *Dallas,* July, 1942.

16. Restricted Monthly Field Operations Report for Dallas Area for January and February, 1944, Records of the War Manpower Commission (WMC), Record Group (RG) 211, Federal Archives and Records Center, Fort Worth, Texas.

17. E. C. Barksdale, *The Genesis of the Aviation Industry in North Texas* (Austin: Bureau of Business Research, University of Texas, 1958), p. 3.

18. *Dallas Morning News,* July 5, August 18, 1940; "North American Comes to Dallas," *Southwest Business* 19 (October, 1940): 9.

19. *Dallas Morning News,* August 18, 30, 1940; Barksdale, *Genesis of Aviation Industry,* pp. 1–7.

20. Barksdale, *Genesis of Aviation Industry,* pp. 1–7. "North American Tells 30,000 about Dallas Plant," *Dallas,* November, 1941, p. 36; Employment Trend in Selected Establishments by Primary Area and Industry, WMC Records, RG 211; "Report of Current and Required Employment," WMC Records, RG 211.

21. George L. MacGregor, "Democracy's Arsenal Needs Trained Workers," *Dallas,* March, 1941, p. 9; *Dallas Times-Herald,* July 25, 1943.

22. Mr. McNutt's statement to the Truman Committee regarding Dallas labor market situation, November 10, 1943, WMC Records, RG 211. Statistical summary of the Dallas–Fort Worth Area, January, 1944, ibid.

23. WMC, Restricted Monthly Field Operator's Report, February 1944, WMC Records, RG 211; McNutt's statement to Truman Committee, WMC Records, RG 211.

24. Dave Williams, "Defense on the Home Front; Avion Village," *Dallas,* May, 1941, p. 18; "Dallas Plans New Units," *Dallas,* June, 1941, p. 11. Under the public housing program initiated in 1938, the DHA built approximately 900 units for blacks, 450 for whites, and 100 for Mexican Americans. Even before the DHA completed the two projects for whites, federal officials designated them Defense Housing Projects and allowed over-income war personnel to move in. Much of the personnel transferred with the Eighth Service Command used these projects. Minutes, DHA, September 29, 1942, DHA office.

25. McNutt's statement to Truman Committee, WMC Records, RG 211.

26. Ibid.; Clyde V. Wallis to James H. Bond, May 1, 1943, WMC Records, RG 211.

27. McNutt's statement to Truman Committee, WMC Records, RG 211; Homer A. Hunter, "Ingenuity and Small Outlay Greatly Increase Dallas Water Supply," *American City,* April, 1945, p. 81.

28. Harland Bartholomew and Associates, "A Master Plan for Dallas," Report No. 8, "Land Use" (October, 1944).

29. D. A. Wood, "Master Plan for City of 670,000 by 1970," *Dallas,* December, 1943, p. 12; Bartholomew and Associates, "A Master Plan for Dallas," Report No. 2, Scope of the Plan" (September, 1943).

30. Bartholomew and Associates, "A Master Plan for Dallas," Report No. 1, Character of the City" (September, 1943); "A Master Unification and the Greater Dallas Master Plan," pamphlet, Dallas Historical Society.

31. From 1945 to 1952, the city annexed 119.4 square miles of suburban territory: William Neil Black, "Empire of Consensus: City Planning, Zoning, and Annexation in Dallas, 1900–1960," Ph.D. diss., Columbia University, 1982, p. 286.

32. Bartholomew and Associates, "A Master Plan for Dallas," Report No. 10, "Housing" (December, 1944).

33. Ibid., pp. 12–13.

34. Ibid., p. 31.

35. Ibid., pp. 27–29.

36. For more on the homogeneous approach to better housing, see Robert B. Fairbanks and Zane L. Miller, "The Martial Metropolis: Housing, Planning, and Race in Cincinnati, 1940–1955," in Roger W. Lotchin, ed., *The Martial Metropolis: U.S. Cities in War and Peace* (New York: Praeger, 1984), pp. 197–209; Howard Gillette, Jr., "The Evolution of Neighborhood Planning: From the Progressive Era to the 1949 Housing Act," *Journal of Urban History* 9 (August, 1983): 421–23.

37. "Reconversion Contrasts—Buffalo and Dallas," *Business Week* (September 1, 1945): 17; Barksdale, *Genesis of Aviation Industry,* pp. 13–16.

38. Shortly before the company started its move to Dallas, a Chance Vought official called D. A. Hulcy, head of the Citizens Council, and informed him that nearby municipally owned Hensely Field's runways were too short and had to be extended if the aircraft builder were to come. That same day, Hulcy got the City Council to meet and appropriate $256,000 for runway expansion. Work started the following Monday: Leslie, *Dallas: Public and Private,* p. 70.

39. "Meeting Problems of Uprooting an Industry," *Business Week* (August 14, 1948): 26–30; Barksdale, *Genesis of Aviation Industry,* pp. 17–20.

40. *Dallas Times-Herald,* October 29, 1947.

41. *Dallas Morning News,* December 25, 1949; *Dallas Times-Herald,* February 23, 1948, September 10, 1950.

42. *Dallas Morning News,* December 25, 1949, February 26, 1950.

43. DHA, "Dallas Public Housing Market Review," June, 1947, p. 22.

44. Quoted in *Dallas Morning News,* April 21, 1948.

45. *Dallas Times-Herald,* January 10, 14, 1950.

46. *Dallas Morning News,* January 18, 1949.

47. "Text of Negro Housing Survey Report," *Dallas Times-Herald,* May 28, 1950.

48. *Dallas Times-Herald,* July 3, 1951.

49. *Dallas Housing Authority. What Is It and How Does It Work?* (Dallas: DHA, n.d.), p. 3; *Dallas Morning News,* October 31, 1962; "West Dallas," *Journal of Housing* (February, 1954): 54–55.

50. "Text of Negro Housing Survey Report," *Dallas Times-Herald,* May 28, 1950, November 26, 1951.

51. *Dallas Morning News,* March 25, 1962; Richard Austin Smith, "How Business Failed Dallas," *Fortune,* July, 1964, pp. 157–63; Martin V. Melosi, "Dallas–

Fort Worth: Marketing the Metroplex," in Richard M. Bernard and Bradley R. Rice, eds., *Sunbelt Cities: Politics and Growth since World War II* (Austin: University of Texas Press, 1983), pp. 183–84.

52. *Dallas Times-Herald,* June 6, 1950; *Dallas Morning News,* October 4, 1962. For more on the changing focus of the Dallas leadership in the mid-fifties, see my "Metropolitan Planning and Downtown Redevelopment: The Cincinnati and Dallas Experience," *Planning Perspectives,* forthcoming.

53. Gillette, "The Evolution of Neighborhood Planning," pp. 421–44; Zane L. Miller, *Suburb: Neighborhood and Community in Forest Park, Ohio, 1935–1976* (Knoxville: University of Tennessee Press, 1981), pp. xxiv–xxv, 3–27.

CHAPTER 9 — BUILDING A NEW URBAN INFRASTRUCTURE

1. Douglas Tomlinson and David Dillon, *Dallas Architecture, 1936–1986* (Austin: Texas Monthly Press, 1985), p. 119. I would like to acknowledge the assistance of Sylvia Arredondo, Don Arispe, Lorah Tidwell, and Diane Miller in the collection and analysis of the bond voting data.

2. Kenneth Gray, "A Report on the Politics of Houston" (Cambridge: Joint Center for Urban Studies of MIT and Harvard, 1960), pp. VI-36.

3. Susan MacManus, *Federal Aid to Houston* (Washington, D.C.: Brookings Institution, 1983), p. 1.

4. See chap. 6, this volume.

5. Ralph Maitland, "San Antonio: The Shame of Texas," *Forum,* August, 1939, p. 53.

6. Ibid., p. 52.

7. *San Antonio Express,* March 7, 1930, p. 17.

8. Ibid., April 2, 1930, p. 14.

9. Ibid., May 1, 1930, p. 14.

10. Ibid., May 7, 1930, p. 10.

11. Ibid., January 25, 1925, p. 16.

12. Ibid., October 15, 1934.

13. Ibid., December 16, 1935, p. 14.

14. Ibid., November 11, 1936, p. 20.

15. *San Antonio Light,* November 11, 1936, p. 1.

16. San Antonio 1951 City Plan, pp. 182, 206.

17. *San Antonio Express,* October 23, 1945, Local, p. 1.

18. Ibid., editorial, May 30, 1946.

19. Ibid., October 6, 1949.

20. "Persistence Pays," *National Municipal Review* (May, 1955): 237.

21. *San Antonio Express,* January 24, 1954.

22. Ibid., July 4, 1954.

23. Ibid., editorial, November 28, 1955.

24. Ibid., November 29, 1955.

25. Ibid., editorial, November 27, 1955.

26. The simple correlation between the "yes" vote on the expressway bonds and the north side dummy variable is a statistically insignificant 0.10, based on seventy precincts. The correlation between a positive vote on the aquarium bond issue and

the north side measure is only 0.08, indicating no real difference in the average positive percentage between the north side and the balance of the city.

27. City of San Antonio, "Progress for San Antonio," November, 1955, p. 61.

28. *San Antonio Express,* October 21, 1970, special section.

29. City of San Antonio, "Progress for San Antonio," p. 8.

30. *San Antonio Express,* October 21, 1970, special section.

31. Gray, "Politics of Houston," pp. VI–31.

32. *The Albuquerque Citizens' Committee Reports,* 1955, p. 1.

33. George Starbird, *The New Metropolis* (San Jose, Calif.: Rosicrucian Press, 1972), p. 5.

List of Contributors

AMY BRIDGES, a member of the Department of Political Science at the University of California at San Diego, is the author of *A City and the Republic: Antebellum New York and the Origins of Machine Politics* (1984).

ROBERT FAIRBANKS is an assistant professor of history at the University of Texas at Arlington. His *Making Better Citizens: Housing Reform and the Community Development Strategy in Cincinnati, 1890–1960* is forthcoming from the University of Illinois Press.

ROBERT FISHER, author of *Let the People Decide: Neighborhood Organizing in America* (1984), is an associate professor of history at the University of Houston–Downtown.

DAVID R. JOHNSON, author of numerous essays on the history of crime and urban history and coeditor of *The Politics of San Antonio: Community, Progress and Power* (1983), is a professor of history at the University of Texas at San Antonio.

CHAR MILLER, a member of the Department of History at Trinity University, San Antonio, is author of *Fathers and Sons: The Bingham Family and the American Mission* (1982) and *Missions and Missionaries in the Pacific* (1985), among other works.

HEYWOOD T. SANDERS, who is coeditor of *The Politics of Urban Development* (1987) and has completed work on a study, "The Politics of Urban Infrastructure," for the Twentieth Century Fund, is an associate professor of urban studies at Trinity University, San Antonio.

ELIZABETH TURNER, associate editor of the *Journal of Southern History,* is completing her Ph.D. dissertation on women in Galveston at Rice University, Houston.

CARY D. WINTZ, a member of the Department of History of Texas Southern University, Houston, has published a number of books and articles on nineteenth- and twentieth-century urban and social history.

Index